Management Relations with Organized Public Employees

Theory, Policies, Programs

Edited with a Preface and Introductory Notes by

KENNETH O. WARNER

PUBLIC PERSONNEL ASSOCIATION

1313 EAST SIXTIETH STREET   CHICAGO 37, ILLINOIS

Library of Congress Catalog Card Number 62-21432

Printed in the United States of America

Preface

Whether public official or government worker, you know this monograph deals with a crucially important--but controversial-- subject. In these pages I have collected statements of facts and opinions. I hope they will widen areas of understanding and narrow areas of disagreement in a field of great importance to management, public employees, and the general public.

For many years this Association has been interested in employee relations. Twenty years ago the Public Personnel Association (then the Civil Service Assembly of the United States and Canada) recognized the personnel man's obligation to provide leadership in employee relations by publishing the first substantial study of the subject. In 1942 a 246-page book entitled Employee Relations in the Public Service presented fresh concepts and laid a solid foundation for efforts to resolve problems. Public officials who want to understand the many facets of this complex subject can still read that volume with profit.

In the last two decades the Public Personnel Association has dealt frequently with various aspects of employee relations. Its journal, Public Personnel Review, has carried many articles on the subject. The topic has been discussed in featured talks and panel sessions at the Association's Annual International Conferences, at numerous Regional Conferences, and in many meetings of PPA's twenty Chapters.

In 1960 two Association Chapters prepared special reports on collective bargaining. The Vancouver (British Columbia) Metropolitan Chapter issued a report on joint efforts of public agencies in the Vancouver area to deal collectively with unions; the San Francisco Bay Area Chapter published a report entitled "Collective Bargaining in the Public Service." Both of these reports were studied by the Executive Council and the PPA staff.

While the Public Personnel Association has had long and intensive concern for employee relations, I want to emphasize that PPA holds no official position on most aspects of the subject. Specifically, PPA does not take an official stand on collective negotiation with organized public employees.

Sound reasons support the position of PPA's governing board in these areas on personnel administration. The Association is composed of close to 600 public personnel agencies in all levels of

i

government in the United States, Canada, and elsewhere. Varied legal, administrative, and political arrangements govern these agencies. Working within such diverse circumstances, the 2,500 individual members add another dimension to the problem of getting a consensus of thinking. To reconcile such wide divergencies among agencies and individuals in a policy statement acceptable to all, or even most members, becomes well nigh impossible.

It is not surprising, then, when I say that editor and authors accept sole responsibility for facts and opinions in this monograph. Neither the Association nor its Executive Council endorses what we say or imply.

Let me make perfectly clear one point: This Association does not close its institutional eyes to differences of viewpoint. The diverse character of Association membership actually increases the need for exchange of information. When the Council authorized publication of this monograph, it took a positive step toward increasing the tempo of the Association's effort to give public officials facts, opinions and experience. This action follows a well established policy: The Executive Council charges the staff to give members and other public officials information so they can make their own policy decisions. If public officials have a body of facts about employee relations, know varied practices and experience, and see examples of success or failure, then they can apply such knowledge to conditions at home.

I regret that circumstances keep me from covering management-employee relations in Canada. In Canada, by rule, rather than exception, provincial laws accord city employees full trade union rights. Well established employee organizations exist in provinces; in one (Saskatchewan), government workers receive rights and privileges and exercise responsibilities that go with regular trade union practices. In the Canadian federal service "staff associations" operate actively and press for more opportunities to work with federal officials.

But collective negotiation in Canada deserves separate and full treatment. A number of publications of high quality, written from intimate knowledge of the Canadian scene, appear in the Bibliography. The public official who wants to be well informed and who wants to profit by the experience of others must know about employee-management practices in Canada.

A collection of essays on a single subject may suffer for two reasons. First, it never covers the subject to the satisfaction of all. I know some of the gaps here, but I wanted to make a start, and not compile a collection that would serve for all time. Second, it inevitably repeats material. But even that has its value; it gives readers unabridged thinking of the authors and preserves their phrases. This feature often contributes to a better understanding, particularly on subjects in controversy.

I want to expressly thank a number of individuals and organizations. Almost one hundred of the largest personnel agencies in the United States furnished statements of their policies and practices in dealing with organized employees. The Executive Council gave advice and criticism. PPA's Vancouver (British Columbia) Metropolitan Chapter and the San Francisco Bay Area Chapter each provided a report. Research staffs of the American Federation of State, County, and Municipal Employees and the Building Services Employees International Union kindly furnished reference material. The authors, identified in the Table of Contents and also with their individual chapters, through their willing cooperation brought this monograph into being.

Mrs. Eleanor R. Batson, former Director of Publications, Public Personnel Association, served as editorial consultant and wrote Chapter 11, "A Survey of Current Practice"; Miss Sadie J. Doyle of the PPA editorial staff edited the manuscript and styled it for publication; Mr. J. J. Donovan, PPA Associate Director, designed the cover and counseled the editor; Mr. George Young, PPA Staff Assistant, served as research assistant.

My sincere thanks to all of you.

Kenneth O. Warner
Editor

October, 1962

Contents

v

PART I

imate for Management-Employee Cooperation

in the Public Service

Chapter I

Climate for Cooperation

KENNETH O. WARNER

The purpose of this monograph is to give public officials an over-view of current thinking and events that bear on management relations with organized public employees. To this end I gathered a number of essays, statements, and illustrative documents. They come from public officials, consultants, union representatives and academic authorities. The material appears in six parts:

Part I.   Climate for Management-Employee Cooperation in the Public Service.

Part II.   Role of Management-Employee Relations: Four Points of View.

Part III.   Management-Employee Relations in Action: Five Programs in Local Government.

Part IV.   Management-Employee Relations in State and Local Government.

Part V.   Management-Employee Relations in the Federal Government: A New Program.

Part VI.   Selected Bibliography.

The purpose of this book is not to convince you that any one system of management-employee relations is superior to another. Instead, it is designed to give a setting in which you can consider management relations with organized public employees . . . to give facts and opinions that will help you make your own appraisal of the central theme. If the essays stimulate your thinking and help you view the subject with fresh perspective, the Editor and this Association will be amply repaid for their efforts.

When I say this book is for public officials, I mean all public officials. No category of official can avoid being involved in the problem of how management deals with its employees. Members of law-making bodies, elected and appointed administrative officials, and career civil servants all share concern. They have the responsibility and obligation to work out ways of dealing with employee groups.

Kenneth O. Warner is Director of the Public Personnel Association.

3

This chapter is intended to show the kind of climate in which management and organized employees work. As used here "climate" obviously does not refer to the weather. Rather, it describes the intellectual elements that pertain to management-employee relations.

What determines intellectual climate? Primarily the attitudes and concepts held by a given group of people. What people think and what people believe make up the intellectual climate of their particular group. In this case the group is a composite one: public officials, organized employees, and the general public.

We can better understand and appreciate the "climate" if we know what causes people to hold their attitudes and concepts. For that reason I review in the following pages some background factors intended to show why people think as they do about employee organizations in government.

The Bugaboo of Semantics

The first obstacle to be surmounted is the bugaboo of semantics. It's not easy to choose words that convey the same meaning to all people when you talk about negotiating with employees in the public service. But why?

Perhaps the most important reason is that the literature of employee-management relations deals primarily with practices in private enterprise. To some public officials the terminology of industrial relations conveys semantic overtones which produce both emotional reactions and stereotyped thinking. Words like "negotiation," "collective bargaining," "exclusive recognition," and many more, impart special meanings because of their use in private employment. Such terms imply to some that public and private enterprise are the same or similar. Persons of this persuasion might tend to automatically apply industrial labor relations to government employee-management relations. That is stereotyped thinking.

On the other hand, persons who believe public and private business differ often recoil when they think of "collective bargaining" being carried on in the public service. Their minds do not easily entertain the thought of applying to government ideas about employee-management relations developed in the private sector. That is an emotional reaction.

Words can produce fear and worry. That's why they are a bugaboo. And that's why they obstruct understanding and decrease communication. If you recognize that some words cause people to react with

emotion and some words cause people to think in stereotypes, you
thereby take the first step toward surmounting the bugaboo of semantics.

Why Do People Join Employee Organizations?

Here's a subject that hits people in their emotional-plexus. If you
oppose unions and employee associations, you probably see no reason
why anyone should join them. If you favor employee organizations
you probably believe it's absurd to raise the question.

Since this monograph deals with organized public employees, I
summarize here the explanations offered by supporters of the idea:

-- Public managers are not perfect, so employees must find a
   vehicle that will represent their interests, speak to management and protect what they regard as their rights.

-- Civil service merit systems are also imperfect. They fail
   to give employees all the benefits and protection they believe
   they deserve. Quite apart from benefits, employees believe
   they should have some say about day-to-day activities at
   their work place. Personnel policies and procedures apply
   unevenly between departments, employees contend. They say
   some administrators are good, others are bad; the latter
   create one need that can be met by an employee organization.
   Individual employees often feel it is almost impossible to
   gain a fair hearing when their opinions differ from management's view of work performance, discipline, classification,
   and similar matters. Through an organization, they contend,
   protests can be made without fear of reprisal and with greater
   chance of success.

-- Many employees dislike unilateral decisions, even when benevolent. Besides having a voice in solving bread-and-butter is-
   sues--such as wages, vacations, and sick leave--they want to
   help formulate all personnel policies. Sometimes they go
   further and want to shape the program of their department.

-- Merit systems cover only a fraction of the governments in
   this country. Where no merit systems exist, employee organizations offer a practical opportunity to improve working conditions.

-- Employee organizations render services often unavailable
   elsewhere. Included are: social activities, recreation,
   health service, insurance, and the like.

You and I may deny the merits of one or all of these reasons.
Our denial, however, does little to make them less real to persons
who embrace them.

How Many Organized Public Employees?

Opinions differ about the number of organized public workers in the United States. This situation exists because not all organizations keep or release accurate membership records. The Bureau of Labor Statistics and the U. S. Census Bureau issue the most reliable statistics on the subject.

In 1960 the Bureau of Labor Statistics reported employee organizations in all U. S. governments had a membership of 1,070,000. At that time there were 8,908,000 civilian public employees in all U. S. governments, including education. In round numbers, roughly one out of nine employees belong to unions or unaffiliated associations -- approximately 11 per cent.

The membership statistics of independent employee associations, included in those just mentioned, can be singled out. In Chapter 13, Joseph Krislov's study of state and local associations shows that they account for fewer than 400,000 dues-paying members. Based on a 1960 study of the California State Employees' Association, approximate figures for "independents" in California show something about the movement in that state. Outside the federal service, all governments in California (except special districts) employ about 575,000 people. Of these, 203,000, or about 35 per cent, belong to independent associations in the state, counties, cities, and school districts. In this light, California ranks high in independent associations.

What About Trends?

If one wants to evaluate the relative importance of employee organizations in public administration, the question of trends arises naturally. Are there more or fewer government workers in organizations now than two decades ago? What is their relative strength in relation to total government employment?

The answer to the first question is very clear: numerically, unions and associations are stronger. But the gains in relation to increased employment are less striking, and differ between levels of government.

Let's see what has happened in the federal service in a little over two decades. When this Association published its 1942 book on Employee Relations in the Public Service, it contained data on 1939 membership in federal employee organizations. At that time 313,000 employees--34 per cent of the total federal service--belonged to unions. Of these, 289,000, or 66 per cent, were in postal unions.

In contrast, the President's Task Force on Employee-Management Relations in 1961 reported 762,000-- 33 per cent--membership in employee organizations. So, in 22 years membership more than doubled; but percentage-wise membership decreased by 1 per cent.

In local governments the picture differs. I could find no data on the extent of growth in actual numbers of organized employees. But accurate figures reveal a substantial upswing in the percentage of cities over 10,000 with one or more employee organizations. Over a period of thirty years that percentage has almost doubled. Statistics in The Municipal Yearbook, published by the International City Managers' Association, show the percentage of coverage (in terms of the number of cities over 10,000) for the years indicated below, as follows:

Year	% of Cities over 10,000 with 1 or more Employee Organizations
1942	41.8
1952	67.6
1962	78.3

If you look at the data on growth of employee organizations you don't get a strong feeling that it has far outstripped the rate of increase in public employment during the past generation. In the last two decades the numerical strength of federal employee organizations has doubled, but their strength in relation to total federal employment remains practically static.

On the other hand, the number of employee organizations in cities over 10,000 has almost doubled in the past thirty years. These observations may be somewhat tentative but they are based on the best available information I could find.

A Basic Element: Restrictions on Public Employees

As you read further you will see clearly that one point of disagreement among contributors to this monograph centers on their idea of the rights of a public employee. This consideration may be elementary but it is likewise basic.

Traditionally public employees have been more restricted in their rights than those in private industry. Sharp differences between employees in government and private enterprise show up in law, opinions of courts, and statements of chief executives.

In 1892 Mr. Justice Oliver Wendell Holmes ruled that, "the petitioner may have a right to talk politics, but he has no constitutional right to be a policeman." This statement has been used to support the view that government employment is a privilege, not a right. In the 1960's public employees can be fired for soliciting political funds in violation of government regulations just as the New Bedford, Massachusetts, policeman was in the 1890's.

The courts also upheld President Franklin D. Roosevelt's view "that the process of collective bargaining, as usually understood, cannot be transplanted into the public service." For example, in 1947 the Missouri Supreme Court barred collective bargaining by a governmental agency on these grounds: "It is a familiar principle of Constitutional law that the legislature cannot delegate its legislative powers . . . . "

When the National Labor Relations Act of 1935 (Wagner Act) gave private employees the right to join unions or assist labor organizations and bargain collectively, public employees were specifically excluded. The Act said: "The Term 'employer'. . . shall not include the United States, or any state or political subdivision thereof."

The federal government, as well as a number of states (for example, New York, Michigan, Texas) forbid strikes and provide penalties should strikes occur. The most recent federal legislation, Public Law 330, passed by Congress in 1955, says: "No person shall accept or hold office or employment in the government of the United States . . . who . . . participates in any strike or asserts the right to strike against the government . . . or is a member of an organization of government employees that asserts the right to strike. . . . "

It is difficult -- but not impossible -- to remove the restrictions set down in law. Laws do change when public opinion changes.

For example, in the early 1900's executive orders of Presidents Theodore Roosevelt and Taft denied the right of individual employees or employee associations to petition Congress for increases in pay or for any other benefit. Employees could only respond to requests for information from Congress through their department head. This "gag rule" lasted for ten years, but it was removed in 1912 by the Lloyd-La Follette Act. Instead of restricting employee rights, the Act granted rights. This "positive" federal legislation spelled out procedures for dismissal of employees. The Act also provided that, "The right of persons employed in the civil service of the United States either individually or collectively, to petition Congress or any member thereof, or to furnish information to any House of Congress, or to any committee or member thereof, shall not be denied or interfered with."

Why Remove Restrictions?

Proponents of removing restrictions on public employees rest their case on three major points.

1. They say anti-strike legislation is unnecessary. Unions of public employees have renounced the right to strike; governments can prevent or stop strikes in other ways. The right to strike, they contend, should depend on the type of service rendered. For example, they ask: Why is it logical to allow employees of a privately owned bus company to strike and deny the same right to employees of a municipally owned transit system?

2. They believe many aspects of personnel administration can be "negotiated." For example, promotion standards, grievance procedures, safety regulations, transfers, and the like. They believe something very similar to or the same as industrial collective bargaining can exist in government.

3. They contend that if employees are given the right to organize, recognition is logical and even exclusive recognition is possible.

Why Continue Restrictions?

Opponents of removing restrictions rest their case on these major points.

1. They say a strike by public employees challenges the sovereignty of government. Representative legislative bodies, not administrative officers or employee representatives, must decide policy in the interest of all citizens. Groups of dissatisfied employees cannot be allowed to curtail or stop government functions. Anti-strike legislation actually protects employees. Since employees do not have recourse to force, management is stimulated to deal with them fairly.

2. They contend the merit system is the fairest way to administer personnel programs in government. Government must treat all employees alike. Collective bargaining can lead to agreements that differ from department to department and therefore result in inequitable treatment of employees within the same government jurisdiction.

3. They believe exclusive recognition fails to protect the rights of individual employees or specialized groups of employees. They point to employees who do not join any organization. They cite the variety of public employees--the blue-collar and white-collar workers, the scientific, professional, and administrative workers. From this they would argue: Many types of employees need to be represented before management; exclusive recognition curtails the rights of some.

These views on "restricted" and "unrestricted" public employees oppose each other almost diametrically. Management and employee groups seek greater agreement on the rights of public workers.

Implications of the New Federal Program

The new federal management-employee relations program attempts one type of solution of the dilemma. Details of the program appear in Chapter 16. There, John W. Macy, Jr., declares: "More progress has been made in federal employee-management relations since June 22, 1961, than was made in any comparable period in the 80-year history of the federal civil service."

Regardless of whether you accept the principles of this new program you will agree that it does represent a significant event in the history of federal personnel management. It may also bear directly on, and influence developments in, state and local government.

Here I want to mention the important features of the new federal employee-management relations program.

-- It gives a positive, official statement of policy which supports collective negotiation and exclusive recognition.

-- It recognizes differences between employee relations in public and private enterprise.

-- It rests on a system of negotiation within the framework of the traditional federal merit system. Thus it removes, or at least reduces, one obstacle to negotiating with employee organizations.

-- It confirms the view, expressed by the President's Task Force-- out of which the new program grew--that a civil service merit system does not in itself solve all personnel problems.

Many factors will determine the extent to which the new federal program will influence, speed up, or alter similar activities in local governments. In any event, other governments now have a model-- they now have a case study to observe.

Views of Personnel Officials

What Contributors Say

First, let's comment briefly on the basic positions expressed by contributors to this monograph. The variations are worth noting.

Charles A. Meyer. In Chapter 6, on the Detroit story, Mr. Meyer states a case for the competitive merit system as a superior method

of dealing with all employees--organized and unorganized. Point-by-
point he gives reasons why he believes industrial-type techniques are
less desirable than those used in Detroit. He emphasizes the importance of protecting the public interest through established features
of representative government, and placing accountability on public
officials after open discussion in which all interested portions of the
public can play a part. He shows what a merit system can do for
employees.

Foster B. Roser. The Philadelphia story, told in Chapter 8, takes
on special significance for two reasons. The Philadelphia experience
has been cited by some public officials and members of employee
unions as a good example of what can be accomplished through collective negotiation that results in an agreement. But, as Mr. Roser puts
it, "every provision of the contract, except one, is contained in the
Civil Service Regulations." He believes the agreement is "largely
an instrument of psychological and prestige value to the union."

Messrs. Sharpe and Freedman. These authors, in Chapter 7,
say municipal bargaining cannot exactly duplicate the industrial
process. They also believe political pressure by unions substitutes
for strikes. The city manager, the council, and the public, they believe, have much to gain "from an orderly bargaining process,"
perhaps even more than labor itself.

Messrs. Heisel and Santa-Emma. In Chapter 9, these authors
cite gains for the City of Cincinnati, despite higher municipal ex-
penditures for increased wages won by unions through collective bargaining. The city now has ground rules to follow. But even more
important than ground rules, they point out, is the increased ability
of the city to demand responsible action from the union. They say
"We believe that management gets the kind of union it deserves."

John W. Macy, Jr. Mr. Macy provides a stage setting in Chapter
16. He notes that only part of private-industry experience applies
unchanged to government. Congress and the Civil Service Commission control basic personnel structure, benefits, and employee rights
which are not subject to bargaining. He stresses that strikes are
prohibited; and, significantly, "Any program of employee recognition
or cooperation must meet and be compatible with the basic principles
of the merit system."

Views of PPA Members

As you might expect, an organization like PPA contains members
with widely divergent views on many aspects of personnel administration. This is natural in an association composed of agency and individual members so widely separated in terms of geography, basic
laws, administrative, social, and political practices.

The range of extreme and middle-ground views appears in such statements coming to the PPA Secretariat as "PPA underrates the most important part of the personnel work; it gives far too little attention to fostering good employee organizations and dealing with ways of making them effective" . . . "I think that this Association should not admit to its Conferences any representatives of employee associations or Unions" . . . "If we're going to invite representatives of employee organizations to our Conferences, let them just listen, but don't put them on panels" . . . "How can we expect to make progress in solving the problems of our employees unless we learn how to work better with employee organizations?" . . . "The Association is to be congratulated for giving such intelligent attention to improving management relations with employees and their organizations."

Regardless of the spread of thinking represented in the quotes above, PPA members are taking positive action in dealing with organized employees. The story appears in Chapter 11, where Mrs. Eleanor Batson tells about a survey of employee-relations practices in larger places. In the Introduction to Part IV, I stress the point that personnel officials are not sitting on the side-lines.

Here I want to emphasize another point. In the main, personnel officials are far less concerned with purely legal aspects of collective negotiation than they are with the practical problem of how to help their governments do a job. As part of the management team they go about that job in a number of ways: through collective negotiation that involves recognition; through two-way consultation with unions and independent associations, without exclusive recognition; through direct dealing with individual, unorganized employees. And here is the significant point: in far more cases than not, whether on an informal or formal basis, public agencies definitely do provide systematic ways to get give-and-take between management and employees in developing and reviewing personnel policy. Furthermore, in a great majority of cases they operate systematic grievance procedures.

Some years ago Professor Sterling Spero asserted that government officials dissipated energy to prove they cannot bargain collectively. He said sound administration would be greatly advanced if half as much energy were devoted to discovering how employees can play a greater role in fixing their working conditions.[1]

I believe great progress has been made in achieving the goal set by Professor Spero. And, remember, he wrote it only fourteen years ago.

---

[1]Sterling D. Spero, Government As Employer (New York: Remsen Press, 1948), p. 348.

Union Views

Union views about collective negotiation were voiced at the 1961 hearings of the President's Task Force on Employee-Management Relations in the Federal Service. Most union leaders agreed on these points: essential features of private and public employment are similar or the same; industrial collective-bargaining practices apply equally well to the public service; union recognition should be definite and clear cut. I believe it is worth noting that presentations to the President's Task Force said very little about how recognition and collective bargaining would improve the quality of service rendered to the public; emphasis was placed almost exclusively on assuring and protecting rights of individual employees.

As a result of my request to union leaders, six responded with their views about the new federal employee-management cooperation program. These views appear in Chapter 17. Here I want to highlight some of their thinking, to reflect concepts and, in some cases, to show rather distinct differences of opinion.

AFL-CIO. Mr. Andrew J. Biemiller speaks for the entire American Federation of Labor and Congress of Industrial Organizations. Like all other union officials he regards the new federal program as a step forward. He struck one distinctive note about those employee organizations that should have the benefit of government protection. They should be restricted, he says, to "those made up in whole or in part of employees of the federal government." He further says they should not "include organizations whose basic purpose is purely social, fraternal, or limited to a special interest objective which is only incidentally related to conditions of employment. Nor should they include any organization sponsored by a department, agency, activity, organization, or facility of the federal government."

National Alliance of Postal Employees. The President of this union, Mr. Ashby G. Smith, opposed exclusive recognition when he appeared before the President's Task Force. He backs up this position with a question: "Do the rights which a union obtains with exclusive recognition compensate it for taking on the responsibility of representing all persons, members and non-members in the unit?"

National Federation of Federal Employees. Speaking for this independent group, President Vaux Owen vigorously opposes the idea of applying industrial bargaining concepts to the federal service. Many of his viewpoints rest on a legal base quite similar to the one expressed by Charles A. Meyer. Mr. Owen writes with much feeling when he predicts the dire results that will flow from "progressive developments of practices associated with collective bargaining in private industry." He questions the proposition that laws against strikes are effective, pointing out that "language doesn't prevent strikes," as illustrated by the recent strike of the New York City teacher's union.

American Federation of Government Employees. In contrast with Mr. Owen's position, Mr. John F. Griner of the AFGE, offers a definition of collective bargaining. He says it means "nothing more than group negotiation over problems of mutual concern." The alternative to collective bargaining of this type, he says, is "unilateral dictation."

American Federation of State, County, and Municipal Employees. Chapter 3 carries a full account of this union's views in the words of its President, Mr. Arnold S. Zander. His statement speaks for itself, but I want to call your attention to his views about strikes. He says this basic weapon in the private field is "the most questioned and the most controversial device in labor relations in public employment. We oppose strikes; they should not be necessary. To outlaw strikes will not eliminate them; bona fide negotiations will." He further declares prohibition of strikes in the public service denies a fundamental and inherent right. Then he sounds this note: "Certainly it is unfair for government to require its employees to surrender the economic weapons of others unless impartial machinery is provided for settlement of employee grievances and for improving labor standards" (emphasis added).

So, we glimpse the viewpoints held by several leaders of employee organizations. Their in-depth ideas, as well as those of other labor leaders, appear in these essays.

From Theory to Action

Theory -- when expressed forcefully and pressed ardently -- often leads to a program of action. But espousal of theory, and pronouncements of policy, can also sharpen a conflict of views and stay action.

These generalizations apply to what's happening over the country in the changing scene of collective-negotiation activities of public employee organizations. Theories find expression as policy statements; some impede enactment of basic legislation while others provide the groundwork for action programs sanctioned by law. Let me illustrate what is happening.

Michigan. In this state the Michigan Municipal League spoke for local governments when it issued a policy statement on employer-employee relations in cities. The basic concepts expressed by Mr. Charles A. Meyer in Chapter 6 are voiced in the League views. The policy statement opposes curtailment of home rule powers of cities. It speaks against removal from municipal officials "to some state board, independent arbitrator or other outside authority" of the responsibility to settle disputes with municipal employees on the local level.

Wisconsin. A state long known for liberal practices in private labor relations breaks new ground in establishing the Employee Relations Board of Wisconsin. Here the practice departs from the policies announced as guidelines for Michigan cities. The Wisconsin experience appears in Chapter 10, by Arvid Anderson; its significance rests in part on the fact that it describes practices followed in a state agency that administers aspects of a municipal labor-relations program.

California. Active efforts in California to get legal sanction for collective bargaining in state and local governments have failed. The independent California State Employees' Association vigorously opposes collective bargaining. At the present time, a policy of employee-management cooperation prevails in California. This policy, set forth in full in Chapter 12, assures consultation and negotiation with employee groups in the broad sense, but does not provide for collective bargaining.

Washington. In the state of Washington, controversy exists. It involves points of law about "collective negotiation" and carries overtones of conflict between two state employee organizations. Briefly, here are the facts.

A new state personnel program was established in 1961 by adoption of an initiated measure. The Washington Federation of State Employees worked hard to get popular support for the proposal. Within less than a year after its adoption, the independent Washington State Employees' Association supported an employee who contested the law and rules proposed to make the law effective.

The law empowers the State Personnel Board to "adopt and promulgate rules and regulations. . . regarding the basis for and the procedures to be followed for. . . : agreements between agencies and employee organizations providing for grievance procedures and collective negotiation, personnel matters, including wages, hours, and working conditions, which may be peculiar to an agency. . . ." During the summer of 1962, James E. Donaldson brought suit against the State Personnel Board. The brief of Donaldson's attorney stated:

> . . . that the State Personnel Board has no statutory authority to make any substantive grant of power to any state agency of the legislative authority to enter into any contract providing for recognition of an exclusive bargaining agency, payroll deductions, etc., that were purportedly enacted in Article XX (of the State Personnel Board's Rules). . . the rule itself contains provisions such as a wage check-off and recognition of exclusive bargaining agents which are clearly contrary to the Constitution . . . .

In early October, 1962, the Superior Court set aside a temporary injunction and threw out the case. In essence, the grounds were: up to that time none of the plaintiff's legal rights had been infringed. Until the provisions of the State Personnel Board's Rules became effective, until actual collective bargaining and a dues check-off exist, Donaldson has no case.

I do not know whether this case can or will be appealed. Regardless, it clearly illustrates how employee groups disagree among themselves.

Massachusetts. Questions about collective bargaining in cities and towns arose recently in Massachusetts. A law passed in 1960 (General Laws, Chapter 40, S. 4-C) permitted cities and towns "to accept" collective bargaining. It said that a city or town may (emphasis added) engage in collective bargaining with labor organizations representing its employees, except police officers, and may (emphasis added) enter into collective-bargaining agreements.

Provisions of the law become effective in cities with a Plan D or E charter by majority vote of all members of the city council; in other cities by vote of the city council, subject to the provisions of the city charter; in towns by majority vote at an annual town meeting. The law remains silent on strikes, determination of representation and a closed shop. Efforts failed in 1961 to amend the law and clarify the matters on which it was silent.

The Massachusetts law was supported by labor. It was opposed by the Massachusetts Federation of Taxpayers and the Massachusetts Municipal Personnel Boards Association. Grounds of opposition were: that since it was "an acceptance law," upon acceptance it might supersede provisions of existing civil service laws, and all matters covered in them would have to be handled through collective bargaining. Opponents also contended the law would take important powers from city and town legislative bodies.

According to most recent information, not much headway has been made in extending collective bargaining to Massachusetts cities and towns. In late 1961, the Massachusetts Municipal Personnel Boards Association surveyed the 39 cities of the Commonwealth and the 62 towns that are association members. Only five out of 26 cities reporting had given any consideration to the statute. Of these, three had accepted General Laws, C. 40, S. 4-C; one had granted petitioners "leave to withdraw the proposal," and in one city the matter was still unsettled. Only one of the 43 towns reporting had even considered acceptance of the new law, and in that case the proposition was killed.

It seems to me that the developments just discussed broaden the spectrum of subjects dealt with in this monograph. Taken in composite, these considerations lift the whole business out of the academic and place it squarely in the practical realm.

The Labor Movement at the Crossroads?

Another phase of the climate for cooperation between management and organized employees involves the status of the labor movement in the United States. Does it sound absurd to say the labor movement in fact shows signs of slipping? If a non-labor man suggested the movement is wasting away, his motives might be questioned. But Solomon Barkin, a labor analyst and advocate, says exactly that in a 1961 monograph entitled The Decline of the Labor Movement.[2]

How do you measure "decline"? One practical criterion might be to determine whether the labor union movement maintains its relative standing in the economic and political order of the country. This idea comes from a statement by Clark Kerr, President, University of California, in his Foreword to Barkin's provocative study. Mr. Kerr says the labor movement "does face a 'crisis,' or, perhaps better, a series of 'crises.' "

I cannot give a fair summary of Barkin's thesis in a few sentences; for that you must consult his full statement. In it, supporters and detractors of unionism will find fodder for their ideological mills; and this may speak well for the impression of objectivity he gives. But a few isolated points in Barkin's account are germane.

Reasons for Decline

In sum, Barkin believes labor is on the decline because of factors and events outside the labor movement as well as within. He believes, however, unionism is essential to a dynamic, democratic society; and he presents a five-point program for its revival.

To all persons interested in the future of public employee organizations, Barkin's case deserves thoughtful reflection. Note the factors outside the labor movement that Barkin says contribute to its decline: shrinkage of employment in organized industries, both relatively and in actual numbers; movement of industry to parts of the country traditionally unfriendly to labor; unwillingness of employers to accept "unions and collective bargaining as an integral part of the industrial system"; management insulation of employees against union influence; increased use of anti-union techniques in unorganized plants; curtailment of free speech of union members by amendment of the Taft-Hartley Act; right-to-work laws in 19 states that bar union shops and prohibit union membership as a requirement

---

[2]Solomon Barkin, The Decline of the Labor Movement and What Can Be Done About It (Santa Barbara, Calif.: Center for the Study of Democratic Institutions, 1961).

for employment; improvement of social and economic conditions; the
sullied image of unions and some of their leaders; failure to tap
workers in textile industries, on farms, and in government because
of the attitude of their respective employers.

Unions themselves, Barkin believes, share responsibility for the
decline of the labor movement. Chief reasons are the failure of
national headquarters to provide adequate funds and manpower to
promote membership, apathy among local members toward recruitment of new blood, outmoded organizing techniques suited to a by-
gone day, inter-union rivalry--reckless attacks of one against another, unwarranted and undignified charges among unions.

Future of Organized Labor Outside and Within
the Public Service

What, if any, relationship exists between the labor movement
outside and within the public service? How does organized labor in
the private sphere affect the future of public employee organizations?
How do stepped-up activities of organized employees potentially affect the public service? How will the merit system be affected if
employee organizations become more active and influential than now?
What policy issues need to be settled to protect the public interest in
the event employee organizations gain wider formal recognition?

Some of the answers to these questions may be implicit in statements of the contributors. But I doubt that you can find them spelled
out in one-two-three fashion. Nor will I attempt to answer them.
But let me state three propositions and raise three other questions,
all of which I believe are urgent.

Proposition: Unions and associations in government, like their
industrial counterparts, achieve their goals through "politics"--a
legitimate use of the political power.
Question: If true, what controls, if any, should be applied to the
activities of public employees who engage in political efforts through
organizations that represent them? Should the organizations be regulated? How?

Proposition: Merit systems seek to take public employment out
of politics and put selection and tenure on a basis of demonstrated
competence.
Question: If true, will political activities of organized employees,
unless carefully controlled, defeat the purpose and principles of the
merit system?

Proposition: Public employee organizations, particularly where
no merit system exists, stand for and seek many objectives common
to merit systems: redress of grievances, better working conditions,
pensions, insurance and hospitalization, position classification,

opportunity for personal development and training, tenure, uniform and equitable arrangements for sick and vacation leave, adequate salaries, hours of work comparable to private industry.

Question: If true, should management deal with these matters through collective negotiation or try to install a merit system?

Enough of propositions and questions. But it takes good propositions and good questions to give durable answers. The questions raised here serve only to suggest many other critical ones that must be considered by management and employee organizations as they forge their working relations in the public interest.

Unions and Employee Associations

Up to this point I've given the impression that unions and employee associations are the same kind of organization. This could be misleading.

Unions are affiliated, national, craft, industrial. Associations are independent, local (state, and/or county, and/or municipal), and across-the-board. But the differences go deeper. Barkin characterizes them like this:

> Civil service employee associations have scorned unionism. Dominated by supervisors or employees allied with them, or even by politicians, they rely upon lobbying and representation techniques, and upon the grievance procedures prescribed by governments, rather than genuine bargaining. The supervisors. . . are interested in raising standards and protecting the individual employees. In some cases, including teachers and policemen, the opposition emphasizes the professional character of the employment which, it is argued, would be downgraded by union organization. Numerous "employee associations" have built up insurance or benefit programs and valuable educational facilities to attract a greater following.[3]

Administrators and Employee Organizations

Frankly I've found little objective evidence that the attitudes of administrative officials are cast in one mold. It would almost appear from Barkin's statement, quoted above, that administrators and civil service employee associations are bedfellows. But, he says, the attitude of administrators toward unions differs from their attitude toward associations:

---

[3]Barkin, op. cit., p. 34.

> . . . the administrators continue to resist unioniza-
> tion and conspire with other anti-union groups to dis-
> courage its appearance. . . . Even in communities where
> the principle of collective bargaining has been accepted
> for public employees, administrators of individual de-
> partments and agencies invariably seek loopholes to avoid
> putting the principle into practice. Administrators at all
> levels of government are improving personnel and griev-
> ance practices, hoping thereby to forestall unionization.[4]

Barkin offers a solution; simple to state but harder to get. Just
persuade "administrators to accept the right of workers to join unions,
either through conversion, public and political pressure, or forceful
action by employees."[5]

I have drawn heavily here on Solomon Barkin's monograph. His
views give ballast and balance to some of the irresponsible comments
about how public officials over the country "sell out" to employee
organizations. Also, Barkin's testimony is provocative to all con-
cerned--officials, unions, and employee associations.

Responsibility of Public Officials

At the beginning I said all public officials share some responsibility in dealing with management's relations with public employees.
How widely they share this responsibility becomes more and more
evident as you read these essays. Here are just a few what's and why's
of official responsibility.

-- Legislators (at all levels of government) need to know the
   issues involved, both to fix public policy in law and to estimate the impact of their acts.

-- Administrators need to advise legislators about what will
   work and what may fail.

-- Legislators and administrators need to look on themselves as
   only one side of the triangle of management-employee relations; the other two are employees (organized and unorganized)
   and the public.

-- Career civil servants need to know what they can and should
   do to improve effectiveness of government.

The advice of one public official to his colleagues runs like this:
"If you're considering a new policy or revising an old one, don't make

---

[4]Barkin, op. cit., p. 35.
[5]Ibid., pp. 35-36.

a move until you talk it over with the employees themselves." This can be done whether employees are organized or not; some believe it's easier to deal with employee organizations.

A Final Word About Climate

In this essay I have dealt with some of the attitudes and concepts that make up the climate of management cooperation with organized employees. It is not now a stable climate. But the essays that follow argue convincingly that there is an intellectual climate of management-employee relations in the making. They suggest, moreover, that management and organized employees--if they want to share an intellectual climate in which more attitudes and concepts are jointly held--may well consider acceptance of three basic tenets:

1. Each group -- management and organized employees -- should first systematize its own ideas about what in reality are its pervading attitudes and concepts about collective negotiation--- about the precise role of each in dealing with the other.

2. Neither employer nor employee group alone determines the climate of management-worker relations. It is a joint affair. Otherwise the climate is turbulent, never calm.

3. Changes in climate come with a fresh breeze; so a change for better management-worker climate comes when fresh ideas are permitted to displace old, stale ones.

4. There may be no "perfect" climate, but joint management-employee organization action may bring a "better" climate.

There you have the setting. Finally, as you read these essays may I suggest a point of view. As you look again at the issues, firmly held positions, sharply different opinions, contested facts, and near-imponderable questions, note how often attitude emerges paramount. And may I also suggest that attitudes toward ideas and toward people, when more tentative and less dogmatic, may create a climate for cooperation which will speed progress and gain more durable relations between management and organized employees.

Albert Camus once wrote some words that epitomize my own views on this subject:

To feel absolutely right is the beginning of the end.

PART II
The Role of Management-Employee Relations: Four Points of View

<hr>

Introduction

In Part II, each of the four authors views the public service from a different background. Louis J. Kroeger is an officer of a management consulting firm that serves governments in all phases of administration. Eli Rock, formerly a labor relations consultant in a large eastern city--Philadelphia--now serves as a professional labor arbitrator. Arnold S. Zander is International President of the American Federation of State, County, and Municipal Employees--the largest union in the local government field. Rollin B. Posey, a professionally trained political scientist who specialized in employee relations in the public service, is now Editor of the College Department of Harper & Row, Publishers.

These men hold two things in common. In one way or another each has worked to improve the U.S. public service. Each believes that organized employees have a legitimate role to play.

Their opinions differ about how much unions should participate in decision making and the best rules for management cooperation with organized employees. Thus one man believes that negotiation can, and should, include wages and accompanying fringe benefits. Another believes that matters affecting taxation cannot be delegated to public executives and union representatives; nor should unions bargain directly with the legislature. One man believes that exclusive representation is desirable to secure a continuous management-worker relation and to assure joint consideration of problems. Another thinks that, because government employees perform so many different jobs, multiple representation is justified.

The Kroeger and Zander articles deal primarily, but not exclusively, with theoretical questions, legal difficulties, problems of satisfying conflicting interests not only between management and employees but also between different types of employees. Messrs. Rock and Posey offer practical advice to union and management officials to improve both their formal and informal relations.

These articles provide background for an evaluation of the six different approaches to management relations with organized employees in municipal government and the new federal management-cooperation program described later.

K.O.W.

Chapter 2

What Management Needs To Know About Approaches to Collective Negotiation

LOUIS J. KROEGER

Public management approaches collective bargaining like a young man approaches fatherhood -- in an attitude of joy mixed with misgiving, regarding his experience as unique, not realizing that despite the pacing and fretting, nature will take its deliberate course.

To the extent that public management has prepared for this ordeal (negotiation--not fatherhood), it has tended to follow the precedents of private enterprise, has been bewildered by their variety, and has sometimes followed the wrong examples.

Public management's approach to across-the-table personnel relations has often been fearful. It has had something of the resigned atmosphere of preparing token defenses against an invasion that everyone is convinced will succeed, with all the dire consequences of surrender to follow.

A Grip on the Facts

Let's shed those attitudes. Let's erase the apprehension. Let's relax and open our minds to a fair and objective examination of where we are and where we are going in personnel relations in the public service. In doing this, we can keep an eye on the record of collective bargaining in the private sector, not to copy what has been done there --for much of it has been wrong--but to benefit from whatever lessons are to be learned.

Public management, by its nature, must be sensitive and responsive to social and economic forces about it. In part, government shapes those forces; but in far greater part, it is their creature.

It should be clear by now that collective bargaining has become

Adapted from an address before the Public Personnel Association's 1961 International Conference on Public Personnel Administration, Denver, Colorado.

Louis J. Kroeger is Executive Vice President of Griffenhagen-Kroeger, Incorporated, management consultants, San Francisco, California.

a widely accepted practice, as a result of the growing strength of the organized work forces in our economy. I am well aware of the foul tactics and unbending attitudes of some managements and some unions at the bargaining table; and equally aware of the general attitudes in some places where hostility toward organized labor still exists.

Notwithstanding the exceptions, we cannot escape the generalized observation that as a part of the social and economic development of the last quarter century, collective bargaining has established itself as a force to be reckoned with.

It's Later Than You Think!

Collective bargaining has been slow to reach the public service for several reasons:

1. Because of concepts of sovereignty which raise the question of whether "we the people" can stoop to bargain;

2. The public service has not been considered a fair target for the most potent weapon in labor's arsenal--the strike;

3. Civil service laws have often been so paternalistic and public personnel administration often so protective that there has been little left on which organizers can base their appeal to public employees; and

4. Up to now organized labor has had bigger and richer fields to conquer, so has regarded the public service as one of the pockets of resistance to be taken care of in the mop-up relations after the main campaign has succeeded.

Let us re-examine these conditioners of our attitudes and practices in the clear light of the times.

Starting from the fourth reason given above, if labor has concentrated on more promising fields first, it has been making steady progress in them. Hence, we can expect that greater attention will soon be focused on the public service. We are running out of time in which to prepare a position. I assume that is why the subject has become of such vital interest to us at this time.

Intent of Present Laws

It is true that civil service laws have been paternalistic and personnel administration has often been protective. It is not true, however, that these laws say all that needs to be said about terms and conditions in public employment.

They neither prohibit nor pretend to substitute for the benefits of give-and-take bargaining. Nor do they necessarily provide the kinds of protections to both employee and employer that might be assured by a bargained agreement.

I think it wrong, in fact, to argue that the protective features of our civil service laws are meant to protect the employees in ways substituting for devices commonly found in industrial relations. Instead, the protective measures are intended to save the public from the consequences of poor selection or of political manipulation. The employees are only the incidental beneficiaries.

Strike Myths

The argument that strikes cannot be directed against the public reflects confused thinking on at least two counts.

First, we need not assume that the strike is an inherent part of labor relations. It is often an effective last resort. Some unions resort to it freely; but in some industries, labor relations have been based on enlightened understanding, with scarce use of this extreme measure.

Second, we are wrong in reasoning that strikes against government may not be permitted because the government represents the public and the public is not to be struck against. When the public tolerates strikes in industry which tie up transportation and communication or other operations vital to whole communities, it concedes that the strike can be used against the public.

Sovereignty Makes the Difference

The nature of sovereignty affects the limits of collective negotiation in the public service. It does not preclude it. In a democracy, the sovereign power is in all the people. It is exercised in their behalf by duly constituted governments -- national, state, and local.

In a democracy, the sovereign cannot abdicate. In a democracy, the sovereign people may delegate to their agents the duty to represent and act for them with wide discretion in specified fields, but the essence of sovereignty remains with the people.

We cannot substitute government by contract for government by law. That still leaves room for negotiation and agreement on a host of details that do not reach the sovereign functions of government.

Granting that sovereignty is the basic difference between the character of government and that of private industry, we should seek solutions to problems of labor relations in the public service within the limits of that difference rather than use the difference as an excuse for doing nothing.

We have a choice between arguing the fine points of rights and obligations based on constitutional theory, or using common sense in terms of the times in which we live. The right decision is suggested by the mere statement of the choice.

Seven Important Elements

"Collective negotiation," like many another phrase, has many meanings and it embraces many parts. It would help public management determine its approach if we consider its parts separately.

Included in what we are talking about are seven elements. They ought to be considered separately because the whole subject can be better understood by understanding its elements, and because public practice cannot parallel private practice in the same degree on each point.

The seven are: organization; affiliation; recognition; representation; negotiation; agreement; and sanction.

Organization

There should be no doubt about the right of the public employee to organize. If any number of people want to form an organization for any purpose of common interests, short of overthrowing the government, it is their clear and unmistakable right of citizenship not to be impaired because they happen to be on the public payroll.

Affiliation

The natural extension of the right to organize is the right to affiliate with other organizations of like purpose. Just as the individual is entitled to decide whether or not to belong to an organization, and which organization it should be, so do organizations of such individuals have the right to determine whether they will ally with other groups.

Some have been concerned whether organizations of public employees affiliating with others will confine themselves to groups having interests in common with them. It would be a misguided effort if we prevent public employee organizations from affiliating with other groups for fear they might fall into the wrong company.

Individuals or groups whose freedom of choice is respected are sufficiently sobered by that trust and responsibility that they usually make the right choice.

Recognition

When we turn to recognition, the problem gets a little more difficult -- but not much. If employees have the right to form an organization, it logically follows that its existence should be acknowledged. There may be several organizations competing for members and clamoring for recognition.

The question, then, is whether we are to recognize all or some of these organizations, and by what standards; or whether we are going to recognize only a single bargaining body.

I doubt that a single bargaining unit for the employees of a given government will usually be the answer. A government's employees do so many different kinds of work that there may be enough legitimate differences of interests along occupational or departmental lines to cause the employees to want several organizations.

Those in occupations having exact counterparts in industry may want to affiliate with organizations representing both public and private employees. Those having jobs peculiar to government may have other ideas. Why require an unnatural combination of diverse interests where coexistence might serve better?

There may be substantial differences among public employees about what they want to accomplish. It may not be practical to have a single organization try to represent diverse views by advancing both the majority and the minority views. It makes more sense to let those who have common objectives form their own organization and advance their own program.

Some will argue that this confronts government with too big a problem in treating with too many organizations. This will take care of itself. Numerous small and independent organizations are not a potent force. If they form because of initial differences in viewpoint, it will be only a matter of time before they find they must reconcile and unite to gain the strength they need for effective representation. This is the employees' own problem. Management should not intervene.

Representation

This should be no problem. When we concede the right of a group to organize, we must concede its right to have spokesmen. In fact, there are clear advantages to management in dealing with a few articulate spokesmen rather than with individual employees.

Some fear that the chosen representatives will be so busy representing that they won't have time for the job for which they are hired. We ought to be able to deal with any abuse of a privilege by more intelligent means than by denying the privilege.

Moreover, some managements could reduce the time spent in discussions with employee representatives by working toward reconciliation of viewpoints and agreement rather than prolonging the discussion by holding stubbornly to the position they first happened to get stuck with.

Negotiation

When we turn attention to this element, the going gets a bit thicker. We must distinguish between two senses of the word "negotiate." In one sense it means nothing more than to confer and exchange viewpoints in search of mutual understanding. In its other sense, as usually used in labor relations, it goes beyond this and means bargaining to the point of reaching a binding solution.

Agreement

We should be quick to concede that there is no question about the right to confer and argue and reach a common understanding of a course of action to be taken within the limits of existing law and procedures. The harder question is whether, in the public service, we can bargain to the point of binding agreement. The answer is not either yes or no, but rather, both yes and no, depending on what we are negotiating about and who does the negotiating.

The principal subject of negotiation in the industrial field is wages and the accompanying fringe benefits. Labor negotiates these points directly with management, which is authorized to agree in behalf of the owners. In doing so they may create the need to raise prices or reduce profits.

As we know, in government there are no "profits" to be reduced. Increased salaries and other costs, unless offset by such corresponding economies as the reduction of staff, can be met only by increasing "price" -- in this case, taxes.

Under the concept of sovereignty we cannot delegate to negotiations between administrative representatives and the employees the right to increase taxes. Neither is it feasible to have negotiations directly between employees and the legislative bodies, which have the responsibility for levying taxes.

There remains much to be discussed and agreed upon about the terms and conditions of employment. The problem immediately before us -- the subject, if you please, for the first negotiation -- is to agree on those subjects normally within the control of public management, which can be the proper subject for negotiation, while reserving other issues to the discretion of the constituted representatives of the sovereign people.

Sanction

There is little gained in acknowledging the right to organize, to affiliate, to be recognized, to be represented, to negotiate, and to agree if, in the end, the employees are deprived of all means of pressure to support their position against the attitudes and actions of management's representatives.

So we return again to the question of whether the public employee can be permitted to strike. I hope we shall never see the day when a strike will suspend the enforcement of the law, the fighting of fires, the combating of epidemics, the safeguarding of our resources, the care of the mentally incompetent, the incarceration of the evil, the care of the needy, or any of the countless other activities involving care of the public interests that we have entrusted to government.

By the same token, it is unfortunate that strikes in the private sector can so extend a controversy between management and labor as to affect the public by halting transportation or communication, blocking the sale of food, closing hospitals, or by the use of any other means to paralyze our economy or society.

The strike issue is not sharply divided between public and private employment. Governments first engaged in activities which were a direct exercise of their sovereignty. Now they also engage in enterprises.

Private enterprises, in turn, engage in services vital to the welfare of the people, as well as in some that are quite remote from any general public concern. In seeking more satisfactory sanctions for both public and private employment, we should concentrate more on the nature of the service than on who is the employer.

At the Bargaining Table

The purpose of bargaining is to resolve matters about which there are differences. If we could somehow reach inspired, mutually satisfactory agreement about everything, there would be no issues -- hence, no need to bargain. We should hope that all concerned will remember that there are at least two sides to every issue, and there are usually some valid facts or reasoning to support each side.

It requires an understanding mind to approach the bargaining table effectively. It requires from a person the kind of mind that seeks to grasp the other fellow's viewpoint -- not necessarily to be persuaded by it, but to see it in perspective and to weigh it in the balance with his own viewpoint.

Each side of the bargaining table is entitled to full and effective representation. The big remaining questions are: Who in government is to represent management? What is to be the limit of his authority? What are to be the rules of his conduct?

By the nature of government, responsibility for representing management has to be divided. Every government has a legislative body elected by the people to express its will. They make policy after balancing principle with the practical realities.

Each has an elected chief executive or professional administrator, or both. They are advisers to the legislative body on policy and the chief implementers of what it decides. They can and should stand closer to principle, letting the legislative body do the necessary compromising of principle with reality, and administering the compromise impartially.

Role of Personnel Administrators

In the immediate field of collective negotiation a major part has to be played by the personnel administrators. This group needs to clarify its own thinking about its role. Some regard themselves as representing management, some as representing employees, and some as representing a sort of public conscience and morality, the exact nature of which depends on their own definition and interpretation.

There must be no doubt that the public personnel administrators represent management. They must work with and for the public policy as declared by the legislative and the executive and administrative arms of government.

Boundaries of Authority

The limits of authority are pretty well defined by what has already been said. The legislative body sets policy subject to the limits imposed by the nature of sovereignty, subject to the general attitudes of the people it represents, and subject to the more specific limitations imposed by constitutions, charters, or other organic law.

The chief executive or administrator or personnel director designated to represent management should have his authority defined by the policy-making body. If management's approach to the bargaining table is to be effective, that authority must be broad enough to permit some latitude in reaching agreement on negotiable points.

It will have to stop short of final decision on matters which will affect service to the public or add to the cost for altering the levels of service or the appropriation of money, with its implied effect on the levying, if taxes must remain with the legislative body.

Within these somewhat clumsy limits, however, the legislative body and its executive and administrative agents can have an understanding of a workable plan of representation in negotiation.

Right Attitude Important

The rules of conduct are suggested by what has been said about attitude. Representatives of public management should approach the bargaining table with an open mind and a relaxed attitude.

They are to represent the best interests of the public as an employer. They are to offer the terms and conditions of employment that the legislative and executive bodies believe just. They are to hear the requests of the employees. They are to explain their own position clearly and listen patiently and understand fully the points of the employees. They are to seek to reconcile the views as far as possible.

On points where they are persuaded that the original public position was wrong, they may make concessions or return with recommendations to the legislative body, depending on the nature of the points. At the conclusion of the negotiation they may make a binding agreement or make a tentative agreement, subject to approval of the legislative body, again depending on the nature of the points involved.

Need Not Threaten Merit Principle

There were some weasel words in what I just said about "negotiable matters." What are these? To what extent do they imply substituting negotiation for personnel programs prescribed by law and rule?

The law will need to remain to create the personnel agency and define the personnel program. The principle of merit should continue to rule. Competition to determine merit need not be abandoned.

All I am saying is that many details of working conditions should be subject to discussion and agreement, and the machinery should be created to adjust the grievances that arise in any work situation. Collective negotiation need not be considered a substitute for merit systems. It should be regarded, instead, as a useful supplement to them.

To the extent we can transfer some subject from law to agreement we can gain a desirable flexibility. Agreements can be rewritten more easily than laws can be amended.

The Opportunity Knocks

In short, public management's approach to the bargaining table should recognize that the civil servant is an economic being, entitled to the same considerations as his colleague in industry.

Here is an opportunity to work out concepts and practices of labor relations which may be a model for industry to follow. In industrial relations we tend to think of issues in terms of capital or management versus labor. In government the shareholders are all the people, including many who, in their private capacity, are part of labor.

This circumstance itself may help create an atmosphere in which governmental employee relations can be founded on cooperation toward common objectives, rather than controversy and conflict.

Chapter 3

A Union View of Collective Bargaining
in the Public Service

ARNOLD S. ZANDER

Why does the union in the public service want collective bargaining? The union wants collective bargaining because it is concerned with the general welfare of the public employee, raising
wage levels in public employment, improving working conditions,
and providing job security, and because it is equally concerned with
improving the public service. The one is dependent on the other.
The union wants to represent and bargain for all employees in the
unit involved in order to secure a continuous relationship and joint
consideration of problems arising out of the bargaining contract.
It wants more than meetings prior to the adoption of the annual
budget; it wants consideration of day-to-day problems. The union
wants collective bargaining to help do away with the spoils system,
to correct the lag between the economic position of the public employee and that of the industrial worker.

Collective bargaining is the mutual participation by management and labor in the determination of the terms of employment and
of the obligations and responsibilities of both management and the
union. It is accomplished through negotiations in conferences between representatives of the employer and representatives of the
employees, and it terminates in a collective bargaining agreement
between the parties. It is a continuing process of bilateral accom-
modation on the part of labor and management. Collective bargaining is concerned not only with the economic status of the
employee but also with the protection and extension of his rights
and freedom. Constructive collective bargaining is based on

Reprinted from Public Administration Review, Winter, 1962, by
permission of the American Society for Public Administration.

Arnold S. Zander is International President of the American
Federation of State, County, and Municipal Employees, AFL-CIO,
Washington, D. C.

peaceful negotiations, mutual understanding, and agreement. Constructive collective bargaining tends to reconcile the respective interests of management and the union. Without this relationship, there may result tension, quarrels, and bitter conflict between the parties, with their ultimate effect on the public.

Traditionally, public employee unions in the United States have not attempted the same collective bargaining procedures and techniques as have developed and continue to be developed in the nongovernmental areas. They reacted to bad conditions with public appeals and if pressed hard they walked out in disorganized strikes, for which they were later sorry; they wrote letters to newspapers, they met privately with those presuming political influence. They worked for the enactment of legislation regulating their conditions of employment. They exercised in a very elementary way the right of assembly and petition. They were ineffective and they did not prosper.

The American Federation of State, County and Municipal Employees started out in the tradition of other public employee unions. Today, it is the dominant union in the state and local government field with 220,000 members in forty-eight of the fifty states, the Commonwealth of Puerto Rico, and the Canal Zone. Its success is clearly the result of not having accepted the traditional forms of relationships between the sovereign government and its employees. It decided to discard the traditional techniques and through organization, the development of political effectiveness, and the development of new tools to bring collective bargaining to the public service. It found early that statutory regulation of conditions of employment was inadequate in the complex operation of government. AFSCME advocates the merit system at all levels of government, and the promotion of civil service legislation and career service in government is one of the objectives stated in its constitution. But civil service laws and rules were found to be too broad to care for the day-to-day problems of employees. Even a good civil service system must be policed through the collective bargaining process.

Collective bargaining and the civil service merit system are complementary. A growing number of civil service jurisdictions have found it expedient to enter into collective bargaining agreements covering their employees because they have discovered that the medium of the agreement is increasingly valuable in dealing with questions within the general framework of civil service law and rules. Many points of conflict and misunderstanding arise in the day-to-day relations of employees with their supervisors. These problems are much more satisfactorily handled at the departmental level through a procedure involving the employee union than through formal civil service appeal. Public officials are well aware that a more or less detached central personnel agency is much less apt to secure a satisfactory settlement of an employee's grievance than is a system which gets to the problem at its very inception and gives the employee assurance of representation from the outset. Even in those instances where the grievance comes to the civil service board, the employee needs the assurance of union representation.

Collective bargaining holds other advantages for the public employer. The union serves as a channel of communication. When conditions of work have been determined through collective bargaining, the union feels a responsibility for enforcement of the regulations which have been agreed upon. Employee morale is higher and efficiency greater if employees have had a voice in formulating policy. Improved standards and higher productivity brought about by employee participation result in economic gains not only for the employee but for the employer. Collective bargaining is a time-saving device for employers because it eliminates the process of never-ending individual bargaining. It insures a stable relationship between the employer and employees and it helps promote an orderly administration of government affairs. Collective bargaining when practiced in good faith has tended to reduce conflict and strife and has brought harmony in place of disorder. Collective bargaining is a vital and essential part of a healthy and democratic employer-employee relationship. The process of collective bargaining in the public service gives to the public employee social status and a sense of dignity essential for sound human relations. Moreover, employers by bargaining in good faith with the leadership and membership of democratic unions strengthen the mature and responsible leadership of the union and encourage the better employees to seek leadership positions, thus helping to insure the continued success of a responsible collective bargaining relationship.

The Instruments of Collective Bargaining

Most of the union devices used successfully in private employment can and are being projected into the public service. Despite the fact that the National Labor Relations Act exempts from its provisions federal, state, and local government employees, and despite the fact that no state or municipal government has yet adopted for public employees a thorough comprehensive code of labor relations, there has been increased legislative activity in the last few years in this area and a growing favorable climate is found in opinions of attorneys general and municipal attorneys throughout the country.

Union Recognition

The right of public employees to organize is a generally accepted principle in the public service. Formal union recognition,
which is guaranteed employees in industry by the National Labor
Relations Act, is gaining increasingly greater acceptance in the
public employment field by law, by contract, by administrative or
executive order, and by court decision. While AFSCME takes the
stand that public employees have the right to organize and bargain
collectively through unions of their choice in all areas, the position
is, of course, strengthened by favorable legislation. Its goal is a
well-drawn comprehensive code of labor relations governing public
employees in each of the fifty states.

Dues Check-Off

Another union device which is used in industry has now become
fairly widespread in state and local government, namely the check-
off of union dues. Presently, there are thirty-eight states and the
Commonwealth of Puerto Rico where the check-off for state or local
government employees has been authorized either by legislation or
administrative arrangement. More than 80 per cent of AFSCME
membership pays dues by the check-off method.

Exclusive Representation

In industry, exclusive representation by the union of all employees in a bargaining unit in negotiations on wages, hours, and
working conditions is almost universal. While most public officials
appreciate the practical advantage of exclusive representation by a
majority union in achieving orderly relationships with their employees, many are hesitant to grant this full recognition to the union.
However, exclusive representation elections are part of the New York
City labor relations program covering city employees and are authorized by statute in Minnesota for the state and local governments; exclusive bargaining rights are granted AFSCME unions by collective
bargaining agreement in 214 state, county, and city jurisdictions.

Grievance Procedure

The formal grievance procedure which is given great emphasis
by unions in industrial employment is also found in an increasing
number of public jurisdictions. The employer-employee relationship, whether in public or private employment, inevitably gives rise
to disagreements which produce grievances. Civil service regulations, although they are important to such matters as appointment,
classification, promotion, and discharge, are not so comprehensive

that they dispel all causes for employee complaints. Grievance procedure in the public service is frequently inadequate because it is often part of the civil service mechanism which does not lend itself to quick, practical settlement of day-by-day irritations and complaints. Public employees need representation by their union at every stage of the grievance procedure and if it becomes necessary, final settlement of their grievances by outside neutrals. When part of the collective bargaining process, the grievance procedure is jointly determined by the union and the public employer and then issued as an administrative regulation by the employer or it may be part of a formal signed working agreement between the employer and the union. A multi-step grievance procedure, setting forth various steps for the orderly settlement of grievances of the employee, is found in 351 agreements negotiated by AFSCME locals.

Mediation

Mediation, or third party intervention in disputes in an effort to secure voluntary agreement of the parties, while common in industry is found to a lesser extent in the state and local government field. Several of the states have by legislation made available to public employers and public employees the facilities and services of their state labor mediation and conciliation departments. In Wisconsin, New York, Connecticut, and Massachusetts, there has been some use, on a voluntary basis, of state labor relations facilities despite the lack of specific statutory authorization for such use.

Arbitration

Arbitration, the terminal step in the grievance procedure, by which an unresolved dispute or grievance is submitted to a third disinterested party for final settlement, is used commonly in industry. Despite the general feeling in government that arbitration is an improper compromise of the government's sovereign position, arbitration of grievances has achieved some acceptance. AFSCME unions have collective bargaining agreements with 159 jurisdictions which provide for binding arbitration as the final step in the grievance procedure. Arbitration awards have been made under these agreements in a number of instances.

Union Shop

The union shop, whereby the employer agrees to keep only union employees on the payroll but may hire non-union persons provided they join the union within a designated period of time, usually thirty days, is fairly widespread in industry, except of course in the states with so-called "right-to-work" laws. The union shop is making some

headway in public service with eighty-eight contracts negotiated by
AFSCME locals containing this strongest form of union security
provision.

Negotiation

Negotiation between the union and management on wages, working conditions, and grievances is practiced to varying degrees in
public employment. The ultimate objective, collective bargaining,
has been negotiated by AFSCME unions in well over 400 state,
county, and municipal jurisdictions.

Strike

The strike, the basic union weapon in union negotiations in private employment, is the most questioned and the most controversial
device in labor relations in public employment. We oppose strikes;
they should not be necessary. To outlaw strikes will not eliminate
them; bona fide negotiations will. Government is expanding and
government functions are mushrooming; the line of demarcation between government and private enterprise is becoming more shadowy.
Many services are performed interchangeably by public employees
and by employees in private industry, and there is no logic in depriv-
ing such an employee of his right to strike simply because he is employed by a governmental unit. We recognize that in certain services
restrictions may be necessary; for example, AFSCME charters to
police locals contain a no-strike provision. However, the outright
prohibition of the right to strike by public employees is a denial of
a fundamental and inherent right. Behind almost every strike in
public employment will be found refusal by a shortsighted, irresponsible public official to meet and discuss with organized public employees and their chosen representatives grievances and other matters of concern to both the public employee and the public. Certainly, it is unfair for government to require its employees to surrender
the economic weapons of others unless impartial machinery is provided for settlement of employer grievances and for improving labor
standards.

Meaning of Collective Bargaining Misunderstood

The greatest obstacle to organization and collective bargaining
in public employment is the lack of clarification of the legality of
officials dealing with unions and the failure of the government employer to spell out the right of employees to organize. Except for a
few state and big city governments which are more attuned to
present-day realities and show a more progressive approach to the

problem, the area in large part is a no-man's land. Legislation is
needed which will permit collective negotiations and contracts.
Even in a collective bargaining situation, there is often a lack of
clarification as to which city officials are responsible for conducting negotiations, for example, the legislative and executive branches.

This failure to spell out the rights of the worker in public employment is due to the timeworn and outmoded parochialism of many
public administrators who cling to the theory that government is a
sovereign employer. These administrators fear that the collective
bargaining principle constitutes a delegation of power incompatible
with their concept of sovereign government. At the roots of the attitudes expressed by these public officials is the complete misunderstanding of the meaning and essence of collective bargaining. Collective bargaining does not involve the surrender of sovereignty or
the delegation of authority from the governmental body to the labor
union. The government cannot in good conscience dodge its responsibility to face its problems simply on the grounds that it is the
sovereign and that the assertion of any right by public employees is
the delegation of its sovereignty. If it does so, public employees
are then faced with extensive lobbying to secure piecemeal relief,
litigation before the courts, and living under conditions autocratical-
ly and arbitrarily imposed until they become demoralized and either
leave the service, lose all incentive for efficiency, or strike.

Actually, sovereignty resides in the people who have delegated
its exercise partly to the government. The question is not one of
surrendering sovereignty; the problem does not involve giving up
something which the government has but rather is to create something which we have not had but which we imperatively need in employer-employee relations in government. When the government
employer fails to keep abreast of conditions, some method of handling the situation must be devised. If the people who are the real
source of sovereign power conclude that a new method should be
devised, they are not surrendering anything; rather they are requiring law and order in a field where such law has never existed and
an institution which will guarantee the rights of employees in public
employment.

Obstacles to Collective Bargaining

Here then are two great obstacles to collective bargaining. One,
the refusal of public officials to bargain because to do so would
oblige them to surrender some of their "sovereign" authority and
two, the refusal to bargain because they claim they do not possess
the authority.

A third obstacle is no-strike legislation which has been enacted
in eleven states. We have already discussed the failure of no-strike

laws to solve the problem of strikes, and the use of substitute measures. A fourth obstacle is restriction of political activities on the part of public employees. Another limitation on occasion is that the union must not be affiliated with the labor union movement. In some instances workers have been denied by law the right to organize; in other instances the right to organize has been forbidden to certain occupational groups, e.g., policemen.

Another obstacle is refusal of the public employer to recognize the union as exclusive bargaining representative for employees even where a majority belong to the union. Many public officials refuse to submit unresolved grievances to arbitration or to call in outside neutrals even for the purpose of fact finding or making recommendations. Another difficulty in the way of orderly development of public employee unionism is the existence in almost half our states of the spoils system which spreads fear among the workers and results in high turnover with higher cost and poorer service to the citizens.

A further obstacle to organization and collective bargaining is the presence of company unions sponsored and aided by management. They usually take the form of state, county, and city employee associations. We find in practice that these associations are dominated by supervisors who invariably align themselves with the employer in any showdown over employee demands and grievances.

Still another problem is the psychology of public employees. Fear is still amazingly widespread. Without any guaranteed protection of his right to join a labor union, the employee fears discrimination by the employer. Other obstacles are refusal by the employer to grant the union shop, refusal to grant check-off of union dues, insistence on the right of individual bargaining, all of which undermine the union and deny the union stability and security as a permanent institution with the result that the union is not free to devote enough time to constructive work which will benefit both the employee and the employer. Without these securities, namely, union recognition and a formal contract with security provisions for the union and the employees, the union tends to disintegrate as a benefit is won.

The Mechanics of Collective Bargaining

How do public service unions bargain? The collective bargaining relationship in public service may range all the way from participation in annual budget meetings to full scale collective bargaining on all matters relating to wages, hours, working conditions, and fringe benefits, culminating in a written agreement. Let us look at two areas where labor management relations have been well developed and where public officials have taken an open positive attitude to collective bargaining and have attempted to establish their relations in a pattern approaching that practiced in private industry.

Philadelphia Experience

Philadelphia is probably the outstanding example of such an area. There, a collective bargaining relationship has developed over the years to the point where in 1958 a contract was signed giving AFSCME Council 33, with which are affiliated ten separate locals, exclusive bargaining rights over all non-uniformed city employees. This year approval was given to a modified union shop agreement. This latest agreement establishes three categories of city employees—12,000 who must join the union as a condition of employment (10,500 of these were already members of the union at the time the agreement became effective), 4,800 for whom membership is voluntary, and 1,200 for whom union membership is prohibited.

Now what does all of this mean in Philadelphia? It means that Philadelphia instead of dealing with a multiplicity of unions, as is common in other cities, deals with only one union, AFSCME Council 33. The personnel director is directly in charge of labor relations and has been authorized by the civil service commission to engage in negotiations and to enter into agreements with District Council 33. Each department or other sub-unit of government of Philadelphia is considered a separate bargaining unit. However, these individual units do not bargain directly on major items such as wages, fringes, and general working conditions. In these areas, centralized negotiations are conducted between the city and our union.

The major participants on the city's side of the negotiation table are the personnel director and the labor relations consultant, the finance director, the managing director, who is the city manager, and the mayor's assistant. Prior to negotiations, preliminary meetings are held between the labor relations consultant and the union to clarify issues, to present data relating to the matters to be negotiated, or to explore matters of a detailed nature.

You may ask how the city council and the civil service commission fit into this picture. Neither of the two is directly involved in the bargaining and yet both must give their approval to various items, for example, the budget, and certain provisions in the form of civil service regulations. There is then a liaison activity between the participating city officials on the one hand and the members of the city council and civil service commission on the other.

Negotiations are on a continuing basis and are not limited to annual demands. Some negotiation takes place at the department or local unit level with regard to work rules and practices which are solely in the jurisdiction of the particular department or unit. The labor consultant is an important part of the collective bargaining relationship. His function is to provide advice on labor relations problems and handle grievances and special problems. He is responsible to the personnel director of the civil service commission.

Looking beyond the union security provisions of the agreement
—exclusive representation and the modified union shop—we find the
very important area of employee security and fringe benefits.
There are generous provisions for holiday, vacation, and sick leave
as well as a grievance procedure and job security provisions, but
the most significant employee benefit provided by the contract is
the health and welfare fund. This provision, improved constantly
since its initial adoption, sets up a health and welfare program financed by the city with a $120 a year contribution by the city for
each employee. The contribution covers the cost of ambulatory
service provided by the AFL medical service plan in Philadelphia
as well as health, surgical, and maternity care with some limits.
Hospital benefits are paid for members and dependents at the rate
of $11 per day up to a total of seventy days. Full costs for matern-
ity benefits are paid for members and their wives at the medical
center, with pre- and post-natal care included. If a member pre-
fers another hospital, maternity benefits are paid up to $135.
Surgical and medical benefits and medical services are paid for
members, their wives, and their children up to the age of 19. Retired members receive the entire hospital, surgical, and medical
coverage at a cost of $10.75 per month.

City officials in Philadelphia are happy in their relationship
with the union. They have found that collective bargaining does work
in the public service and they have repeatedly declared the value of
Council 33 as an organization of "strong and responsible leadership,
an excellent medium of communication and interpretation from
management to employee as well as vice versa, and a continual
source of strong support and sympathy for our program of ever-
better government."[1] The pioneering of Philadelphia and our union
in the exclusive bargaining relationship and the modified union shop
was accomplished "in an atmosphere in which the paramount interest of the public and the need for efficient, good government has at
all times been recognized and respected on both sides."[2]

Cincinnati Experience

The collective bargaining relationship which developed over a
period of twenty-two years in Cincinnati emerged from a policy of
tacit recognition of unions to culminate in a union-management
agreement in April 1960. When AFSCME unions were first organized in Cincinnati, recognition by the city was provided only in the
sense that if a business agent appeared he was allowed to talk. The

---

[1]Foster B. Roser, Personnel Director, City of Philadelphia.

[2]Richardson Dilworth, Mayor of Philadelphia.

city council first formally recognized unions in 1951, when the city
council passed a resolution which declared a city wage policy and
defined a system of collective bargaining between the city manager
and employee representatives on all matters pertaining to wages
and working conditions. The 1951 resolution came as a substitute
form of recognition granted after labor unions had requested a formal collective bargaining agreement. The resolution declared it to
be the policy of the city council, through the city manager, to "bargain collectively with city employees, their unions or other authorized representatives on all matters pertaining to wages and working
conditions before determination is made by the city council." The
resolution further defined collective bargaining as "the process
whereby city employees, their unions or other authorized representatives and the city manager and his designated assistants shall
make every effort to reach an agreement on all matters through
negotiation. . . . "

In 1957 the city manager announced a policy approved by the
city council with regard to unions, which went a step further by providing exclusive recognition of a majority union and written record
of results of agreements, subject to approval by city officials or
bodies where necessary. The new contract signed in April 1960,
after a series of meetings between AFSCME and city personnel officials, is evidence of mature, responsible labor relations in the
city of Cincinnati. The significance of the exclusive bargaining
rights clause is that management has agreed that it will make no
change in the present working conditions or recommend any changes
to the city council which would affect the bargaining unit without
negotiating with AFSCME Council 51.

Immediately after the agreement was signed by the union and
the city, the city manager issued a written statement of his policy
with regard to the union, and meetings were set up with supervisors
at every level in each operating agency affected by the agreement
for the purpose of explaining the agreement and the city manager's
policy statement which declared that recognition of the union is city
policy requiring supervision's support. The city manager also emphasized that the concept of management prerogatives included in
the agreement should not be stretched into a basis for refusing to
discuss anything with unions. The city manager, in his statement,
delegated to department heads the responsibility of dealing with
unions on matters affecting their own agencies and named the personnel officer of the city responsible for review and approval of
agency policy with regard to unions. The meetings with supervisors
served to communicate the city's policy. About 500 supervisors
were reached in thirty meetings. Prior to the meetings, supervisors were furnished a copy of the agreement, policy resolution,
and the city manager's policy.

Political Pressure and Publicity Are Important Methods

What is the role of publicity and political pressure in the public employee movement? The labor movement does not lack for publicity, but unfortunately the press seldom finds space to talk about the public services of labor unions. Its treatment of labor affairs often creates conflict in the minds of the readers and a vague fear that labor unions are a threat, to be viewed with alarm. Somehow we must get across to the public that we are not isolated from the community, but that instead we are part of it. We must convince America that we are not a narrow pressure group, but instead a source for the social good and that we are performing a job for the people by community leadership, service, and by helping solve the economic problems of the community. Only by greater public service and by responsible actions made known to the public can unions build a better public image of themselves.

One of the most important channels used by public employee unions to support their programs is political pressure. AFSCME may have a ten-point legislative program in a particular state. A committee of our union meets with the controlling interests in the legislature, in some cases the political party leaders, in other cases, where one party is not dominant, a combination of people. Then we meet with the executive branch, the governor or his representatives, and we develop a program of what is possible, what the political powers will accept, and in some cases what we can do to support legislative bills in which they have an interest. In almost all instances, we have a legislative representative who follows the course of these bills, can speak for us in accepting adjustments and, where hearings are held, make the proper presentations. Often our legislative process starts at the political convention. We attempt to get the party to incorporate in the platform our program as pre-election commitments.

Seldom do public employee unions engage in direct political campaigning. Rather we are concerned with political education consisting mainly of presenting to the membership and to the public the voting record of legislators. Sometimes the union seeks out the views of legislators or candidates for political office toward pending legislation affecting public employees and gives publicity to the answers received.

Generally, we have found that political designations mean little in judging the fairness of public employers toward their employees. Some of our first and some of our best collective bargaining agreements have been negotiated with conservative New England Republicans. Philadelphia's excellent reform administration is Democratic, but so are some of the large city administrations where the spoils

system still operates. Enlightened public officials of both parties
have recognized and bargained with AFSCME as the union chosen by
the employees.

The labor union provides employees with a democratic vehicle
for representation and articulation of their interests, and the union
contract between the labor organization and the employer, covering
the employee's legal rights in his job, his wages, and working conditions, gives him his bill of rights. It is true that collective bargaining is motivated to some extent by failure of many cities,
counties, and states to provide proper pay, classification, and personnel procedures for their employees and by failure by many administrators to take into consideration the needs and desires of
their employees. But a much stronger motivation is the need of the
employee to have a voice in determining the economic conditions
under which he works and to have job security.

The union movement in public employment has grown through
the past twenty-five years to a position of strength, influence, and
responsibility. In its building public employees are contributing
much to the development of citizenship, to the preservation of
democracy, and to social and economic justice for all of the people
of the United States. Unions are a fundamental part of society and
they are a fundamental part of government service, bringing order
and system to what otherwise might well be chaos in the increasingly complex area of labor relations in government.

Chapter 4

Practical Labor Relations in the Public Service

ELI ROCK

The problem of labor relations in the public service can, I think, be attacked from two separate, broad perspectives. The first would deal with problems of <u>law</u> and <u>theory</u> or <u>concept.</u> This approach might be described as the "conceptual" approach.

What are the permissible limits of bargaining in the public service? What should be the essential theory of bargaining in relation to our concepts of government? Is the written contract legal? Or check-off? Or union shop? Or exclusive bargaining? What should be the rules regarding appropriate bargaining units and how should bargaining agents be determined? What are the "weapons" of the union in the public service? What should constitute unfair labor practices?

These and similar questions urgently require treatment and consideration—on a scale considerably more comprehensive, in my opinion, than has yet been attempted.

The second approach, which deals with the problems of <u>method</u> and <u>attitude</u> or <u>behavior</u> in connection with public service labor relations, might be described as that of <u>practice.</u> Recognizing the wide area of uncertainty and confusion which still surrounds the problems of concept in this field, what should be our methods of handling the concrete, day-to-day or year-to-year problems with which those of us who are practitioners in the field are confronted?

From many points of view, I believe, this problem of attitudes and methods, or <u>practice,</u> can rank at least equally in importance with the problems of <u>concept.</u> I doubt that anyone with experience in the field will suggest that even in that distant Valhalla, when problems of concept will have finally been clarified to a point approaching satisfaction, the factor of methods, attitudes and behavior will still not remain as a major determinant of successful labor relations.

Reprinted from <u>Public Personnel Review</u>, journal of the Public Personnel Association, April, 1957.

Eli Rock is a professional labor arbitrator with offices in Philadelphia. When this article was prepared, he was Labor Relations Consultant for the City of Philadelphia.

Conversely, there can be little question that even under the present state of confusion regarding concept, much could be done to smooth our path through a re-examination of our existing day-to-day practices.

In any case, I have chosen to emphasize the problem of <u>practice</u> as distinguished from that of <u>concept</u>, and this may serve to <u>explain</u> the title "Practical Labor Relations in the Public Service." At the same time, I trust it will be recognized that a sharp line between these two areas may not easily be drawn, and that to some extent I may, here and there, find it necessary to cross that line.

Where Are We Today?

I think a fair way to characterize much of the practice of labor relations in the public service today is by the single word "chaotic." While many administrators or union leaders may dispute the applicability of this term to their own situations, and in some cases they may be justified, I remain convinced that for the bulk of our public service labor relations in this country, that label must stick.

To illustrate the point, I have prepared a kind of composite picture of practices and experiences in the public service, with emphasis first on the problems of the administrator and, second, on the problems of the typical union leader. It is possible that some portions of this picture will not be applicable to individual cases, but it is likely that many if not most of the portions of this picture are characteristic of most of the labor relations situations in the United States today.

Problems of the Administrator

Let us start with the problems of the administrators: Those who are trained professionals have usually, of course, received their training and experience in public administration. Up to now, unfortunately, the field has included little or no reference to problems of collective bargaining. Although many administrators have achieved at least a minimum <u>modus operandi</u> with their unions, this very lack of experience together with the lack of available adequate guidance has often resulted in solutions which are, at best, only stop-gap in nature.

Frequently the administrator is forced, by pressure or by circumstances, to make basic labor relations policy decisions without knowledge of alternatives or probable consequences. Without easily available information he is unable to refute successfully union claims or to propose alternatives. Under such circumstances mistakes of policy may be made which, as so many of us know, once done become extremely difficult to undo.

Many an administrator has come to rely on the "prerogatives" of government and his employees' ability to strike as a crutch to avoid seeking solutions to his problems. When he does engage in some form of bargaining, he does so almost completely unversed in the art of bargaining—for example, the art of proper utilization and proper timing of concessions to achieve maximum union acceptability. Although some of us, on the government side, may regard this as a sort of "evil art," the fact is that it is an art in which the union leader may not be unversed. I believe that many of us, perhaps quite unknown to ourselves, are frequently the "victims" of this art in reverse.

The average local administrator also finds himself at a loss to cope with the tendency of his unions to by-pass him in favor of legislative action, either by the local legislative body or by the state legislative body dealing with local problems. This tendency is often reinforced by the administrator's own reluctance to face up to the "hard problems" posed by the unions' collective bargaining demands.

He may find himself at a loss, also, to cope with the lack of understanding of the fundamentals of government personnel administration which characterize some of the newer union leaders, particularly those from nongovernmental unions. In the face of threats by the unions to invoke political pressure, sometimes fancied and sometimes real, the administrator may give too much or may promise more than he can produce.

Where he seeks sincerely to meet his unions on an equal basis and to erect cooperative relationships, the administrator may find himself confronted by the barrier of rival or minority unionism— with the seemingly simple solution of written contracts or exclusive bargaining often denied him under rulings of the city's law officer.

Lastly, the hard-pressed administrator, even if adequately aware of the importance in collective bargaining of patience and an ability to sit long, seemingly wasteful hours, simply cannot, in the face of his other responsibilities, give the task the time it needs.

Problems of the Union Leader

If the lot of the administrator lines up as a somewhat unhappy one, the lot of the union leader in the public service must be regarded as at least equally difficult: The same lack of guidance and lack of experience may handicap the average union leader in the public service. Many of these leaders have risen from the ranks of the service and sometimes have little knowledge of techniques of outside collective bargaining which might be applicable and helpful to their own collective bargaining problems.

Conversely, as mentioned above, where a union of nonpublic employees has organized public employees, the outside union leader may have little or no knowledge of the special problems and requirements of government which make collective bargaining different in the public service.

The average union leader in the public service is, more often than not, a highly frustrated individual. He lacks the right to strike or arbitrate. He is confronted by the often incredibly complex division of authority and shifting of responsibility between the various branches of government. Because of that division of authority, he may find himself involved in annual negotiations which take as much as eight months out of each year, by the time his requests have channeled through each of the various executive and legislative branches of government which may be concerned.

He may frequently be forced to deal, particularly insofar as grievances are concerned, with management representatives who have little knowledge and small compulsion in the direction of compromise as a necessary ingredient of collective bargaining. In the face of these, and other barriers, there is perhaps small wonder that the union leader may be lagging in the development of a sense of responsibility to the other side of the bargaining table.

Because the union leader tends, sometimes by inclination and sometimes because of circumstances, to rely on political activity rather than accepted union activity to advance his cause, he, as well as his members, fall prey to the whole culture of easy pre-election promises or to the risk of retaliation which comes from too close involvement with what may eventually turn out to be the losing side. Yet staying out of politics has its problems, not the least of which is that in an atmosphere of extreme politics, particularly at the local government level, the ward committeeman becomes, in effect, the shop steward of his appointees. Under such circumstances the union leader may encounter resistance and small interest in his organizing efforts.

The union leader may also be faced by employment practices which tend to perpetuate the attraction, particularly to municipal employment, of the politically favored and the inefficient. These not only hinder his organizing drives, but offer serious obstacles to union requests for higher wages and wages which will coincide with those in private employment.

Together with his frustrations, the union leader is often guilty of other practices and omissions which denigrate the collective bargaining process. Regularized grievance handling, in the manner practiced by outside industry, tends to be side-tracked in favor of quick and frequent visits to the "front office"; training of stewards, assuming stewards exist at all, is a need almost ignored.

Playing off one branch of government against another—the legislative against the executive, the state government against local government, and one department against another—are temptations seldom shunned. Widespread use of the press for personal attacks on government administrators, threats of removal from office directed against administrators, appointive as well as elective, who do not see eye to eye with the union position are frequently used weapons.

Lastly, there is the problem of the union taking in supervisors as members, with its implication, in some instances, of divided loyalty and possible favoritism in connection with grievances brought before those supervisors.

The fundamental interest of the public in this entire problem should, of course, be toward the achievement of a dignified and efficient employment relationship in the public service, which at the same time recognizes the legitimate aspirations of the public employee for collective representation, where those aspirations exist. From the public point of view, no less than from the viewpoint of government management or government unions, the existing state of collective bargaining cannot, I submit, be regarded as satisfactory.

If it does nothing else, the often depressing combination of evaded responsibility and broken promises on one side and indiscriminate resort to every shade of pressure on the other cannot help but produce collective bargaining "solutions" which are either hastily contrived, legally improper, or wasteful. The effects on the sought-after "dignity" of the public service and on the attempted professionalization of the service are obvious.

If this picture seems overdrawn, as indeed it will be for some situations, I shall insist again that for many, many situations, substantial and significant portions of the picture are an accurate reproduction of the facts.

Significance of Union Growth

Having painted the picture I have no doubt that I will be expected to point out answers or solutions. In this connection, let me say first what is of course obvious: there are no easy answers. In part this is so because the whole problem is so dependent, almost desperately dependent, on the much-needed answers in the area of concept. Until some of the basic and very difficult questions, such as those at the beginning of this article, are comprehensively examined and clarified, we shall never be able to achieve truly satisfactory labor relations in the public service.

Nevertheless, if I may repeat myself, the matter of practice, or attitudes and method, will not remain as an important factor after the questions of concept have been answered, but it furnishes a most important opportunity for substantially reducing our present difficulties and heartaches, even while the conceptual problems remain unresolved.

Let me also say this about our present sad situation in general: The existing state of affairs cannot, in my opinion, continue much longer. Unions are growing steadily in the public service. Although no accurate or complete set of data is available regarding total union membership, the growth of membership in unions which recruit exclusively in the public service (and these figures are available) supports this conclusion.

Of particular significance are data in the Municipal Year Book for 1938 which showed that of 960 cities reporting, 319 or 32.2% indicated the existence of one or more employee organizations. By 1945, this figure had risen to 57.9%, by 1950 to 66.2% and by 1955 to 70.3%, or 692 cities out of a total of 985 reporting the existence of one or more employee organizations.

What is perhaps even more important, unions are growing increasingly more assertive of what they regard as their legitimate rights. The bill introduced by Congressman Rhodes in the last session of Congress providing for government employee union recognition and arbitration of grievances is but one case in point.

The administrators' argument that "we in the government are different and therefore don't need collective bargaining," while it may still be acceptable in a few areas of the public service, is no longer acceptable in the great majority of the areas of public service—either from the point of view of administrators, union leaders, large numbers of government employees, or from the point of view of many, many legislators, particularly those who, rightly or wrongly, regard union political strength as significant.

According to the Census Bureau figures for March, 1956, there were 7,000,000 civilian public employees in the United States as of that time, or 11% of the total of gainfully employed in the whole country. It is inconceivable to me that so substantial a portion of our total working force can long remain as separated as it now is from the mainstream of collective bargaining in this country.

I do not mean to imply that labor relations in the public service belong squarely in the middle of that stream. Obviously not. There are unavoidable differences of concept, and to a lesser extent, of practice which will always separate the public service and private industry. Nevertheless, the gap which has up to now separated them is unnecessarily great and, in my opinion, will not long remain unreduced.

Some Suggested Do's and Don'ts

With all of this in mind, I have taken the liberty of preparing a list of "Do's and Don'ts" in the area of practice—addressed both to union leaders in the public service and to administrators. I will plead guilty at once to the count of presumptuousness, and can only say, by way of defense, that while these suggestions reflect, to a considerable extent, some experience in private industry labor relations, I trust that they will also reflect my experience during the past four years in which my day-to-day efforts have been largely devoted to laboring in the public vineyard and to the study and observation of labor relations problems in that area.

Much of what I suggest will be equally applicable to private industry labor relations; this, in itself, does not render it inapplicable to the public service. At the same time, I have attempted, wherever possible, to recognize the distinguishing features which characterize the public service.

For Labor Leaders

Insofar as the methods and attitudes, or practice, on the part of union leaders in the public service are concerned, the following represent what I regard as major contributions that union leaders can make toward an improved level of labor relations. Some of these suggestions, I recognize, are dependent on a reciprocal change in behavior by the other side of the bargaining table, as are some of the suggestions which I shall shortly make in the case of the administrators. The fact is that the obligation to change is very much a mutual and interdependent one in all sorts of things, in labor relations no less than in marital relations.

Go Through Channels

First and foremost, in my list of suggestions, is a strong admonition against the over-free tendency by so many unions to by-pass one branch of government in favor of another, and in some cases, to play off one against the other.

I recognize, of course, that the division of authority between the executive and legislative branch is a very real factor. However, even this division varies from place to place, and each branch has more or less power over personnel matters depending on local circumstances. But whatever the division, there is almost always a clear area of matters, be it no more than grievances, which belong to the executive branch or some subdivision of that branch. On these, both sides, unions and management alike, have a clear responsibility to face up to the problems realistically and fairly and to recognize that the very essence of any good union-management relationship is mutual respect.

Assuming an honest acceptance by management of the principles of collective bargaining, union leaders must, for the sake of their own long-run welfare, give up the temptation to go over the heads of their opposite numbers, or to run to the legislative body every time they receive a decision which may not suit their wishes or precisely meet their needs. This, I regard as basic to good labor relations in the public service.

Be Realistic and Reasonable

Closely related to the latter is the matter of annual wage negotiations, or similar items, where the division of authority between executive and legislative is, however, clear and sharp. On these matters, the union leader may well ask: "Recognizing that even from my own point of view it is much better to have one centralized authority with which to deal, what am I to do here, where the executive branch can only recommend and the legislative branch must appropriate? Surely only a fool will argue that the union should not deal with both."

Rising at once to the latter invitation, I will cite a recent negotiation in Philadelphia with our largest single union. There, following lengthy negotiations between the union and a city team made up of the Personnel Director, Managing Director, Finance Director, and Labor Relations Consultant, an agreement was reached on all points.

This agreement has now been incorporated in the Mayor's budget message to Council, and I think the chances are excellent that the money will be appropriated. Should the Mayor's recommendations require some advocacy before Council, I am confident that the executive branch and the union will present a united front in their efforts to obtain approval of the amount (no more and no less) which is required to finance the program agreed upon. Thereafter, the same united front will be presented when the program is presented to the Civil Service Commission.

True, the agreement reached with the union could not have been a final agreement with the "City," and the right of Council not to appropriate or the right of the Civil Service Commission to reject the whole program and to embark on an entirely different program point up some of the inherent difficulties of bargaining in the public service.

Nevertheless, in the face of all these problems, a substantial degree of collective negotiation with the executive branch was and is possible. Assuming a true willingness by the executive branch to face up to its responsibilities, it is very much incumbent on unions in the public service to respect the position of the executive branch and to meet it half way.

I recognize the difficulties which may still present themselves in many or even most individual situations and the difficulties which may stand in the way of an agreement at the executive level, even where there is the best of good will on both sides, and a maximum of mutual respect. I suspect, however, that there are more than a few unions in the public service who, despite the admitted reasonableness and fairness of an offer by the executive branch, will never consent to be bound by that offer, to the exclusion of their rights to appear and seek upward revision of the offer before the legislative body.

The standard argument presumably is "Why shouldn't we try to 'up' it in Council? What have we got to lose, after all?" My answer is that they have a great deal to lose—possibly their only chance to encourage, once and for all, a real collective bargaining pattern on the part of the executive branch of government; possibly their only chance to begin to improve on what the unions themselves so often refer to as the pattern of "buck-passing" which can make bargaining in the public service so very frustrating. For the executive branch, too, may be quite willing to pass the problem on to the legislative branch, and may readily use the opportunity which is provided by the union's insistence on going before the legislative branch to avoid any real bargaining between itself and the union.

My second major word of unsolicited advice to the unions in this field, therefore, is that even in connection with such matters as annual wage increases, true long-run stability of bargaining can only be achieved by an approach which (1) will keep the union's essential demands vis-à-vis the executive branch within reasonable limits, (2) will emphasize at all times the importance of reaching an "agreement" with the executive branch even if this may mean in some instances the acceptance of an offer from the executive branch which, while "reasonably reasonable," may still fall a bit short of what the union regards as a minimum figure, and (3) will rule out efforts to obtain an "upping" of the amount by the legislative branch except in those extreme cases where the recommendation of the executive branch is truly unreasonable and truly impossible of acceptance.

All of this, to repeat my earlier statement, is part of a reciprocal pattern. It depends on a true willingness by the executive branch to face up to the hard problems of collective bargaining and to adopt an approach which is both realistic and reasonable vis-à-vis the demands of the union.

Shun Pressure Politics

If any one phrase could be used to describe the two situations which I have listed, I would say that the phrase is "greater sense of responsibility" by union leadership. Another phrase which could be applied is the importance of "mutual respect" in any successful collective bargaining relationship.

These phrases are equally applicable to what I have previously described as "indiscriminate resort to every shade of pressure" by some union leaders in the public service field. I fully appreciate that in the absence of the strike weapon or the right to go to arbitration, a union would be virtually helpless in the face of an adamant management position, were it not to have recourse to these various pressure weapons. At the same time, I believe I have pointed out and many union leaders themselves recognize the dangers and disadvantages of over-involvement in the game of "pressure politics."

Moreover, I believe that more than a few union representatives are guilty of a certain "trigger-happiness" in connection with this game of pressures, attacks, and job threats, and have a tendency to resort to it in situations where it is clearly uncalled for. Many administrators who are relatively new at the business of collective bargaining and who are feeling their way, are nevertheless men of honesty and reasonableness and will be temperamentally well-equipped to deal with the problems once they have learned their way.

Union leaders dealing with them can play a major role in educating such administrators to the concept that perhaps collective bargaining is not such a bad thing after all. Bluster and threat in these and many other situations, particularly where they are directed against a man's job, can only have an opposite effect. Recognizing that political pressure may have its place in the absence of the other, normal weapons which are available to outside unions, I feel that a considerably greater degree of restraint in the exercise of these various pressure weapons is nevertheless very much indicated for many of the union leaders in the public field.

Re-examine Grievance Procedures

Many government union leaders, I believe, have a great deal to learn from union leaders in private industry in connection with the operation and handling of a grievance procedure. I have already referred to the tendency to run to the "front office" with everything, rather than to follow the orderly processes of the grievance procedure.

There is a lack of understanding, still, of the importance of reducing grievances to writing. Designation and training of shop stewards is often overlooked. Most important of all, some union representatives, and this is equally true in private industry, have yet to learn how to say "No" to an unreasonable grievant.

Reduce Strife

The problems of jurisdictional spats and minority unionism, which has long kept many of the government unions weak, will be reduced somewhat as a result of the AFL-CIO merger, but only somewhat. The administrator, like so many private employers, may continue to find himself caught in the middle of these fights, or he may, in some cases, regard the union strife as not entirely unwelcome.

In either event, this inter-union strife and rivalry very much hamper the growth and development of collective bargaining in the public service, prevent the appearance of that much-needed greater sense of responsibility by union leaders in the public service, and represent a continuing problem to which the unions themselves must soon address themselves.

Regarding Supervisors

Relatively little recognized, but a major problem for the future, I think, is the matter of membership by supervisors in unions of their subordinates. Unlike private industry, where the Taft-Hartley Law dictates otherwise, I suspect that there is a considerable amount of this in the public service.

The problem is not an easy one, and a good deal can probably be said on both sides. But I think the time has come for government unions themselves to re-examine this entire question and to ask themselves quite candidly whether some of their present practices in the recruitment of supervisors as members add to or detract from their own long-run objectives of a sound and stable collective bargaining level in the public service.

For Public Administrators

Turning now to the methods and attitudes, or practice, on the part of administrators charged with labor relations responsibilities in the public service, I have broken down my suggestions into two categories—first, certain general principles, the acceptance of which I regard as essential to good labor relations and secondly, certain specific "do's and don'ts" for particular situations.

If my overall list here is somewhat longer than in my discussion of union practices, this is not necessarily indicative of a more critical attitude on my part. It may simply reflect my own association with the administrative side of the table during my experience in this field. Under the heading of general principles, I think the following items of philosophy and attitude might be regarded as first essentials to a satisfactory collective bargaining relationship, insofar as the administrator is concerned.

Give Official Recognition

If you have unions and if you want labor-management rapport, then recognize officially that the maximum, permissible amount of collective bargaining is desirable and essential. Recognize and accept that collective bargaining, properly exercised, can be good for morale, that it can give employees a sense of outlet and a sense of dignity; that it may be very necessary if the employees are to offset, even in part, other pressures for the taxpayer's dollar.

Recognize that unions and collective bargaining may legitimately be regarded by an employee as his best means for taking up grievances, particularly in connection with some of the more technical aspects of government personnel procedure, which at best are not always easy to understand. Recognize that unions that have been led to feel and believe that they have a stake in the merit system have become great salesmen and strong defenders of that system.

Recognize, also, that many employees, in the absence of a satisfactory collective bargaining arrangement, will otherwise run to a ward leader for representation. Finally, union recognition should be officially declared and enforced.

Make It Work

Closely related to this official recognition of collective bargaining must be a sincere desire to make collective bargaining work. This is largely a matter of heart and spirit, but I believe strongly that without it, collective bargaining can never really be satisfactory. If you regard collective bargaining only as a necessary evil, you will never have truly good union relations.

The sincere desire to make it work means, among other things, that you don't stand on legal technicalities and barriers if you can possibly help it. It means that you strive, really strive, for agreement with your unions, and regard it as a real personal failure if you have to ram something through.

Incidentally, if a union has agreed to a program, it will usually help sell it. The reverse will be true if the program has been rammed through.

Be Honest, Flexible, Tolerant

It is important to recognize also that the essence of good labor relations is no more than good "human relations." This means, among other things, a scrupulous observance of promises. Break your promises, if you must, to your wife or children, but never, never break a promise to your union.

It means an attempt to understand the other fellow's problems—for example, the problems of a union official vis-á-vis his members. It means a realization that the union officer also can have good ideas.

It means an attitude of tolerance and flexibility. The bane of collective bargaining anywhere is the over-perfectionist on the management side of the table and the individual who regards any form of compromise, whether basic or not, as a virtual sell-out to the devil.

Face Up to Responsibility

I have already referred to the barriers posed by the division of authority within government and the responsibilities of union leaders to seek means for at least reducing the difficulties which this places in the path of successful collective bargaining. Those opportunities and responsibilities apply equally to the administrator.

The nature of the problem might be further illustrated by the following quotation from the 1955 report of the Committee on Labor Relations of Governmental Employees of the Section on Labor Law of the American Bar Association:

> Injustices in public service often result from the complexities and confusion of divided authority confounded by political manipulation. The tendency of administrative officials to avoid their full responsibility by shunting the blame for inaction or inadequate action to the fiscal authorities or the legislature places the public employee in an unenviable position contrasted to private employees in dealing with their employers.

Quite clearly, the administrator must face up squarely, himself, to the difficult problems and responsibilities posed by the union's collective bargaining demands, thereby making any further recourse by the union unnecessary, in at least some cases. If further steps are unavoidable, as in the case of necessity for a legislative appropriation, management and the union are at least able to present an agreed-upon program for approval by the legislative body.

Incidentally, ultimate approval can be considerably facilitated by a judicious amount of liaison between the administrator and the legislative branch during the time the administrator is negotiating an agreement with the union.

Tips on Improving Labor Relations

In addition to these four general matters of principle or philosophy, the following brief list of suggestions for specific situations may prove helpful to an administrator seeking to improve his labor relations:

Always call the union leaders in for discussion before you do something which may conceivably be of interest to them.

This one little rule, we have found in Philadelphia, has literally done wonders toward improving our overall labor relations. It has engendered a feeling of mutual confidence and trust. More often than not the union, anxious to prove the value of such prior consultation, has leaned over backwards to be reasonable about our proposal; and once having been consulted about a matter, it has been in a position to back us up should complaints or questions arise from its membership.

Let the union get some of the credit for new benefits which are to be instituted.

This may mean, instead of putting the benefits through unilaterally, saving them up for annual bargaining negotiations, at which time, incidentally, the particular benefit can perhaps be traded off against some other, perhaps much more costly request of the union. If the benefit cannot be postponed that long, then it is wise to immediately negotiate any possible changes that may be indicated and announce the benefit as a joint agreement.

It is important to know the "red flags" in labor relations, the things that union leaders really are touchy about.

Sometimes nothing can be done to avoid an explosion. Nevertheless it is well to keep in mind always that union people are extremely touchy about such things as the firing or disciplining of a union official, unilateral action by an administrator, interference in internal union affairs, attempts to influence the choice of a union leader, a suggestion that the union does not accurately represent the views of its members.

It can be extremely helpful to find out or try to sense what is really important to a union in its bargaining requests.

An accurate discovery in that direction can lead to an agreement sometimes on a lesser point which will cause the union to give up on a more costly item; furthermore, the concession on the lesser point can on occasion engender as much as, or even more labor relations good will, than some major concession, considerably more expensive.

Another item, which needs no elaboration here, is the pressing need for better training of supervisors and personnel officers in labor relations matters.

Last, and by no means least, is the importance of being patient and of being prepared to sit for long hours in connection with union discussions.

Avoid, if at all possible, giving the union the impression that its problems are less important to you than others. If this objective is simply unattainable, because of the pressure of other matters or because you feel you are not trained for it, then I strongly suggest adoption of the idea which has been accepted for some time in private industry and has recently been adopted by some governmental jurisdictions—namely, the designation or appointment of someone, on a full-or part-time basis, whose primary responsibility will be labor relations. Such a person must, it is important to remember, have sufficient standing and prestige so as not to leave the union people the impression that they are being passed off on some mere lackey.

In Summary

My list, I am afraid, has been overly long; and yet it is only a partial list of what, in my opinion, is needed in connection with behavior, or practice, of both administrators and union leaders in the public service.

I would like, however, to address one last word to the administrators: I am sure that much of what I have said will clash with some of the basic thinking and feelings on which many administrators have been brought up. I am sure, also, that not everything I have said is necessarily the best answer. I am equally sure, however, that the time has come for some basic rethinking on all of these matters.

In more than one sense, the position and attitudes of some administrators today are not altogether different from those of private industry management twenty years ago when unions were first getting a real foothold in this country. Yet I am sure that a considerable segment of private management, in candid moments, will concede that collective bargaining has not been the unadulterated evil which they had anticipated it would be. In one sense, the government administrator has a major advantage over private industry—the fact that, in most cases, his union cannot strike; this will always enable the administrator, when he feels that something basically and fundamentally wrong is being urged, to say "No."

Before he says "No," however, let him keep in mind that most employees in that portion of the world which practices democracy today have an acknowledged and open right to participate, really to participate, in the policy-making processes which determine their working conditions, and that this has now come to be a very basic ingredient of the democratic system. In many democratic countries this applies to government employees even more than to the employees of private industry. True, government is, and I think always will be, at least somewhat different from private industry in the United States, but is it and need it be as different as some of us have made it?

To the union leaders, I say only: Remember that there is a difference, but not always the same differences which the unions themselves have sometimes brought to public service labor relations. Remember also that if the collective bargaining process is to be better adapted and made to work more satisfactorily—from the viewpoint of all concerned—in the special framework which is government, a major share of the responsibility for bringing that about must rest squarely on the shoulders of the unions.

Chapter 5

How To Negotiate with Labor Unions

ROLLIN B. POSEY

The membership of governmental employees in labor unions has been growing steadily during the last twenty years. Governmental employees have been joining three kinds of unions: those composed primarily of employees in private industry, such as the Teamsters Union; those affiliated with organized labor but open only to governmental employees, such as the American Federation of State, County, and Municipal Employees, or the International Association of Fire Fighters; and independent unions for governmental workers only, such as the National Federation of Federal Employees, or the United Public Workers of America.

The increasing unionization of governmental employees has led, in one governmental unit after another, to the introduction of the union as a participant in the determination of personnel policies. To participate in making personnel policies is, in fact, the fundamental reason for the existence of a labor union. In nonunion employment, the employer, whether private or public, decides personnel policies. The individual applicant for employment accepts or rejects the conditions specified. In practical effect this is unilateral determination of the conditions of employment. On the other hand, where employees are organized the conditions of employment may be jointly determined by the employer and by the employees through their instrumentality, the union. In an ever-increasing number of governmental units, joint determination is being adopted.

Under such circumstances the executives of the employing organization no longer determine personnel policies, leaving to the employees only the one decision of whether to accept or reject the policies. Authority over personnel matters is shared by the employer and the union. This authority is exercised in negotiation conferences

Reprinted from Public Personnel Review, journal of the Public Personnel Association, January, 1953.

Rollin B. Posey is Editor, College Department, Harper & Row, Publishers, New York City. When this article was prepared, he was Chairman of the Department of Political Science at Northwestern University.

between representatives of the employer and representatives of the union. In these negotiations the making of personnel policies is concentrated. Negotiation becomes a new and important technique in personnel relations.

Negotiation Objectives

If the public officials look upon negotiation as a condition to be tolerated only until an opportunity arises to eject the union, it is obvious that no constructive results will be produced. Unfortunately this has often been the attitude of employers. A governmental executive, such as a mayor or department director, who has been fixing personnel policies pursuant to rules enacted by the legislative body, often resents a labor union coming in to take over part of the authority he has been exercising. The executive may conceive that his authority has been challenged and that ultimately there must be a showdown. To this kind of an executive, the negotiating process is warfare rather than an opportunity for constructive relations.

In other situations the employer may accept the facts of union life, but he may distrust the sincerity of the union representatives. If so, the union will listen to the executive's statements with matching suspicion. Both sides then try to negotiate an agreement covering every possible contingency. They look upon the agreement as iron-clad law which will prevail in all circumstances. The negotiations become a contest, with each side trying to trap the other side into an agreement, the ramifications of which are not at the time fully apparent.

The primary objective of management-union negotiations should be, of course, to arrive at an agreement that will enable the employer and his organized employees to work together constructively and cooperatively, with regard for the interests of both sides. If this objective is sincerely accepted by everyone, the agreement that results will implement the objective.

It is especially important for the executive side to approach negotiation with a determination to be constructive and cooperative. This is so because of the effect of management attitude upon union leadership. Union negotiators rarely have full authority to enter into an agreement. Usually they must go back to the membership to ratify the agreement they have made. If the union negotiators have been unable to get a constructive agreement, then, or later, the membership will change its negotiators. If management has been aggressive and combative, the membership will select aggressive and combative negotiators of its own. If management has been clever and tricky, the membership will find clever and tricky negotiators too. But if management approaches negotiation with a real acceptance of the new way of doing business, determined to make the new arrangement work, management will assist the reliable, steady, common-sense elements within the union to gain ascendancy. In labor-management relationships, management usually gets exactly the kind of union leadership it deserves.

Preparing to Negotiate

Preparation for negotiations must begin long in advance of the initial bargaining conference. Unions fully realize the crucial importance of these negotiations, and so they prepare themselves carefully and thoroughly. A governmental official, sitting for the first time in a bargaining conference with union representatives, is often astonished at the excellence of the preparation of the union people.

The union will have collected a great amount of factual information about wages, hours, and working conditions to back up its demands. The information will cover other local governmental employers, local private employers, and governmental employers elsewhere. From among these data, the union will select those that tend to support its demands. Let us assume for the moment that one union demand is for higher pay. If wage rates in other local governmental units are higher, these rates will be presented to back up the demand. If wage rates in local private employment are higher, these will be the data selected. If wage rates among governments elsewhere show the local rates to be low, then the rates elsewhere will be stressed. The data the union presents will be selected to support its demands. The union will not reveal the data it withholds.

The employer representatives must have assembled such data too. Otherwise the counterposition of the employer representatives is weak.

In addition to data about other jurisdictions, the union will have made an exhaustive catalog of employment conditions within its own jurisdictional unit. The negotiating executives must be careful that they do not proceed upon the assumption that they already know everything there is to know about their own personnel policies and practices. This is an easy and common assumption, which is unfortunate, because the assumption is almost always an erroneous one. The written rules and regulations are usually incomplete; some practices and customs have never been reduced to writing. The personnel rules are not always followed, invariably and exactly, but are modified by tacit understanding or agreement. Employer negotiators may find themselves in an indefensible position if the union people demonstrate that they are the only ones who really know local conditions and policies. A compulsory rule for employer representatives in preparing for a bargaining conference is to make an accurate and complete inventory of personnel policies and employment conditions.

In making the inventory, the most important step is to find out from the foreman and other first-line supervisors how they are administering the personnel policies currently in effect. This is especially important if the policies already in force were decided by a negotiated agreement. The good and bad points of the agreement, as appraised by the foremen, should be cataloged and made ready for presentation when negotiations begin. Foremen make or break personnel policies. To check with them in preparation for negotiations will give a realistic basis for negotiations which is otherwise impossible.

The employing unit's negotiators, furthermore, should learn everything they can about the union. Are union meetings well attended? Does there seem to be a ruling clique within the union? If so, does the clique rule by default, or through high-handed methods in spite of discontent? Is there intense factionalism within the union? Are its relationships with national headquarters satisfactory? Does there seem to be a Communist cell within the union? Has the union made any local political contacts or alliances? How does the union seem to get along with other local unions? Knowing union affairs helps management negotiators to do their job better. While management observes the union, the union will have been observing management too.

This is not to suggest, however, that a spy be planted within the union. If information about the union does not come normally on a voluntary basis or through the union's house organ, then the information should not be secured. No under-handed method should be used to secure information about the union.

Subjects and Demands

A full-fledged agreement between a public employer and a union of its employees may contain the following five categories of subjects: (1) wage rates, including base rates and policy for applying individual differences; (2) working hours, including length of the work day, the work week, holidays with pay, and starting and stopping times if such times are required to be unusual; (3) a grievance machinery to handle the many small grievances inevitably arising in human relationships; (4) the type of union recognition agreed to—union shop, agency shop, or exclusive bargaining shop; and (5) other important conditions of employment, including, for example, policy on layoffs and recall, eating facilities, insurance and other benefit plans, leaves of absence, etc. A discussion of these subjects is not the purpose of this article. The subjects are listed only to show the categories within which demands may be made.

Commonly the union makes proposals to the employer asking for changes which will benefit the employees, in as many as all five of the categories. Many employers believe that the union is always asking for more, and that the employer's role in negotiations is never anything more than to beat as reluctant a retreat as possible. This need not be so. If management has polled its foremen thoroughly, there is no reason why management cannot start negotiations with a few proposals of its own.

The position of the union will ordinarily be presented in the first meeting of a series. The union demands should then be thoroughly analyzed. Just exactly what would the effect be of each demand? What demands have been included simply for their trading value—included only to be bargained out? What demands have been included as an educational device for presenting them seriously in later years? On the other hand, what are the demands the union really wants now? Of these, which ones seem to be the most important from the standpoint of the union? How does this rating compare with management's rating of the importance of the demands? While the employer's negotiators address themselves to questions like these, the union committee is doing the same thing with the demands the employer has presented to the union. Both sides ask for more than they expect to get. This seems to be the invariable practice.

Techniques of Negotiation

There are a number of do's and don'ts to be observed in the bargaining conferences. One of the most important is what should be said and what should not be said in the initial conference. In this meeting the original proposals of both sides are presented, of course, and the meeting adjourns soon after so that both sides can study the proposals they have received. In the meantime the proposals will be hastily scanned—if they are in writing—and a question or two asked, if any individual point is not clear. It is important, however, that the negotiators make a statement of good intentions in the first meeting, if only to lay a psychological foundation for the bargaining to ensue. Under no circumstances should any flat declaration be made, like the observation, "I want you gentlemen to understand that on such-and-such a point there is nothing that we can do for you." An adamant stand taken early is surely not the way to eventual agreement.

The physical conditions of the meeting room are important too. The room should be well lighted, well ventilated, quiet, and equipped with reasonably comfortable chairs. There should be another room nearby, preferably two rooms, so that the representatives of the two sides can separate for private conferences. Some unions object to meeting anywhere except on "neutral" territory. They believe that meeting in the city manager's office, in the governor's reception room, or in some other room closely identified with the management side, tends to oppress the union representatives. In such a case a suite of rooms in a local hotel may have to be used. This union attitude is by no means universal. Some unions, indeed, feel exactly the opposite. They want to meet with management in management's own quarters—bearding the lion in his den, as it were.

In a negotiating conference, progress cannot be made by long, uninterrupted sessions. Yet the tendency is to want to keep right at it, if a conference seems to be making progress. The reasoning is that if the negotiations are running in high gear, any halt will make difficult resuming negotiating speed. There are two dangers to this, however. One danger is that as sessions grow long and men become weary, tempers inevitably tend to grow short. A bargaining session carried on to the point of fatiguing the participants may flare up into a squabble that will undo everything hitherto agreed to.

The other danger is that the points of agreement will not stick. There should be frequent breaks to permit each side to talk things over confidentially among themselves. If either side feels that they have been pressured into an agreement in a prolonged bargaining session, they will find a way of repudiating the concessions they have made. A "yes" uttered in desperation is no excuse for moving in on the kill. There is nothing constructive about employee relations conducted by high pressure.

A related admonition is never to gloat over a point that has been won. It is painful enough for any human being to have to give in, without having the fact of his defeat waved in his face. A point won should be left alone. A negotiator should never say, "I knew you'd let us have that one, Charlie. On that we were right and you knew it."

In several instances personally known to this writer, negotiations have been broken off completely because the public officials have issued derogatory statements to the press about the union officials with whom they were dealing at the time. Whether the published quotations were accurate or not is beside the point. Certainly they were lifted out of context. Reporters are always anxious for news, of course, and they cannot be blamed for trying in every which way to get a story. But a negotiating conference, like the constitutional convention in Philadelphia in 1787, should be carried on secretly. Statements to the press during a negotiating period should be confined to the bland generality that everything is getting along just fine. Otherwise what has been accomplished in the conference room may be undone in the public press.

Another bit of advice is--stick to the particulars! Two men can disagree quicker and more violently over principles than over particulars. One man may believe, for example, that wage rates should be tied to the cost of living by means of an escalator clause. Another may believe that such a tie is most unwise because it tends to defeat the very purpose for which it was created. These two men could get into a violent argument over this principle, and the argument would tend to drive them apart, when what they need to be doing is to find a common ground on which they can agree. Two men can agree on a five-cent-an-hour increase even when the principles upon which they rely in their two minds may be quite antithetical.

This bit of advice should not be mistakenly applied. To stick to particulars does not mean to stick to technicalities. An obsessive preoccupation with technicalities impedes the progress of negotiations. This is primarily a matter of relative values. A negotiator who hangs on to a minor point like a bulldog probably does so because he is unable to distinguish the minor from the major points. If so, he should not be a negotiator.

No factor in negotiations is more important than the factor of timing. A sense of timing is primarily a shrewdly accurate appraisal of the state of mind and emotion of the negotiators. It is the ability to size up the situation at any point during the negotiations and consequently to know what matters can at the moment be fruitfully discussed. A sense of timing comes only from long experience in conducting negotiations. One reason why professional mediators are a constructive influence is that they have acquired an excellent sense of timing.

A little trick of timing is the interjection of a spot of humor now and then. Negotiators are engaged in important business, and they know it. They concentrate in deadly earnest upon what they are doing. This tends to make the affair a most serious one, with tensions mounting gradually and imperceptibly. A break easily and casually introduced is helpful in relieving nervous tension and consequently in keeping up the progress of negotiations.

Both sides should always tell the truth. No expert skill in the conversation of negotiation is great enough to mask the lie, the half truth, or the evasion. No slicker can ever be slick enough to do a better job of negotiating than the honest man of integrity, however awkward in negotiation the latter may be.

Even if both sides stick to the truth at all times, it must also be recognized that in the atmosphere of negotiation, points are usually made with some degree of exaggertion. It is only human nature for a person to resort to intensified colors as he paints the picture he wants the other fellow to appreciate. The Supreme Court has called this tendency "puffing," and the word is an excellent characterization of earnest exaggeration. Management negotiators should have a skeptical—but not hostile—attitude toward arguments advanced by the union representatives.

It has been said that an index of the competency of joint negotiation is the proportion of time spent beyond the stage of discussing facts. Disputed facts should be cleared up at the outset of negotiations, if this be possible. If both sides are thoroughly and competently prepared, then the only factual discussions that are needed are the ones devoted to determining what the result would be if one alternative or another were to be adopted.

In the give and take of negotiation, the term "final offer" should be avoided. Agreements do not come from ultimatums, and for a negotiator to say that something is his "final offer" is for him to issue an ultimatum. Even if an offer is final, the word "final" should not be used. A mediator with a sense of humor once said that the phrase "final offer" should be used only when a negotiator is uttering his "final final offer."

This leads me to a few observations about mediators. Mediators are not like arbitrators, for they do not have any authority. Mediators are talkers who intervene between the two sides in a negotiation that seems to have gotten stalled. Mediators would be excess baggage if every participant in a negotiating conference were always completely logical and intellectual, never emotional or prejudiced. Mediators can be a lubricating oil for the machinery of negotiation. If negotiations have been going on a long time without getting very far, the chances are that antagonisms will have been built up between the two sides. A mediator can inject himself between the participants, talking to one group in one room, then alternating with the other group in another room. He can draw from each group the verbal expression of the antagonisms that seem to be blocking agreement—in simpler words, he can induce each side to blow off steam. Never does he inform one side of the unkind things the other side has been saying about them. With the antagonisms having been vented, it is possible for negotiations to get back on the track.

The competent mediator, furthermore, is able rather quickly to size up each side's evaluation of the importance of individual issues. The skilled conciliator can sense just how far the union representatives are willing to go, and the limits of concession the employer representatives are willing to make. He then divides the total task into its component issues, taking up just one issue at a time. Thus the total job is divided into smaller, more easily attainable segments. Progress can be made on one point and then another, and soon, everyone's attitude changes from hopelessness to the feeling that maybe agreement can be accomplished after all.

Bargaining for the First Time

Bargaining for the first time is the most difficult bargaining of all. Not only are a number of the participants inexperienced in the techniques of negotiation, but the events leading up to the negotiations may have been stressful and even reckless. The union in order to win members has probably said some pretty unkind things about management. Surely the weak spots in the unit's personnel program will have been hammered at time and again. The union will have been telling the workers that unilateral determination of the conditions of employment has not worked, and that with a union, the employees may expect a number of improvements. And so promises or half promises will have been made, and the union leaders will do their level best to deliver upon the promises.

The management will have been hearing first- or second-hand the criticisms the union organizers have been making of the existing personnel program. Blood pressures will rise a bit at these tales. Some of the criticisms will have been plainly untrue; they may have been uttered out of sheer ignorance or possibly from malice. Some of the criticisms will have been valid, for no personnel program is perfect. But the justice of a criticism does not prevent resentment over the criticism's having been made. Quite the opposite—the sting from a just criticism is greater, because the criticism is true. Who likes to have his shortcomings revealed?

The first negotiating conference, then, may be approached by the management representatives with inner resentment and hostility. The union representatives may feel cocky and confident, and at the same time just a little timid, as they enter the conference room. If the national office of the union has sent out a representative experienced in negotiating terms of employment, he may be the only person in the room who is able from the outset to represent his side skillfully.

The Negotiation Agreement

Eventually the play of forces in the negotiating conference will result in an agreement upon the conditions of employment which have been in dispute. Can one generalize upon the nature of agreement? Is it possible to say that both sides strive for, and eventually reach, an agreement that is "fair" or "just" or "reasonable"? Unfortunately it is not. These words cannot be translated into specific conditions of employment. People in public life know that reconciling opposing points of view on public questions is not a question of reasonableness or fairness. Compromises are reached on the basis of the relative power of the opposing elements. In private businesses the power is economic. In public jurisdictions the power is partly economic and partly political. In public businesses the employees are part of the business's "stockholders," for they are voters as well as employees. In negotiating agreements in governmental units, the employees sit, figuratively speaking, on both sides of the table.

When agreement has been reached, whatever it is, the next question is whether the agreement should be put into writing, or whether an oral agreement is enough. Oral agreements can be more easily misinterpreted, of course, and yet there is a curious reluctance on the part of many public officials to put into writing the terms they have agreed to. This reluctance is likely to make the union insist upon a written agreement.

The written language should be clear and unambiguous. This should not have to be stated, yet ambiguous, easily misinterpreted clauses are quite common.

Some experts maintain that the length of the written agreement is in inverse proportion to the amount of mutual trust existing between the union and the management. A long agreement, ordinarily referred to as a legislative agreement, tries to cover every situation that could possibly arise. Neither party to the agreement is willing to trust the other party. A short agreement, which is called an administrative agreement, leaves most matters to later joint determination. The process of negotiation is not concentrated into a periodically repeated battery of conferences. Negotiation goes on all the time. Certain it is that if both parties are interested primarily in solving each problem or issue that arises, constructively and with everyone's interests at heart, the contents and the overall length of the written agreement are not of great importance.

Personal Qualities of a Good Negotiator

The principal management negotiator ought to be a person who is skilled in conducting give-and-take discussions, rather than a person who by temperament and experience is best in making decisions and giving orders. This is a natural opportunity for the staff personnel administrator. Yet many personnel administrators have sat back and let others take the lead in dealing with unions. The line administrator should look to the personnel man to exercise leadership in this respect.

A good negotiator should have a lively and realistic imagination. He should be able to put himself into the positions of other people, so that he can properly appraise the effects of the proposals he makes. He should be able to visualize and to appreciate the positions of both the employees and the first-line supervisors, for they are the people who are going to have to live with the terms of the agreement from day to day.

That sincerity and honesty are essential to constructive negotiations has already been said. These personal qualities are vital. To them we may add the quality of friendliness. A negotiator should be a person who likes people. Otherwise his personality will tend to impede negotiations. Friendliness does not imply that the management negotiator should try to become a bosom friend of the union representatives. There is a distinction between friendliness and friendship.

Oftentimes the union representatives consist of a skilled negotiator sent in by the national headquarters of the union, plus the elected officials of the union local. The elected officials are employees; the headquarters representative is not. The management spokesman may feel that things would get along very much better if the union "outsider" were not there. The management spokesman may try, consciously or unconsciously, to disregard the outsider and attempt to deal only with the local officials of the union. Perhaps there may be in his mind the thought that he can drive a wedge between the outsider and the local union men. If so, he had better abandon the idea. The only result of any such attempt will be to close solidly the ranks of the union against him.

In conclusion it may be said that learning how to negotiate effectively with representatives of organized employees is a challenge and an opportunity for personnelists. The trend in personnel relations is away from unilateral dealings to dealings with unionized employees. How to deal with unions is the emerging frontier in the fascinating field of public personnel administration.

PART III
Management-Employee Relations in Action:
Five Programs in Local Government

Introduction

Part III gives five different approaches to management relations with organized employees in local government. All authors have taken part in shaping or carrying out policies they describe and evaluate.

Detroit's employee-relations program appears first because its policies are most typical of present practice in larger U.S. cities. Also, the Detroit story offers a classic statement of the competitive merit system as a way to deal with both organized and unorganized employees. The four other municipal programs appear in order of their adoption.

Detroit, Michigan. Charles Meyer tells about Detroit, a "union town" with a story. In Detroit, city government in the past used almost all the tactics and devices of trade unionism. But now the civil service merit system holds the key to the "open-door policy." The city deals unilaterally with individual and organized employees. It has no written agreements or signed contracts, there is no arbitration, strikes are prohibited.

But the "open-door" prevails. Before any personnel policy is adopted, individual employees, representatives of employee organizations and interested citizens can state their views in open meetings. Such meetings may be held by the civil service commission, departments, the city council, the mayor and the controller. Each employee — individually or through representation of his choice — can bring grievances, and any other matter affecting his employment, to supervisors at all levels.

Mr. Meyer describes Detroit's current practice in terms of the basic philosophy on which it rests. He stresses differences between workers in private and public enterprise and the importance of preserving tenets of representative government. These tenets, he believes, are set aside in collective bargaining typical of industry.

Hartford, Connecticut. Since 1945, Hartford has been experimenting with ways to structure the relationships between employees, administrators, and the city council. Carleton Sharpe and Elisha Freedman report some successes and some unsolved problems. For

example, after a series of meetings on a new pay plan, the city manager and heads of both employee councils signed a memorandum of
understanding. Negotiation efforts were nullified when fire and police
unions went directly to the city council and won special benefits.

Philadelphia, Pennsylvania. In 1958, Philadelphia signed its first
agreement with the American Federation of State, County, and
Municipal Employees. The contract recognizes the union as exclusive
bargaining agent for all non-uniformed civil service employees except supervisors. Collective bargaining covers wages, hours, working conditions, and grievance procedures. There is no provision for
arbitration; strikes are banned.

Foster Roser says every provision of the contract—except exclusive bargaining—also appears in Philadelphia's civil service
regulations. To unions, however, the contract is important. Employees want to participate in decisions affecting them. Collective
bargaining provides the opportunity for give and take with management in reaching a bilateral agreement.

Cincinnati, Ohio. Cincinnati entered the written-agreement stage
of union-management relations in 1960. A policy issued by the city
manager said: "willingness on the part of administration to explain
and to listen does not mean that the union is necessarily entitled to
participate in the decision-making process. Negotiation is proper
in some areas: determination of these areas is a function of the
written agreement. It is the opinion of the city manager that formalization of our relationships with unions through the medium of a written agreement will help to clarify these areas of mutual concern."

Cincinnati, like Philadelphia, recognizes AFSCME as the exclusive bargaining agent for city employees. Results of negotiations
must be approved by specified officials or bodies before written
agreements are made. There is no arbitration; but if city and union
representatives fail to agree, a board of review makes recommendations. If agreement still is not possible, the city council makes a
decision.

Wisconsin. Arvid Anderson tells about a labor-relations code
for local governments passed by the Wisconsin legislature in 1959
and amended in 1962. The code contains several features that approach private industry practices. For example, the procedure for
enforcement of prohibited practices is the same as that applicable
to private employee disputes. Also, insofar as applicable, the procedures to determine bargaining representatives are like those for
private employers. A fact-finding provision may be invoked by either
local governments or the union in case of deadlocks. Recommendations, however, are advisory. Mr. Anderson believes it will be
several years before the effects of the arrangements can be evaluated.

- - - - - - - -

Comparison of these five programs shows some common features. All recognize the right of employees to form or join organizations. All accept the legitimate interests of employee organizations to help shape personnel policies. Representatives help employees adjust grievances and petition about working conditions. Strikes are banned.

But there are differences. They stem from contrary views about the legality of such matters as exclusive representation, signed agreements, arbitration, and the merit system as an adequate protector of employee interests.

These five programs are not presented as models. Procedures for dealing with organized public employees—fully satisfactory to all interest groups—have not yet been devised. These accounts provide both factual information and counsel based on experience.

K.O.W.

Chapter 6

The Detroit Employee-Relations Story

CHARLES A. MEYER

Detroit's employee-relation policies and program have been built on the following premises:

1. That employer-employee relations programs in the public service should be based on the needs, problems, purposes and experiences of representative government;

2. That policies and procedures of such program should be consistent with the principles of the competitive civil service system;

3. That policies and procedures must be controlled by the framework of laws established to protect the public interest;

4. That employment policies must equitably affect all public employees and be non-discriminatory on any basis other than merit and fitness; and

5. That programs so constituted serve the interests of public employees, individually and in organized groups, more effectively than would programs applying practices found in private industry.

These policies and program have evolved in a municipality which is known as a "union town." The headquarters of several international unions are located in Detroit. Solidarity House is only a short distance from the City-County Building and other union offices are also housed nearby. In all municipal elections, organized labor endorses candidates for membership on the Common Council and the Office of Mayor.

Adapted from a paper presented to the Public Personnel Association's 1961 International Conference on Public Personnel Administration, Denver, Colorado.

Charles A. Meyer is Assistant Secretary and Chief Examiner of the Detroit Civil Service Commission and Past President of the Public Personnel Association.

Although Detroit has a strong mayor form of government, there are lay citizen boards associated with all city departments. Practically every such board has at least one member who in private life is directly associated with or employed by a labor organization. Since 1947 there has been a union officer serving on the Detroit Civil Service Commission.

Background of Detroit Program

In 1913, the City Charter was amended to provide for a competitive civil service system. Employees already working were "blanketed" into civil service status. Most of the employees in skilled trade occupations were union members. Other employee groups began to organize approximately at the end of World War I. In 1919, an independent employees' association was formed and has been active ever since.

Over a period of years and particularly beginning in the mid-1930's, other unions and organized groups of employees were formed so that today there are approximately 34 organizations, some representing trade and occupational groups while others are more general organizations which cut across occupational lines. Each of these groups, sometimes separately and sometimes jointly, are continuously active in the employer-employee relations programs of the City of Detroit.

Policies Product of Experience

Detroit's policies and programs are the result of years of experience, observation, and study by city administrators, attorneys, and elected officials.

The city government has had intensive first-hand experience in all patterns and phases of employer-employee relations. Over a period of years, these have included: formal signed bilateral agreements (eliminated in 1951); recognition of specific unions as exclusive "bargaining" representatives of large groups of employees; formal negotiation; arbitration of disputes by "outside" arbitrators (thirteen different disputes); dealing with affiliated and non-affiliated organizations; formal and informal grievance procedures; strikes (none since 1951); mediation; political maneuvering by employee groups; negotiation with large unions representing both shop and office employees, craft unions, unions which include supervisors and those which exclude supervisors, etc.

City officials who have had this cumulative experience have been in a position to observe industrial and private business experience and to study policies and programs of other governmental units. Observation and evaluation of all such facets led to acceptance of the stated basic premise and to the city's current policies and program.

The premise, policies, and program recognize that patterns, framework, and procedures of employer-employee relations developed for a government should be established on the foundation of, and be consistent with, basic principles of representative government in a free society, rather than derived by casual reasoning from industrial precedents which were created in a completely different environment.

Public vs. Private Employment

In Detroit's labor environment, city officials have recognized basic differences between public and private employment which necessitate significant differences in employer-employee relations programs for government. Some of these are discussed below.

Civil Service laws giving clear-cut and definite responsibilities to civil service commissions, laws providing definite responsibilities of the executive and legislative bodies, as well as definite responsibilities being lodged in the many departments of government, create a situation completely different from that found in any private industrial organization. There is no direct counterpart in government of "management" as found in private industry.

Motives and Responsibilities

Another major difference is that there is no profit motive in government.

Continuity of private business is contingent on economic success. Accordingly, management representatives in private industry have a significant personal financial stake in the outcome of bargaining in that an inadequate performance may well result in economic failure and end of the business as an entity.

Government is continuous. Accordingly, "management representatives" in government are not faced with the same economic risk as industrial management. An inadequate performance in a collective-bargaining process, even though it resulted in excessive costs or inefficiencies, would not terminate the governmental unit as an entity.

Moreover, there are inherent dangers in introducing private-industry-type bargaining processes in government. For example, in the public service, "management representatives" may yield to demands because of personal benefit, i.e., benefits sought by employee groups may be matters that would directly and personally benefit the management representatives, or they may yield for political reasons. A second danger is that elected officials might tend to give in to demands of employee groups for short-term personal, political benefits.

Government responsibilities extend to all groups, organizations and individuals, and the public in general.

Elected officials of government have substantive responsibilities for making decisions which determine the types, quality, and quantity of public service. Decisions as to pay of public employees and working conditions must be made only after consideration of all phases of the government programs and problems and consideration of the general public interest. This means discussion and consideration of all problems--financial and otherwise--that are involved.

Such decisions must be made openly, with due consideration being given to the view of other segments of the jurisdiction, such as any of a variety of civic groups, business groups, etc., in addition to public employees. Collective bargaining as it is carried on in private industry precludes the active participation of such other groups in the processes involved.

A system of representative government must provide a means whereby elected officials can be held accountable for their decisions. If a policy was developed under which public officials could in effect abdicate their responsibilities by saying that they were helpless to act in the general public interest because of commitments made to a private labor organization or a decision made by an "outside" arbitrator, there would be no effective means of holding such officials accountable.

On the Government Side

In representative government, any public employee has a right of petition to his government and is entitled to speak for himself or use a counsel of his own choice in matters that affect his own employment welfare.

Legislation providing for only collective representation would in effect require that all employees organize in order to have their interests represented to the duly constituted officials. This would be in marked conflict with civil service laws and practically all of the concepts of a system of representative government.

The fact that government is organized on a departmental basis facilitates the technique of playing one department against another in a "see-saw" fashion in the collective-bargaining process.

The responsibilities of government employees are not identical with those of private business. The public employee in accepting public employment accepts an obligation which is distinctly different from that of the employee in private business.

There are many more protections and forums for recognition, and more consideration of employee needs, desires, and problems, provided by law to public employees than are provided to employees in private industry.

Right To Organize and Be Represented

The city's personnel policy manual, which reflects the considered judgment of all general operating departments, provides that "an employee may become a member of any organization of his own choice so long as that organization does not seek to overthrow the Constitution of the United States. This right includes the right of an employee to join a union or other employee organization." (Police officers are governed by other regulations which prohibit "affiliation" but which permit an independent association.)

The city has consistently practiced its policy that employees have the right to form or join employee organizations and should have maximum opportunity, both as individuals and/or through organizations, for open communication with supervisors and administrative and elective officials.

Provision is made for the payroll check-off of employee organization dues where authorized by the individual employee.

Insofar as principal career, appointive, and elective officials are concerned, the City of Detroit maintains the "open-door" policy. Any employee or representative of any employee or any officer of any employee organization without appointment and very little waiting can see any administrator or elected official at almost any time on any problem.

Grievance and Review Procedures

In the general city departments, provision is made for an employee to represent himself or be represented by the business agent, steward, or committeeman on any grievances or problems resulting from decisions of supervisors or administrators.

Any matter in question is referred first to the immediate supervisor and then through subsequent levels of supervision in the operating department. Most of the larger departments have a personnel officer who will review a case and meet with the employee and his representatives if the administrative chain has not produced a remedy.

If the personnel officer upholds the supervisor, the employee and/or his organization may then apply for a review to the department head. Where there is a multiple board or commission, the matter may be reviewed at that level. The vast majority of problems are handled promptly at the lower administrative levels without the necessity of being reviewed at higher levels.

Under the City Charter and Ordinances, the Civil Service Commission is given certain authorities with respect to classification of positions, review of promotions and disciplinary actions, veterans' benefits, working conditions, and layoff benefits. Where Civil Service staff decisions are made on any of the items covered by Civil Service laws and rules, an employee either individually or through his organization may appeal the staff decision to the Civil Service Commission which holds a public hearing on the requested review.

Pay and Fringe Benefits

On matters of pay and fringe benefits and related working conditions, provision is made annually for all employees and organizations to present their cases to the City Controller's Office and/or Civil Service Commission, where it may be involved, and to present their requests for changes in existing rules, regulations, and ordinances.

The Mayor regularly schedules hearings so that every employee organization may present its request and arguments and discuss the matter with him. The Common Council, which has final authority in making certain types of decisions, particularly with respect to pay, vacations, sick leave, etc., holds similar hearings. Although the term "hearing" is used, there is actually considerable discussion and interchange of ideas between employee representatives, the administrative agencies, and elected officials involved.

Decisions affecting the fiscal operations of the city are primarily made once annually. However, there are continuing discussions throughout the year with union representatives and employees on matters relating to working conditions and other rules and regulations that affect individual employees and groups of employees.

The city policy consistently is to let each employee either individually or with representation of his choice discuss matters of employee concern with the persons whose acts or decisions are questioned. This may mean departmental personnel, representatives of the City Controller's Office, the Civil Service Commission, the Mayor, or Common Council.

Changes in Policy

When major changes in policy and regulations are made by line departments, the Civil Service Commission, or the City Controller's Office, they are reviewed with the employee representatives. It is the policy of the city and its principal staff agencies, as well as the operating departments, to discuss completely all policy questions with employee groups so that there may be full and mutual understanding.

Obviously this does not mean that there is always complete agreement; but in a system of responsible and accountable government, city officials have uniformly acted on the premise that they must make their ultimate decisions unilaterally in the interest of all the people, including the employees.

To clarify this aspect of the program, illustrations of two important policy changes made after the discussion and review procedures just described may be helpful.

Seniority

At the end of World War II it was apparent that, although the Civil Service rules provided a general definition of seniority and required its application in layoff and re-employment, for other purposes, including demotions due to lack of funds or lack of work, departments were applying somewhat different definitions and policies. It was also apparent that with the number of persons returning from military service that many employees would be displaced from the positions they had occupied during the war.

An intensive survey was made of different policies that might be adopted to apply uniformly in all departments with respect to displacement on a seniority basis and the various policies were discussed with every employee group, and every city department. Although initially there were some divergent opinions among the unions, ultimately a compromise regulation which won approval by all employee groups in the city service was adopted at a public meeting of the Civil Service Commission.

Layoff Benefits

This is a plan patterned in part on the State Unemployment Compensation Law, but one financed by the city and administered by the Civil Service Commission rather than the State of Michigan Employment Security Commission. All employee groups were called in to discuss the matter.

A public hearing was held by the Common Council and then the matter was referred to a team composed of staff members of the City Controller's Office and the Civil Service Commission which met with all employee groups who cared to participate. A plan was developed which was acceptable to all employee groups as well as the city administration. This plan was approved after public meetings of the Civil Service Commission and Common Council.

Facts Made Public

In Detroit's type of program, the law and public policy require that where facts are concerned, they are revealed and discussed in open public meetings. Employee groups are heard by supervisors, department heads, departmental commissions, civil service commissions, and the executive and legislative bodies.

All petitions can be and are aired openly and in public. Any disputes are brought to the attention of the public by press, radio, TV, etc. There is seldom, if ever, any question as to the facts involved. Few, if any, employee organizations in private industry have as much opportunity for formal and informal presentation and consideration of reviews and requests.

All major decisions on employment matters and policies are made in unilateral form by responsible and accountable public officials after adequate discussion with the employee organizations and after public hearing.

Variations from Industrial Pattern

The city does not have signed contracts with any employee organization. No employee organization is certified as an exclusive bargaining agent. Collective bargaining, in the sense of the term as applied in private industry, is not practiced. There is no arbitration by third parties who would not be accountable to the citizens of Detroit. Strikes are forbidden by law.

These industrial precedents have been excluded from the city's program after careful examination of their implications and significance to the public service.

Contracts

So-called contracts, and bargaining pursuant thereto, actually are not the most significant but merely the most publicized phase of labor relations. The many phases of personnel management involved in labor relations, including such items as selection, safety, training, promotions, merit ratings, working conditions, and employee representation, can be effectively administered within the framework of law without contracts or what is called "formalized bargaining."

By devoting continuous attention to these problems the city can and has evolved programs more effective than are the programs in industry.

Contracts are limited documents and tend to represent largely an intermittent or sporadic attention to personnel matters. Effective public personnel administration which attracts and retains competent personnel and maintains high morale of the working staff is accomplished only by continuing attention being given to personnel problems.

It is sometimes argued that a written agreement providing for exclusive bargaining is essential to insure union security. This can readily be repudiated insofar as public service is concerned by an examination of the facts. In a city such as Detroit, and many others, there have been strong unions for literally scores of years without either written contracts or so-called exclusive representation.

More Form than Substance. Contracts are more a matter of form rather than substance. In those instances where municipalities have gone through the motions of signing a contract, it is often admitted by both sides to the "contact" that the agreement as a practical matter is a unilateral statement of policy signed for purposes of form by union representatives and public representatives.

Such emphasis on form rather than substance is not only window-dressing but is fundamentally a dishonest approach in that the contract is not actually bilateral. The individual union member may think that he is protected by the all-important contract and yet the conditions granted by the "contract" may be revoked at the will of the legislative body or responsible board.

Time and money are consumed in "negotiating" and formalizing a "contract" with attendant publicity to government and union officials and the resulting document merely duplicates provisions properly established by action of responsible government officials.

Even though it be true, as alleged by contract advocates, that changes are not likely to be made because of possible group political reactions, this in itself is bad. If agreements are made that are unrealistic or improper, then when it is determined that changes should be made in the public interest, such changes should be made whatever the political reactions of a limited portion of the public may be.

It is considerably more appropriate for administrators, executives and legislative bodies to discuss thoroughly all matters affecting the public welfare, and, after weighing the public interest, accept their responsibility for making a decision by adopting whatever ordinances, rules, resolutions, or regulations are found appropriate.

When this is done, the general public has an opportunity to pass on the wisdom or propriety of the actions of the officials, which cannot be done if the public official has the "out" of collective bargaining which resulted in the substitution of a private interest for the public interest.

"Union Tradition" and "Management Rights." Those who advocate "contracts" sometimes state that they are largely concessions to what is called "union tradition." Quite obviously, they are not union tradition in the public service. The number of so-called contracts is relatively small with respect to the number of governmental jurisdictions existing, at least, in the United States.

There is, however, an important tradition in the basic concept of representative government which does not exclude recognition of the rights of employees to form associations for their mutual benefit but does establish a framework of law established for the public interest in which such employee associations or organizations must operate.

Some advocates of the signed contract have argued that in its absence there is no recognition of "management rights." This argument ignores completely a great body of law, including the United States Constitution, State Constitutions, City Charters, Ordinances, Civil Service Rules, judicial decisions, legal opinions, etc., that very clearly establish a framework of law under which public services are to be administered.

Actually, there is a greater body of law relating to the public services and the legal powers and duties of public officials and agencies with respect to public employment than exists with respect to management rights in industry.

Multiple Representation

Detroit does not provide for certification of any group as an exclusive collective-bargaining agent recognizing that such certification would involve an illegal delegation of power or discretion of public officers. It also would mean, in effect, that the officials would be expressing a preference which is incompatible with a system of representative government.

Such recognition would materially lessen, and could completely eliminate, the opportunity of the general public to express itself directly on any matter relating to the public employment which involved a difference of opinion between the employee organization and the administrator or other public official who might be involved in the discussion.

Furthermore, such recognition would be incompatible with the typical civil service law which clearly provides an opportunity for, and emphasizes, recognition of the individual as such in employment matters. Preferential recognition for members of any organization in employment matters would be as invalid as discrimination based on religious belief, political affiliation, race, or creed.

Multiple Unionism No Problem. Many times the argument is advanced that dealing with one union representative or one committee is much more simple and efficient than dealing with more than one representative or more than one group. This type of thinking violates the principles of representative government and the constitutional provisions which, in our free society, provide for the recognition of the individual and his rights. It also negates the concept of a competitive merit system which also emphasizes the importance of the individual and his qualifications, rights, and equities.

In the practical employment situation there are many occupational groups which want separate representation. Responsible public management, whether it be a civil service board, personnel officer, manager, mayor or other official, must daily be thinking in terms of multiple services and a great variety of occupations.

Moreover, even if there were only one large union, there would be factions, occupations, or groups each having a unique interest requiring or deserving just as much or perhaps more attention than if there were different groups.

Public officials and administrators must deal with a multiplicity of services and people in all other relationships. Experience in Detroit has proven that there are probably fewer complications from any viewpoint because of dealing with a number of different employee representatives than there would be if all negotiations were with a single union. Multiple unions need not cause confusion in anyone's mind, nor need there be confusion in the program.

Significant Parallel. In considering this matter of multiple groups versus a single certified bargaining agent in employee relations in the public service, one finds a definite parallel between this and comparing the concepts of a free society and a totalitarian state.

In the United States, citizens can organize and associate freely and voluntarily. In a free society, leadership is voluntary and multiple. In a totalitarian state, leadership is assigned. Imposing a requirement that there be only one union in any given jurisdiction in the public service would have the net effect of assigning leadership. This not only could endanger the merit system but could lead to dictatorship.

Arbitration

After considerable experience with arbitration with the "third-party" arbitrator, mutually selected by union and city representatives, Detroit officials concluded that it is not compatible in principle or practicable in a system of representative government. In principle, compulsory arbitration is completely inimical to a system of representative government. A primary and basic concept of representative government is that elected officials in government are essentially arbitrators in the public interest. Any attempt to introduce an outside arbitrator is a clear negation of this concept.

In addition to the elected officials, provision is made in Detroit's Charter and in many other similar laws for responsible quasi-independent boards, such as civil service commissions, to serve as mediators and arbitrators in the public interest on matters affecting both individuals and employee groups in the public service. If there is to be accountable and responsible government, it must be recognized that elected and administrative officials of the jurisdiction involved have a responsibility to the public for making decisions on all aspects of governmental programs.

The incursion of arbitration, where the arbitrator has no responsibility with respect to the overall problems and seldom, if ever, is in a position to consider the instant problem as only one phase of a complex of operation, would inevitably mean that a private interest would be substituted for the public interest. The statement that public service is a public trust for all the people is more than a cliché. Elected officials at any level of government are the responsible trustees. Third-party arbitration reduces the trustees' authority and assumes the trusteeship is limited to the welfare of the public employee group involved.

Strikes Prohibited

State law prohibits strikes by public employees in a statute intended to implement the common law and stimulate officials to take action in the public interest in the event of a work stoppage which attempts to substitute the private and personal interest of the employees for the public interest.

In representative government in a free society, no activity that is established by law as a function of government must cease merely because an individual employee or group of employees feel that personal interests are not being acceptably handled. No single group can substitute its private interest for the public interest in a system of representative government.

Apart from this basic philosophy, some local officials have argued cogently that a strike which is basically an economic weapon is completely unrealistic if used against government in that a local union would be entering an economic contest with government.

Proprietary and Governmental Functions

The city does not differentiate in its employee-relations program between proprietary and governmental functions. It recognizes that the original distinction between these two was developed largely for tort actions and that even in this area the distinction is largely disappearing.

Organization Not Panacea

None of the foregoing detracts in any way from a positive and effective employee-relations program. Evidence of the effectiveness in the program is attested by the fact that on numerous occasions in policy discussions in open meetings of public officials, including the State Labor Mediation Board, employee organizations representing employees in the Detroit Municipal Service have expressed the view that they are satisfied with the Detroit program as it relates to relationships with organized employee groups.

Fiscal problems have prevented pay adjustments, not only in amounts requested by employees and their organizations, but to amounts recognized as justified by city officials. Formalized collective bargaining could not, under existing fiscal problems, have resulted in any larger pay adjustments.

It is sometimes argued that invariably the activities of public employee unions result in better wages and fringe benefits in the governmental unit involved. This does not necessarily follow, particularly with respect to fringe benefits. Quite frequently, in public jurisdictions, the fringe benefits relating to vacations, sick leave, hours of work, and holidays have been substantially more generous than such benefits provided in private industry.

It has happened that, when employee organizations, basing their approaches on those found in private industry, insist on a precise definition and spelling out of fringes, the result has been at least a much tighter administration and on occasion a reduction of benefits, such as holidays. A number of public jurisdictions have allowed unlimited sick leave for employees with extended periods of service. Where a precise definition of sick leave accumulations has been insisted upon by employee groups, the amount of sick leave accumulation has been specifically defined with a limit.

Administration's Responsibility Prevails

Another argument advanced is that one of the important reasons for individuals joining a union lies in the satisfaction of participation and personal recognition obtained by union membership. Persons advancing this argument also say, somewhat sardonically, that public employers typically may claim that they recognize the individual but that actually such recognition is not provided. There is probably an element of truth in some jurisdictions in this charge, but to assume that the only solution is participation through a union reflects on the administration which accepts the assumption.

In other words, acceptance of the belief that the employee should have his free choice of belonging to an employee organization does not mean that that right takes away any responsibility from the administrative organization for developing and creating a human relations climate where the individual can with assurance know that he is actually being recognized as an individual and treated with dignity.

Individual Recognition Not Guaranteed

A third argument is that if the average employee, by joining a union, becomes an officer or steward, he will get personal recognition and his opportunity to meet with administrative officers and others will give him a feeling of participating in policy.

Actually, the average employee does not become an officer or automatically get any recognition other than being an average employee through membership in unions, either public or private. The average employee may be submerged as an individual in the union just as he may be in a large work organization.

Employee Reaction to Organization

A substantial portion of the United States' total work force is employed by one governmental unit or another. Only a relatively small portion of governmental employees are organized. A still smaller portion of these are in jurisdictions where employer-employee relations are patterned after industrial precedents. If governmental working conditions were as unpalatable or unfair as sometimes alleged, it appears reasonable to assume that many more would seek other employment than has been the case.

Actually, many employees have entered government service to avoid the highly structured employee-relations programs in industry.

Summary and General Comments

In the Detroit program, employees organize in unions or associations with restrictions placed on affiliation in only a limited number of instances. Employee representatives have access to supervisors at all levels in a pattern of progressive review of grievances or petitions provided for on all matters affecting employment. There are several public forums, including hearings before departmental boards, the Civil Service Commission, the Controller's Office, the Mayor, and Common Council. There are never any questions of facts because all facts are available to individual employees, employee groups, and the city administration, as well as the general public.

The major points of emphasis are that, in representative government, the public interest is paramount and decisions—particularly economic decisions, including fringe benefits—should be made by responsible and accountable public officials after public discussion in which all interested portions of the public can have a part.

Formalization is neither an end in itself nor a good in itself. In a free society, true democracy is not completely formalized nor can it be so formalized. Where employees of all levels, singly and in association, are using intelligent, constructive self-interest to further the interests of the agency with which they are connected as well as their own, most problems find a reasonably ready solution. Where intelligent, cooperative good will cannot find the solution, it should be obvious that compulsive formalized approaches will be even less effective.

Detroit's program insures the maintenance of accountability and responsibility on the part of elected and other public officials. It also recognizes the practical fact that, in any government in a free society, standards of governmental conduct are higher under full public scrutiny. It avoids the problem of any governmental officer becoming unduly obligated to one segment of the population, and refrains from blurring both private and public responsibilities in the public eye.

Advantages in Public Service

It appears that those who ardently advocate directly transplanting all union activities and practices found in private industry to the public service have refused to recognize the many advances made in the public service as compared to private industry with respect to all phases of personnel management. Some of these are enumerated below.

1. The public service developed position classification plans long before such plans were found in private industry. These plans had for one of their major purposes equal pay for equal work.

2. Standard pay plans stemming from position classification plans were developed first in the public service.

3. The work week and work day were shortened in the public service much earlier than in private industry.

4. Civil service merit laws, established to insure that employees would be selected, retained, and promoted on the basis of merit and to prohibit discrimination on the basis of religion, race, etc., developed in the public service much earlier than comparable developments affecting private industry.

5. Vacation and sick leave plans developed earlier in
    the public service and for the majority of employees
    the benefits are greater than in industry.

6. Pension plans found their way into the public service
    much earlier than such plans were developed in
    private business.

7. Tenure systems which recognized seniority as a
    factor in employee protection and retention found
    their way in many public service jurisdictions much
    earlier than in private business.

8. Procedures for providing opportunities for the in-
    dividual employee or groups of employees to be
    heard by responsible administrators, legislators,
    executives, etc. developed earlier in the public
    service than they did in private business.

9. Provisions for review of disciplinary matters with
    the employees having clearly established protection
    provided by law were developed in the public service
    much earlier than in private industry and are more
    substantial in public service.

10. The provisions of formalized forums for presentation
    of programs, recommendations for changes in policy,
    etc. have been developed much more completely in
    the public service than in private organizations.

Constructive Services of Unions

As has been indicated, many public jurisdictions without any
employee organization have provided all of the employee benefits
found to date in private organizations. This does not mean that
employee organizations are not worthwhile and desirable. Employee
organizations can be of service not only to employees but also to
administrators and officials in the public service by developing
constructive organizations and supporting improved personnel
programs.

They can audit performance of administrators under existing
policies, audit classification and other personnel policies, and represent those individuals desiring representation on any of many problems before responsible administrators or officials within the laws
of representative government.

They can and do make suggestions for changes in policy and
program. They can provide opportunities for developing leadership
qualities among their members and officers that may well serve such

persons in careers not only within the labor organization but in responsible positions in the public service.

They should never be permitted, however, to substitute themselves for the established essential processes of our system of representative government or to ignore the differences between public employment and private employment.

Must Stem from Own Needs

It is my personal belief that as professional public personnel administrators our primary concern should be that there be competitive merit system laws, in and for every governmental jurisdiction in the United States.

It is my belief also that we should develop our policies and programs on the needs and values and benefits of representative government in a free society and place our emphasis on our collective experience in government rather than attempt to adapt procedures which were developed in private industry. An entirely different environment exists in private industry and many of the precedents are completely inapplicable in representative government.

Chapter 7

Collective Bargaining in Hartford, Connecticut

CARLETON F. SHARPE and ELISHA C. FREEDMAN

Collective bargaining in municipal government still resides in a vast, largely uncharted sea of experimentation and "do-it-yourself" arrangements. By sharing their mutual experiences in this field, municipal administrators have much to gain from each other. It is in this vein that we have prepared this paper, discussing our experience in Hartford, Connecticut, a nonpartisan council-manager city.

In 1945, three years prior to the inception of the council-manager plan in Hartford, city employees were authorized by ordinance to organize and join organizations of their own choosing for their mutual benefit and advancement. Ever since this right was written into law, ways and means of structuring the relationships between employees, administrators, and council have been discussed and tried, collective bargaining being one of them.

Municipal collective bargaining as used in this paper is a system whereby municipal employees and representatives of the municipal government get together to discuss and decide upon issues of wages, hours, and working conditions according to established procedures. Municipal collective bargaining may have all or some of the elements of collective bargaining as known in industry. A municipal collective bargaining system with more of the aspects of industrial collective bargaining is not necessarily a better system than one with fewer industrial attributes. Municipalities have many features such as merit or civil service systems which compensate for lack of conventional industrial collective bargaining. They also can provide many of the procedures contained in industrial collective bargaining contracts through enactment of personnel rules or civil service regulations, and ordinances. There is no practical reason to scrap these devices if they are working in order to further approach the industrial ideal.

Reprinted by permission of the American Society for Public Administration from Public Administration Review, Winter, 1962, where it appeared under its original title, "Collective Bargaining in a Nonpartisan, Council-Manager City."

Carleton F. Sharpe is City Manager of the City of Hartford.

Elisha C. Freedman is Executive Secretary to the City Manager.

This past year we sat down with a group of Connecticut municipal administrators to discuss legislation that had been introduced in the state legislature to allow municipal employees to organize and bargain collectively. To some this proposed law would only legalize what they had been doing informally one way or another. Others, some of whom had never dealt with unions on any matter, were concerned about what to expect if they should be legally forced to bargain collectively. The bill was defeated as similar ones have been so many times in the past. But this time the state legislature saw fit to refer the whole matter of collective bargaining to its legislative reference commission for interim study and report to the next session of the legislature. Collective bargaining for municipalities finally is receiving recognition as a subject worthy of serious consideration by the state's lawmakers.

The nonpartisan council-manager city of Hartford had a collective bargaining bill of its own also in the legislature for the second consecutive session. This bill failed too. It would have given the city's personnel board (similar to a civil service commission) legal authority to draft collective bargaining procedures which would have replaced the informal and unstructured arrangements that now exist. In other words, it would have allowed the reorganization of the present system in a manner to be prescribed by the personnel board. Whether the state study will recommend specific, uniform procedures for all towns, if this is possible, remains to be seen. Regardless of what the state does, the city of Hartford can profit from its past experience and devise a simple vehicle to improve personnel relations.

Hartford System in General

Hartford's present system for negotiating wages, hours, and working conditions has been called confusing and chaotic. Confusing it is, but chaotic is an exaggeration—for there have been no strikes, no outstanding inter-union fights, and no unwillingness on the part of municipal employees and representatives of the municipal government to discuss problems. In fact, in terms of accomplishments for employees, Hartford's system might be called very successful. Employees have gained frequent raises, longevity pay, three weeks vacation after five years' service, a forty-hour week for policemen, fifty-six hours for firemen, and thirty-five hours for white-collar workers. There are no restrictions on who may join a union (supervisors are included) and what unions can be joined. A dues check-off system, administered at city expense, is provided. Fast and effective grievance machinery has been established by personnel rule with appeals to a permanent three-man personnel board composed of two outsiders and one employee member, an active unionist himself. Close to 60 per cent of all city employees are

union members. Aside from this, employees have been provided
with a merit system containing seniority provisions, a pension system, and a broad insurance program.

Industrial Features Not Found in Hartford System

The devices used in industrial collective bargaining that are
not present in Hartford are exclusive recognition, officially
established jurisdictional lines, binding contracts, third party intervention to settle disputes, the union shop, and compulsory bargaining
legislation. The city's corporation counsel has felt that the city has
no authority in its charter or by state statute to use these devices—
which is one of the reasons that the state legislative action described
above has been taken. The city council has followed his legal opinion
and there has been no pressure by the unions to adopt these devices
as has been done in other Connecticut cities. The situations in other
cities are not always comparable with Hartford and in those towns
where there are no civil service systems or other security measures
provided by local law, more pressure by unions for bargained contracts can be expected.

Generally, the unions do not feel acutely the need for these
devices at this time because of adequate substitutes and because of
their established position in the municipal government. For instance, exclusive bargaining, setting jurisdictional lines, and the
union shop are not burning issues because of no real union rivalry
and few membership problems, the latter due to aggressive leadership and the dues check-off. Compulsory bargaining legislation is
not an immediate necessity because a cooperative spirit prevails.
As all wages, hours, and working conditions agreements are translated into personnel rules by the personnel board, or ordinances by
the city council, and thus become the law of the city, the unions are
not interested in changing this security for a system based on short-
term contracts. With the personnel board, composed of two citizens
and an employee, serving as an appeals board for grievances, the
need for other methods of third party assistance in handling
grievances has never been felt by the employees. Third party intervention on wages and hours has not been demanded thus far because
of the willingness of the municipal government and employees to
find grounds for agreement.

Though employees are forbidden the right to strike by ordinance,
and the unions have adopted no-strike provisions of their own in their
local charters, experience elsewhere has shown that strikes do occur
despite such restraints. The Hartford unions, however, have never
seriously considered using the strike weapon primarily because of
the generous treatment they have received. Union leaders also

realize that a municipal employee strike is only an ad hoc device
which will not gain them long-run advantages. Being oriented to the
political context of municipal government, they know that their major weapons are their votes at the polls and their influence through
local and higher labor councils on candidates and issues.

Weak Points of the Hartford System

The weak points in the present Hartford system revolve around
the definition of the respective roles of the city council, the city
manager, and the unions, and the absence of orderly procedures,
understood, accepted, and adhered to by all. There are two major
recurring areas of heated argument—one dealing with general wage
hikes during the preparation of the annual budget, the second concerning pay hikes for particular classifications throughout the year.
The major antagonists have usually been the city manager and the
personnel director on one side, and the city council and employees
on the other. This alignment has become a tradition—the city council defending and championing the employees against administrators
concerned with the budget and the defense of the "scientific method"
of pay plan administration.

Union Action for Wage Hikes

To gain their objectives on general wage policy during the
preparation of the annual budget, the unions, separately or collectively, bargain or deal with councilmen as individuals, as committees, as factions, and as a body. Meetings are usually conducted in
private. A certain amount of suspicion is generated now and then
among councilmen and unions who are not sure who is agreeing to
what—when and where. Meanwhile, the city manager generally
gains his information about these matters second hand and, in some
cases, after his recommended budget has been sent on its way to the
city council. Though much of this activity crosses the shady area
between legitimate municipal labor relations and political action, no
employee has been charged with political activity under the city's
personnel rules. It is this type of maneuvering that best illustrates
the confusing aspects of Hartford municipal labor relations.

The municipal pay plan by 1955 had been thrown out of balance
by a series of individual pay boosts granted by the city council over
a period of years. Each pay boost for one classification of employees created a clamor from others who saw no justification for not
keeping pace with co-workers. Some adjustments were made upon
recommendations of the personnel director substantiated by technical surveys. Others were made by the city council without the personnel director's recommendations. Political favoritism was claimed
in the latter instance; administrative influence in the former.

The great majority of employees, union and non-union, became fed up with this situation. Councilmen, themselves, began to react unfavorably to the incessant phone calls and button-holing by employees for individual consideration. The personnel director and the city manager, who were constantly in the middle between the city council and the employees, looked for a new system of pay plan administration that would correct the abuses inherent in the old.

Attempts to Systematize

Consultants were engaged in 1955 to recommend a new pay plan and new pay plan administration procedures. The consultants advocated a system of collective bargaining. They suggested that the city try out, as an experiment, some basic bargaining procedures in arriving at decisions on the new pay plan then being prepared. This was agreed. The city manager, the personnel director, and department heads represented the administration. The problem of who should represent the employees was handled pragmatically. Departments that had a union with 50 per cent membership were represented by that union. Other departments sent employee-chosen representatives, especially elected for the occasion. The unionized departments and the unorganized departments sat as two separate employee councils at the same table. Though the police department, which was over 50 per cent organized, was the only department not officially represented, it sent observers to attend the proceedings. (A prior feud with the other unions had not yet healed.) On a matter as fundamental as a new pay plan, union members were willing to negotiate with the administration at the same table with non-union employees.

A memorandum of understanding on the new pay plan certifying mutual administration-employee agreement and support was signed by the city manager and the heads of both employee councils. The personnel director agreed to prepare the new pay plan ordinance for submission to the city council. The city manager agreed to recommend the required appropriations in his budget. Though it was understood that the police union had been working on its own with councilmen for larger increases than recommended in the memorandum of understanding, it became apparent after the budget had been submitted to the city council that both the police and fire unions had made a deal with a majority of council. The end result was that both fire and police won additional step-ups over the scale agreed upon in the memorandum of understanding. The signing of the memorandum meant nothing. It was a defeat for the experiment in collective bargaining. The experiment proved that Hartford was not ready to abandon the all's-fair-in-love-and-war method for a system of "collective restriction." Without the legal framework to enforce it, a memorandum of understanding was worthless. The two trips to the legislature since 1955, noted above, have been efforts to acquire the legal framework necessary.

The usual pattern of individual pay changes ate away at the new 1955 pay plan setting the stage for another survey in 1960. The survey produced a new concept in municipal pay plans, the first of its kind in the United States. The significance of the 1960 pay plan to this paper, however, is in the ordinance the city council adopted governing its administration. The basic intent of this ordinance was to prohibit pay plan changes from being made on the basis of political favoritism by restricting the reasons for making changes to standard criteria prepared by the personnel director and amended by the personnel board. Furthermore, the ordinance provided for the buffering of the city council from employee pay complaints by setting up a new procedure of appeals to the personnel board.

This ordinance and the new pay plan were studied over a period of several months by employee representatives, the city manager, the city council standing committee on finance and personnel, together with the consultants and personnel director. These groups all approved the final ordinance and pay plan. After its formal adoption by council, the corporation counsel ruled that the council was not necessarily bound by the new pay plan procedures. Council has since passed several changes without relating them to the standard criteria or requiring preliminary appeals to the personnel board. The new ordinance which was passed with good intentions now seems doomed to the same fate as previous plans.

The Basic Problems

It is obvious from a reading of the preceding paragraphs that the city council of Hartford, the final authority on all wages, hours, and working conditions for municipal employees, is proud of this authority and aims to use it as it sees fit.

It is equally clear that the employees know where the ultimate authority over personnel matters lies and tend to override any obstacles in their way to place their issues before the elected council.

Not so clear, from the examination of Hartford's experience, is the city manager's role in collective bargaining.

Given this set of circumstances, how does one put the pieces together?

The authors maintain that municipal collective bargaining systems cannot ape collective bargaining practices in industry. The hard, cold, realistic political facts of life in government must be recognized. In order to bargain, you must be able to give something and receive something. There are only two parties that meet this

requirement—the city council and the employees. The city council
can grant personnel benefits and can receive employee support.
The employees can pledge votes and service and receive personnel
benefits. The city manager by himself, on the other hand, can only
make recommendations to the council which may or may not carry
weight, but can receive nothing tangible from the bargaining process.

Recommended Area of Union Action

There is a school of thought which believes that municipal
unions should deal only with the city manager, and will do so, foregoing political tactics, if disputes are turned over to arbitration.
We can accept this position for grievances where an internal personnel board is not available, but not for wages and hours.

We consider it wishful thinking to believe that political pressure
by unions can be stopped. (As used in this paper, political pressure
by unions pertains to ways and means of influencing councilmen to
support union measures.) Political pressure is the one effective
weapon the unions have and to deny them this outlet, if it is possible,
arbitration or no arbitration, is to leave the gates open for the srike.
Remember that, even if there were a method of stopping municipal
union members themselves from using this pressure, it is impossible to prevent their affiliated unions and councils from acting on
their behalf, or individual councilmen from encouraging it.

Regulating union political pressure, however, is essential. Collective bargaining procedures established by law should first require
open city manager-union discussions; second, a memorandum of understanding signed by both parties, covering points agreed and dis-
agreed to; third, open meetings called by the city council to review
the memorandum of understanding with the manager and unions.
These procedures are the minimum that should be provided to promote comprehensive consideration of bargaining issues.

Private negotiations by councilmen, city managers, or unions
cannot be prevented by these procedures if two parties want to get
together. Even the fiery proponents of open diplomacy sometimes
can rationalize the closed-door approach. However, a standardized
system of open meetings legally established for the purpose of collective bargaining assures a platform not only for the unions, but
for the manager and councilmen as well. Furthermore, it allows
public opinion to crystallize, something behind-the-scenes negotiations do not allow.

Should the manager deal with departmental unions separately—
public works at one time, police at another, then fire, etc.? We feel
that the unions should operate as a joint committee and develop a

single comprehensive program to present to the city manager. Not only is this a time-saving and less confusing procedure, but it encourages the unions to iron out their own differences. There is nothing more aggravating to a union leader than trying to keep discipline among his members when they know that other unions, operating independently of them, are bargaining for better terms.

Recommended Role of City Manager

The city manager should have a positive program of his own regarding wages and hours based on information supplied by his personnel director and department heads. Properly his program should have as one of its primary frames of reference the proposed budget for the coming year. He should be aware of pay trends in the community, personnel turnover rates, the ability of the city to attract various classes of personnel, and the quality of personnel it is attracting. His supporting data should indicate at what point it is more economical for the city to contract for various services rather than employ its own help, or to mechanize.

Armed with this information, the city manager has a basis for analyzing union proposals and for gaining union reactions to his own program. Upon conclusion of his discussions with the unions, whether there is complete agreement or not, a memorandum of understanding should be prepared setting forth both the areas of agreement and disagreement and a pledge that no new issues will be presented to council by either the union or the manager without first discussing them with each other. This memorandum should be transmitted to the city council with the manager's final recommendations. These recommendations should be clear, stating the administrative and technical considerations which council will need to know before making up its mind. The city council, on the other hand, cannot be restricted to technical considerations if it is to keep the political process intact, and should be expected to make its decision in the public interest, as it sees fit.

Recommended Role of City Council

Some observers will argue that the city manager and city council are, or should be, a team just like the company manager and the board of directors and that separating their roles is unrealistic. They will argue that the 1955 episode where the city council disregarded the signed memorandum of understanding could have been avoided by the manager if he had sought tacit approval from the city council before signing, or if he had requested the city council committee on finance and personnel to be co-signers to the document. If the committee members had signed, it would become their job to defend the agreement before their fellow councilmen. It is contended that this method would have distinct advantages for a city manager by buffering him from union as well as councilmanic attacks. However, there is a real question as to whether a committee of council would want to support such an agreement prior to consideration by council-as-a-whole.

We believe that the city council should stay clear of negotiations until the city manager-union discussions end for three reasons.

First, the city council should consider the results of the discussions in the same way as any other legislative matter, deciding on them in the public interest as it sees it. A certain amount of objectivity is required to perform this exercise which cannot be obtained by teaming up with the manager versus the unions. By sitting back and letting the manager and unions discuss the issues openly, the city council can get the feel of public opinion as well as of administrative and labor viewpoints. This procedure can shield councilmen from making premature commitments before all the facts are digested.

Second, by remaining independent of both the manager and the unions during their discussions, the council can serve as a kind of arbitration board. If the council and manager were to team up against the unions and failed to reach an acceptable agreement, for instance, where would the unions go next? They could not appeal to the same council with which they just finished negotiating. As far as this paper is concerned, calling in outside arbitrators on matters of wages and hours could set a pattern which might eventually disintegrate orderly governmental process. We are old fashioned enough still to believe in the principle of "no taxation without representation." An internal two-step procedure in the bargaining process with a reasonable time lapse between union-manager discussions and city council review provides a built-in cooling-off period and a safety-valve. Both are needed to avoid hasty and drastic actions.

The third justification for keeping the council clear of manager-union discussions is our belief that the political considerations, which are council's, and the technical-administrative considerations, which are the manager's, should not be intermingled.

Conclusion

The points made in this paper are largely based on our experience in Hartford. We have attempted to illustrate that municipal collective bargaining in the council-manager city at least, may be a three-cornered affair. Unlike industrial bargaining which involves labor on one side and management on the other, bargaining in a council-manager city must consider the separate functions of the city council, the city manager, and the unions. Council's fundamental role is legislative. Its considerations must be in the interest of all citizens. Correspondingly, the elected representatives know that they will be held responsible for their decisions by those citizens at the ballot box.

The city manager's power in collective bargaining varies with the weight given his recommendations by the city council. Because of changing membership, the council will react differently from term to term. No two cities will have councils which will react identically to the same set of circumstances. Though the manager's role is that of an intermediary between the unions and the city council, the only parties that have something tangible to give and take in municipal bargaining, he must play his part strongly, setting the facts straight, if there is to be meaning to the bargaining process.

Municipal collective bargaining cannot be an exact duplicate of the industrial process because of the nature of political life and institutions. Political pressure by unions must be recognized as an effective and essential substitute for the strike. However, union access to government must be regulated to allow the council to digest the city manager's recommendations and public opinion, as well as union arguments. Open discussions, as opposed to closed-door discussions, are necessary to protect the public interest.

Collective bargaining is too often talked about in terms of a benefit for labor alone. This is true in those jurisdictions which have fought organization drives and assume a paternalistic attitude towards their employees. Hartford's experience, however, indicates that the city manager, the city council, and the public have as much to gain from an orderly bargaining process as labor, if not more.

Chapter 8

Collective Bargaining in Philadelphia

FOSTER B. ROSER

In the minds of many, the subject of collective bargaining is a controversial one. It is not my intention to approach the subject in the spirit of controversy, but rather to present a factual account of our experience with collective bargaining in Philadelphia.

To accomplish this I want to provide appropriate background information, describe the procedure that we follow, and then offer an evaluation of collective bargaining in Philadelphia. In approaching my task I shall, therefore, not act as advocate, sponsor, or opponent.

Collective Bargaining Defined

What is meant by the term collective bargaining? Precisely what does it involve? To start with, consider four definitions. Recently the following statement appeared in the annual report of the Los Angeles Civil Service Department:

> Public agencies have almost universally recognized the right of employees to organize in unions of their own choosing, but very few have embraced any of the three other elements of collective bargaining: recognition of the right of a majority union to represent all workers, formal negotiations to establish wages and the like, and a written contract as the result of negotiation [emphasis supplied].[1]

Adapted from a paper given at the Public Personnel Association's 1961 International Conference on Public Personnel Administration, Denver, Colorado.

Foster B. Roser is Personnel Director, City of Philadelphia Personnel Department.

[1] "The Right to Strike," in Current Personnel Issues, annual report of the Civil Service Department, City of Los Angeles, for the fiscal year 1960-61, p. 19.

It will be noted from this quote that the definition requires, as one of the necessary elements of collective bargaining, that there be a written contract, in addition to recognition and formal negotiations. Perhaps this is the definition and these are the elements that many of you think of when you refer to collective bargaining.

Now, consider how collective bargaining is defined in the Taft-Hartley Law. It says, in part, that—

> . . . to bargain collectively is the performance of the mutual obligation of the employer and the representative of the employees to meet . . . and confer in good faith with respect to wages, hours, and other terms and conditions of employment, or the negotiation of an agreement . . . and the execution of a written contract incorporating any agreement reached . . . [emphasis supplied].

Under this definition, collective bargaining includes four related but distinguishable processes: (1) negotiations over wages, hours, and other terms of employment; (2) the execution of a written contract; (3) negotiation arising as to the interpretation of the contract; and (4) negotiation over the terms of a new or of proposed modifications of agreement.

You will note that this definition includes negotiation and a written contract, but there is no reference to, or requirement for, arbitration. Perhaps this is the definition you think of when referring to collective bargaining.

Now, let us refer to a definition by Dale Yoder. In his treatment of collective bargaining, with respect to collective agreements, he states, in part:

> The parties propose to conclude a collective agreement, popularly known as a labor contract. That agreement will describe their conclusions with respect to all the major questions on which they have negotiated.[2]

And then he says:

> Negotiation may not, however, result in such a written agreement. It may be concluded without any final written contract. This situation frequently appears in public employment. A union of local, state, or municipal

---

[2]Dale Yoder, Personnel Principles and Policies: Modern Manpower Management, 2nd ed. (Englewood Cliffs, N. J.: Prentice-Hall, Inc., 1959), p. 135.

employees may engage in extensive negotiation without
a resulting collective agreement and without expectation
that such an agreement will result. Negotiation, in such
cases, may be concluded without final commitments by
either party. For many government agencies, a collective
agreement or contract is impossible. Those with whom
employees negotiate may have neither the authority nor
the resources with which to insure performance. Perhaps they can make upward adjustments in compensation,
for example, only if adequate funds are appropriated for
this purpose. They may be able to modify hours of work,
vacations, sick leave provisions, and other conditions of
employment only when legislation or the ruling of a civil
service administrative board approve these changes.[3]

Lastly, I find the following definition in another Yoder text which
states in part:

"Collective bargaining" is used to describe a situation
in which various conditions of employment are determined
by agreement between representatives of a group of employees, on the one hand, and one or more employers on
the other. It is called collective because employees form
an association which they authorize to act as their agent
in reaching an agreement and because employers may
also act as a group rather than as individuals. It is
described as bargaining . . . because the method of
reaching an agreement involves proposals and counter-
proposals, offers and counteroffers.[4]

You will note that this definition makes no reference to a contract or
to formal negotiations.

"By Any Other Name"

I have checked Yoder's definitions with Eli Rock, former Labor
Relations Consultant for the Philadelphia Personnel Department, and
members of the Philadelphia Chapter of the Industrial Relations Association and find that they are acceptable and valid. The act of
collective bargaining in government does not necessarily involve

---

[3]Ibid.

[4]Dale Yoder, Personnel Management and Industrial Relations,
4th ed. (Englewood Cliffs, N. J.: Prentice-Hall, Inc., 1956), p. 356.

formal negotiations or a contract. It does not even require the existence of a memorandum of understanding or any written document.

Collective bargaining in government may consist of no more than discussions, conferences, negotiations, or any other term of meeting you may choose. During the course of review, both management and employee organization would probably indulge in the presentation and rebuttal of employee requests, haggling, bargaining, compromise, and possible agreement.

Assume for the moment that you believe employees may organize. If so, I am certain that you or other officials in your respective jurisdictions would not refuse to meet with employee representatives and, on their request, to be heard or to discuss appropriate issues and requests. My reference to "you or other officials" may be the Personnel Director, Mayor, City Manager, Budget Director, Legislative Body or Committee, etc.

What I am really trying to develop is the fact that many jurisdictions, in reality, carry on collective bargaining in one degree or another, whether or not they recognize it as such. Whether collective-bargaining activities consist of discussions, conferences, hearings, negotiations, adorned or unadorned with all of the trappings of formality including a contract, the fact remains that the only difference is a matter of degree both as to formality and what subjects are appropriate for discussion.

If you sit down with employee representatives and freely discuss some aspect of employment, you are engaging in two phases of collective bargaining. You are, to a degree, giving recognition to, and negotiating with, an employee organization. If you come to a mutually acceptable understanding on an issue, you have the equivalent of a form of labor agreement.

The Philadelphia Program

To support my thesis that collective bargaining may and does take on many variations of form and content, let me now refer to what we find in Philadelphia. By industrial standards, our collective-bargaining provisions would be clearly unsatisfactory. By those of government, they have been adjudged as advanced and sophisticated.

With the many existing and practical limitations which militate against having collective bargaining as traditionally found in industry, I think we have, by any standards, a labor-relations program which is as comprehensive in scope and coverage as can be expected.

Our rather new City Charter contains a provision which provides the authority for the development and operation of a labor-relations program simply through the adoption of a Civil Service Regulation.

Such a regulation was adopted which permits the Personnel Director to enter into collective-bargaining agreements. As a result of such authorizations we were enabled to legally consummate a labor agreement or contract with AFSCME--the American Federation of State, County, and Municipal Employees, AFL-CIO. An interesting legal feature of our labor contract is that with but one exception all of the contract provisions are also found in the Civil Service Regulations.

In accordance with state law the contract stipulates that employees cannot strike. There is no provision for arbitration. There is to be no discrimination between union and non-union employees, and the individual employee still retains the right to present his own requests and adjust his grievances. The contract does not require the payment of prevailing rates. Position classification is not one of the items which may be negotiated.

On the positive side, the contract recognizes the union as the exclusive bargaining agent for all non-uniformed civil service employees, except supervisors. Collective bargaining covers the traditional areas of wages, hours, and working conditions, and the contract in large part is given to covering specific aspects of these three categories.

A grievance procedure is spelled out in the contract. Dues deductions are included. Finally, there are provisions with respect to termination and renegotiation of all or any part of the contract.

Why Collective Bargaining in a Merit System?

I think that by generally accepted standards Philadelphia has a good merit system. I think too, that a review of the various programs included will indicate that it is probably as comprehensive a personnel system as will be found in any American municipality.

With minor variation it would probably have been just as comprehensive, with or without a union or collective bargaining. If you compare the list of 33 ultimate objectives of AFSCME with those presently incorporated in the Philadelphia merit system and other city agencies, you will find that there is only one that we do not have -- that of arbitration of grievances.

Now, if it is contended-- and it is-- that a merit system normally includes all of the necessary ingredients to create a satisfied work force, then why should one of our employee organizations want collective bargaining? Why too, should organized employees working in any merit-system environment, request the right to carry on collective bargaining with the jurisdiction in which they are employed? What are the benefits that accrue to both the employee and the governmental organization as the employer?

In industry, it is recognized that the primary reason for workers joining a union is their belief that the most important single benefit the worker secures from trade unionism is protection against arbitrary discharge, discipline, or grievances. Under a merit system, however, we can quickly discount this argument because of the traditional appeal procedure. But trade unionism in industry has other objectives which appeal to the worker, and these objectives have an equally strong appeal for the government worker.

What Union Members Want

Union members want a strong union, a union which truly represents them with management. In this manner the individual employee feels that he is taking some small part in his own welfare. Conversely, if the union is to remain strong, if it is to continue to keep members and take in dues, and if it is to have any success in gaining acceptance for any of its requests, it must have an appropriate avenue to achieve acceptance. To the union and its members, collective bargaining is an answer in achieving its goals.

A union and its members want collective bargaining because they want some "say" or some participation in the development or determination of their wages, hours of work, working conditions, fringe benefits, and personnel policies. As employees they have a personal concern in their employment conditions and, in these modern times, they want to participate in decisions that affect them, rather than to have a paternalistic employer decide what is good or appropriate for them. Thus, they may ask management to give emphasis or priority on any one or more particular "demands or requests" which they feel are important to them, and about which they ask management for serious consideration and discussion.

Collective bargaining provides the union with an orderly and adequate procedure to present to management what it considers to be important arguments and persuasive points to accomplish its goals. It provides, as an accepted practice, the opportunity to discuss in an unhurried manner those matters which are appropriate for discussion. It provides an opportunity to rebut in detail management's counter-arguments. It provides the opportunity to get management to "give and take" in reaching a bilateral agreement.

I repeat, collective bargaining permits the worker, through his union, to participate to some degree in decisions that affect him.

"Merit System" No Assurance Goals Will Be Met

Certain merit systems, such as in Philadelphia, provide their employees with favorable employment conditions comparable to those found in progressive industrial organizations. These conditions do not exist just because the employees are employed under a merit system, but because the jurisdictions in which they work have the governmental climate and have the leadership who believe it good policy to provide its work force with employment benefits equal or comparable to those offered by its competitors, be they in industry or government.

There are today, however, many civil service jurisdictions in this land of ours, which are considered to be merit systems but whose programs are limited, at the most, to examinations, classification, and performance reports. The term "merit system" in and of itself is no guarantee that the employees' working conditions and benefits are satisfactory by any standards. As a matter of fact, many non-civil-service jurisdictions probably do much better by their workers.

Without collective bargaining in a merit system we must presume that management decides unilaterally what benefits and privileges should be given to its workers. This being so, and aside from financial limitations, what criteria or reasons does it utilize in coming to its periodic conclusions?

The attitudes and aspirations of wage earners in an industrial civilization, whether they work in industry or government, are such that they are striving to fulfill certain needs and to achieve certain goals that are important to them. Which goals are most important to people at work? No simple answer can be given.

Use of Counter-Proposal

From governmental management's point of view, collective bargaining offers one major advantage, if utilized. This advantage lies in the counter-proposals to the union's requests or demands. It further involves the give-and-take of negotiations and compromise. Thus, when the union presents its requests, management offers, in turn, certain counter-requests which it feels to be important.

Let me cite several examples of our use of the counter-proposal approach. One counter-proposal agreed to by the union resulted in a reduction of sick leave allowance from 30 to 20 days per year. At another time, a counter-proposal by management resulted in agreement by the union to increase pension contributions $2\frac{1}{2}\%$ or nearly 40% in the employees' contribution.

Another example was agreement on a wage increase. Here the union wanted additional health and welfare benefits and, to obtain them, agreed to take a pay increase of one-half pay step less than that granted to the uniformed employees. The union could not have both. Management made an offer, and the union accepted.

Collective bargaining has resulted in the adoption of two of our major programs. During years when finances did not permit wage increases, social security and health and welfare programs were negotiated. Management's collective-bargaining advantage in negotiating the social security program was agreement to a 50% social security offset on pension payments, which of course reduced pension costs to the city.

Helps Effect Needed Policy Changes

It is a well accepted fact that once management has granted a benefit to its employees, it is considered impossible to eliminate it, or reduce it to any extent, no matter how justifiable the reason may be. On this point, I am sure that every public agency has a number of personnel policies that could stand tightening up, revision, or elimination but knows full well that it could never obtain voluntary employee or union acceptance of the change.

The only approach I know, in which to cut back all or part of some ill-advised, or too liberal, benefits that were granted in the past, and to obtain employee acceptance in the doing, is through the process of collective bargaining.

Improves Climate

Perhaps the most practical reason for collective bargaining in a given merit system is the existence of a labor-oriented climate in which it operates. With a political-labor-oriented environment there would probably be little or no opposition to collective bargaining-- in fact, there might be a real demand for it. Such has been the case in Philadelphia for years. The drafting of our new City Charter, and the administration which inherited it in 1952, accepted with certainty the principle of collective bargaining.

Your reactions and mine to collective bargaining reflect, in great part, our past personal experiences, or lack of them, with respect to labor-management relations. A government administrator who has not been exposed or accustomed to the technique of collective bargaining can raise many questions as to its propriety. In contrast, an individual who has served on management's side of the bargaining table with government unions will, in all likelihood, be convinced that collective bargaining is not only desirable, but that benefits can accrue from its practice.

Origin of Collective Bargaining in Philadelphia

The American Federation of State, County and Municipal Employees was formed in 1936 and in the same year, at the convention of the American Federation of Labor, was given jurisdiction over all non-federal government employees. The opportunity to establish a Philadelphia local, and to recruit city employees for membership therein, was literally thrust upon the AFSCME.

Early in 1939, the Department of Public Works was paralyzed by a strike of unorganized city employees. Both the striking employees and the Mayor requested the assistance of the AFSCME in settling the dispute. The success of the union in negotiating an agreement, the terms of which were embodied in a formal collective-bargaining contract, assured the union's future in Philadelphia and inaugurated an era of official city-union relationship.

The 1939 collective-bargaining agreement, which even at that time was rather comprehensive in coverage, continued until December, 1939, and from year to year thereafter unless either the city or the union gave 60 days' written notice of its intention to terminate the agreement. As events turned out, the basic features of the 1939 agreement governed city-union relationships for almost five years.

Later Revisions

It was not until 1944 that the first extensive revision of the collective agreement was made. The 1944 contract expanded the union's exclusive departmental representation rights, incorporated the inclusion of wages as a subject for collective negotiation, and a reform of the grievance procedure. Although wages were still to be determined in accordance with the terms of a budget ordinance, the contract provided that the union was to present its wage requests to both the Mayor and City Council, who were obligated to meet with the union to discuss the requests.

The 1944 agreement remained in full force and effect without substantial change until 1953 when an amendatory agreement became effective. This contract was the first to be negotiated under the new Home Rule Charter. Under authority of the City Charter, the Civil Service Commission-- by regulation-- authorized the Personnel Director to negotiate a collective-bargaining contract with the union.

Following the procedure established in the Charter, the Personnel Director proposed for the commission's approval individual regulations embodying in substance the benefit provisions reached with the union.

The agreement of 1953 was amended by appropriate regulations in each succeeding year, after extensive negotiations, to provide additional and increased benefits. Nevertheless, the basic structure of the 1953 contract was unchanged and is retained in the current agreement.

How It Operates

For the sake of brevity, I shall simply list the various steps that are taken in the bargaining process, adding explanatory comments when necessary.

Annual negotiations covering wages and other terms of employment involve a variety of steps to be taken by the city and extend over a period from April or May until November. Agreed-upon benefits become effective on the following January 1, coinciding with the beginning of a new fiscal year.

Following are the major phases of the collective bargaining process:

1. If it is apparent that funds will be available for a wage increase, the Personnel Department conducts a wage survey in April and May and, from data obtained, determines appropriate recommendations.

2. The city bargaining team, consisting of Personnel Director, Managing Director, and Finance Director, confers to exchange views. Counter-proposals are developed. Exploratory conference may be held with the Mayor.

3. On or about July 1, the union submits its requests, in writing, to the city bargaining team. The bargaining team reviews requests and later, during the latter part of July, holds a preliminary meeting with the union simply for purposes of reviewing, clarifying, and understanding what the requests involve. City may submit counter-proposals at this time. No negotiations at this meeting.

4. City bargaining team confers on requests. In light of requests and these involving finances, team determines items on which agreement may be reached.

5. City bargaining team confers with Mayor and Councilmanic Committee representatives on proposal to establish "family understanding" as to what "package" can be agreed upon. Personnel Director advises Civil Service Commission.

6. City bargaining team and union meet in negotiation sessions until agreement on some basis is reached. This usually involves from two to four meetings, during which the Mayor and legislative branch members must be consulted from time to time.

7. Agreed-upon monetary benefits are incorporated in Mayor's budget message to Council. If some advocacy of the recommendations are required before Council, the executive branch and the union present a united front. Passage of any necessary councilmanic appropriations must, by charter requirements, be adopted by December 1.

8. Personnel Director presents, in Civil Service Regulation form, all negotiated benefits at public meeting of Civil Service Commission for approval on or before December 1. Approved actions must, in turn, be approved by the Administrative Board, consisting of the Mayor, Managing Director, and Finance Director, who have already been through the bargaining actions.

9. Negotiated benefits become effective January 1, and are incorporated in amended labor contract shortly thereafter and signed by both parties.

Evaluation

In evaluating our collective-bargaining experiences in Philadelphia, I have come to a number of conclusions which I believe would be applicable, for the most part, to personnel managers at any level of government.

Obviously, one of the more important ingredients that work against having true collective bargaining in government is that of the restrictive statutes on the employees' right to strike. Even in those areas where public administrators strive to develop, establish, and maintain the most progressive and acceptable labor-management relationships and policies, both management and union constantly recognize the inherent limitations that exist because of the inability of the employee to strike.

Consciously or unconsciously, both parties feel the impact of this restriction. Accordingly it affects the tone of any negotiations. Even though this subject may never be outwardly referred to by either party, it is nevertheless inwardly never ignored or disregarded.

The second difficulty in collective bargaining in a governmental setting is that, with no money available, it is -- and this is the understatement of the day -- a problem to find grounds on which to negotiate. I suppose that in union-management relations we could paraphrase an old saying by stating that "No money is the root of most of our troubles."

This lack of money poses a problem for both sides. With no money, management can only negotiate on non-monetary items usually involving minor fringe benefits. The union officials and representatives in such a

situation are figuratively over a barrel and must be frustrated because of their inability to deliver, as their membership has every
right to expect of them.

Another problem relates to the complexities of governmental
administration and confusion of divided authority. Without going into the many gory details, consider the confusion of responsibility for
action or determination in the conduct of negotiations in Philadelphia.
Any other public jurisdiction will present an almost similar picture.
Involved are the Mayor, Personnel Director, Managing Director,
Finance Director, City Council and its appropriations and finance
committees, and the Civil Service Commission.

Each city official and every city body mentioned has prerogatives
which must be recognized and considered by everyone else in the act.
It is under these circumstances that a "family understanding" must,
by necessity, be agreed upon, if negotiated benefits are to become a
reality.

Where several unions are involved, collective bargaining results
in non-uniformity of city-wide personnel policies. In our case, this
is due to the city's willingness, in the spirit of collective bargaining,
to meet the varied interests of three different employee organizations.
The desires and emphasis of each organization as to benefits can and
do result, in a number of instances, in variations in the same overall
policies.

Neither "Give-away" Nor "Cure-all"

There have been some who have expressed to me the belief that
through the collective-bargaining process the city has been, or soon
will be, given away. In turn, certain union leaders are of the opinion
that by the simple expediency of collective bargaining, together with
a labor contract, all of their problems would be solved and all of
their requests would have to be granted.

Obviously, both are wrong. Neither collective bargaining nor a
labor contract, in and of itself, forces management to do anything it
is unwilling to do. In fact, our experience with collective bargaining
clearly indicates that it has not resulted in the granting of any benefits that might not have been given without collective bargaining. The
city may have granted benefits on a somewhat different basis than
would have been the case if granted unilaterally. The one unusual
feature is the exclusive bargaining provision covering all non-uniformed personnel. The city acceded on this point probably as much
in its own interest as for the union's, to prevent future inter-juris-
dictional conflicts.

Just a word on the value of our labor contract. As I have already
indicated, every provision of the contract, except one, is contained in

the Civil Service Regulations. Thus, the document, except for the point of the city's recognition of the union, is largely an instrument of psychological and prestige value to the union.

Collective bargaining as practiced in industry, cannot be carried over to the typical governmental jurisdiction. Industrial collective bargaining in government is impractical for the reason that employees cannot strike. The complexity of the government machinery and hierarchy complicate negotiations. It may be impossible to obtain a "family understanding" on the part of the legislative and executive branches to negotiate as a team in the required give-and-take situations that are by the very nature of collective bargaining bound to arise.

Although the government union will disagree with me, I   claim that it cannot rely solely on collective bargaining for the purpose of obtaining employee benefits. While the union will insist on collective bargaining as a panacea for its demands or requests, experience in most instances will prove that collective bargaining does not create a Utopian situation.

The established government union is accustomed to running to the legislative body, which holds the appropriating authority, to lobby for what it wants, and it has found this approach to be not unfruitful. When a union sits down with an impersonal bargaining team, usually selected from the executive branch of government (which team incidentally may not enjoy the full support and understanding of the legislative body), and, following collective-bargaining meetings, finds that its demands are not to be fully met, it cannot resist the temptation to return to the legislative body for further appeal.

Once this happens, however, collective bargaining in that jurisdiction has ceased to exist.

Merit System Hasn't Suffered

Has collective bargaining made our work force happier and more contented? With respect to tangible results, I doubt it. I think the union and its members look upon collective bargaining as they do any other benefit.

It does permit them to participate in the development and determination of the terms and/or conditions of employment through the process of annual negotiations and those involving the development of new or revised personnel policies.

To me this is a right and privilege to which they are entitled and I do not believe it has done any violence or harm to our merit system.

Chapter 9

Unions in Cincinnati Government

W. D. Heisel and J. P. Santa-Emma

Many public personnel administrators look with distaste on the union-organizing activities of public employees. Some officials have refused to recognize such organizations, and, backed by legal decisions, have stated that employment by government and participation in labor unions is incompatible. In other situations, courts have held against the alleged improper delegation of authority required in the collective-bargaining process.

If this were a learned article, we would by now have dotted the page with footnotes of all the cases arising on this controversial subject. This is not our purpose. We aim only to show that, regardless of laws, regardless of courts, regardless of unfavorable administrative attitudes, you will have unions! We intend to give our reasons why, and, through our own personal experience, also to point out that unions do not necessarily take title to city hall as soon as they are recognized.

Unrealistic Approach Not the Answer

The utilization of such theories as state sovereignty and "improper delegation of authority" may delay unionization but will not prevent it. Unionization is moving ahead at a fantastic rate.

The AFSCME (American Federation of State, County, and Municipal Employees) is the fastest growing union in the labor movement today. It exists in Philadelphia, where it has a contract; and it has members in Virginia and in Alabama (which prohibits unions). It has all forms of recognition, ranging from the contract down to a confused de facto acceptance.

Originally published in Public Personnel Review, journal of the Public Personnel Association, January, 1961, under the title "Unions in City Government: The Cincinnati Story."

W. D. Heisel is City Personnel Officer and Secretary, Civil Service Commission and Department of Personnel for the City of Cincinnati.

J. P. Santa-Emma is Personnel Technician, Civil Service Commission and Department of Personnel for the City of Cincinnati.

Many government units, instead of taking a definite stand, have adopted a "wait-and-see" attitude, in the hope that unions will somehow disappear. Some have fought them openly, but, in the meantime, the AFSCME continues to enroll more and more members.

Of the approaches mentioned above, the one with the worst ultimate implications is the "wait-and-see" approach, which provides an arms-length tolerance but no regulation of the union-management relationship. This permits the establishment of precedents which ultimately will make it more difficult to obtain the type of relationship that is fair to management.

We speak from experience. In Cincinnati, unions had been allowed to exist without formal relationships for a long time. We had quite a problem in getting the kind of restrictions which we considered essential to good relationships, as will be pointed out later.

Why Join Unions?

Why will you have unions in the public service? To answer this question requires answering another: Why do employees join unions?

The first and foremost reason, of course, is the unions' success in obtaining economic benefits. No one can dispute the fact that public employee unions, like their industrial counterparts, have succeeded in getting better wages and fringe benefits. They have acted like any other pressure group in dealing with legislative bodies—and the approach has worked.

Unions have also increased the feeling of security that workers need. True, many public employees get civil service security against dismissal, but the possibility of having a grievance to present or of being involved in disciplinary action in which the penalty could be as drastic as dismissal is ever present. In such cases the employee wishes to have someone more articulate than he to speak for him; someone who is better acquainted than he with the civil service laws; someone who knows what has happened in previous cases. So he turns to the union business agent. The employee thus gains security from union participation.

A third, and perhaps the most important, reason for joining a union lies in the satisfaction of participation—the sense of belonging, the opportunity to be somebody. The average employee has no identity as an individual, especially in a large agency. True, we talk a lot about recognition. Maybe we give 25-year pins, or occasionally put workers' names in the house organ. But day-by-day recognition? We might as well admit we don't provide it.

By joining a union, the average employee gets the feeling that he is participating in formulating policy. Many doors which were

effectively closed to him before now open if he becomes an officer
or steward. He may attend conventions. He may see his name in the
newspaper. He gains a social outlet—perhaps his only chance to join
a social organization. This prestige—sense of belonging, of self-
esteem, call it what you will—is a strong force in the union's organizing drive.

These are three important reasons why unions were created,
and why employees join them. In effect, they are the reasons you
have, or will have, unions to deal with.

Why Recognize Unions?

Once a union organizes, management must then take a position.
We believe there are a number of reasons why management should
willingly recognize unions voluntarily formed by its employees.

The most important is the mere fact that the union exists. It
is unrealistic to say you can ignore your own employees. These
unions are not made up of third-party outsiders but of public employees. Individually, they have the right to appeal to management
about their wages, job classifications, working conditions, etc. If
we recognize these rights of individuals, it is impractical to deny
them to groups of individuals. In fact, it becomes far easier for
management to deal with these individual employees if they voluntarily provide a systematic means of communication through officers and business agents.

Communication with employees is one of the areas in which
good union-management relations can be made to pay off. Management can get information to workers through supervision or through
publications, such as employee manuals or house organs. But unfortunately, when management tries to explain a policy, workers
somehow are more prone to believe their peers than their superiors.
Likewise, in the upward flow of information, individual workers are
more likely to tell supervisors what they think supervisors want to
hear. Collectively, however, they feel freer to speak their minds.

There is a more pragmatic reason for offering recognition to a
newly formed union: the opportunity given management to set the
conditions of representation. Who can the union bargain for? Are
supervisors eligible for union membership? If members, can they
be officers? Can they be included in the bargaining unit? What are
proper subjects of bargaining? What are the rights of management?

Agencies keeping their heads in the sand may find that unions
have enrolled supervisors, or have expressed themselves on matters
far beyond the usual bargaining relationship, or wangled concessions
from one supervisor contrary to the policy of the agency itself. Open,
written recognition provides management with the opportunity to help

set the ground rules of the union-management relationship. In fact, most unions are so anxious to get recognition that management can pretty well write the rules itself.

By grabbing the ball and providing for recognition, the alert management will have less to undo later. We faced that situation in Cincinnati. In the late forties, when unions began to organize city workers, management took no position on unionism, other than a willingness to listen to them just as it would to any taxpayer. The unions enrolled any employee willing to pay his dues.

By the time they became an effective force numerically, much damage had been done. Supervisors talked their employees into joining—a very effective recruitment technique. Unions criticized the city manager's budget—hardly a negotiable item in private industry. Management did not know who was in and who was not in unions. We now have some ground rules, which we will describe later, and feel we are better off for that reason.

Let's Have a Strong Union!

Another effect that denying recognition will have on the union is that it will be weakened. The union won't go out of the picture, but it will be deprived of its strength in two respects: (1) it will be smaller numerically and therefore not necessarily representative, just as a small statistical sample of anything is not likely to be representative of the whole; and (2) it will possibly be of poorer quality, and therefore inclined to be obstreperous, irresponsible, demagogic, extremist, or incompatible with management. If you express disapproval, the better employees may well stay away from unions. Or, if they do join, they may stay out of leadership positions. Thus, by default, its leadership goes to the malcontent.

To be representative of the whole, the union needs reasonable size, adequate leadership, and security. It can't do its job of representing workers if its energies are devoted to staying alive, as a weak union must. It must have a solid financial support--and that means payroll dues deduction.

Although union security is first and foremost financial, it also involves the need for a written agreement providing for exclusive bargaining. This is in part a concession to union tradition. Other unions get written contracts, why not us? But it is more than just window dressing. It is a status symbol in union circles that is a protection against raiding. Our worst union experiences were in those situations where we had two unions competing for the same groups of employees.

Union Relations in Cincinnati

As indicated before, Cincinnati has entered the written-agreement stage of union-management relations only recently. Employees began to organize years ago. We first heard of the AFSCME in about 1939. Recognition was provided only in the sense that if a business agent appeared, he was allowed to talk. Who did he really represent? We had no idea except his own somewhat generous estimates.

During the forties we were well aware of increased union activities, not only by the AFSCME, but also by other unions. They frequently competed for membership in the same departments. The city council first recognized unions in 1951, when it passed a resolution "Declaring a City Wage Policy." This resolution defined a system of collective bargaining between the city manager and employee representatives on all matters pertaining to wages and working conditions. It did not define, however, what a union was, or whether a majority was required before a union could speak for a group. There was no limitation placed upon the areas in which the union could operate.

In 1960, a series of meetings between the AFSCME and management culminated in a modification of the policy resolution and the ultimate signing of a written agreement. The policy resolution amendment required that the union have a majority before it could be recognized. It also permitted the city manager to determine the bargaining unit and whether the union has the required majority. In order to get a written agreement, the union had to delete supervision above the first level from the bargaining unit it wished to represent.[1] It also had to agree to certain other minor exclusions, such as probationary employees, confidential employees, and employees of the personnel department. The right of an individual to represent himself is guaranteed as well as a clause prohibiting discrimination for or against union membership.

The written agreement itself is an administrative type of document. It is very short. Some labor-relations experts consider that the length of a contract is in inverse relation to the amount of mutual trust existing between the union and management. We believe that

---

[1] This requirement has prevented the Firefighters Association and the Fraternal Order of Police from seeking written agreement. They refuse to give up their existing prerogative of representing officers. While this provides two "degrees" of union recognition in Cincinnati, it is relatively unimportant because of the high percentage of membership in these organizations and their relative immunity to "raiding" by other labor organizations.

this agreement sets forth the basis for agreement on any issue, and that it is therefore unnecessary to "legislate" every conceivable matter in the agreement itself.

We also handled the potential problem of delegation of legislative authority by adopting ordinances into the agreement by reference. No working conditions are spelled out in the agreement, no salaries set forth, no fringe benefits described. This not only protects us against possible attack of delegation of authority, but it also prevents possible confusion in case a paraphrase of an ordinance unintentionally changed a meaning.

Management's Policies

Immediately upon the signing of the agreement with the AFSCME, the administration did two important things: (1) the city manager issued a written statement of his policies with regard to the union; and (2) the writers held meetings with supervision of every level in each operating agency affected by the agreement for the purpose of explaining the agreement and the city policy.

The city manager's written statement was primarily a statement of attitude. He pointed out that recognition was city policy, requiring supervision's support. He sought to impress upon management that the concept of management prerogatives, included in the agreement, should not be stretched into a basis for refusing to discuss anything with unions.

The administration's willingness to consult was emphasized. The city manager also delegated to department heads the responsibility of dealing with unions on matters affecting only their own agencies, and gave to the personnel officer the obligation of review and approval of agency policies with regard to unions.

The meetings with supervision did not change policy; they served only to communicate it. About thirty meetings were necessary to reach about 500 supervisors, each of whom had previously received a copy of the agreement, the policy resolution, and the city manager's policy. As a result, this is probably the best-understood policy we have.

What Can Management Now Expect?

Winning a contract is always considered, in union circles, as a great victory. Normally it is won over considerable resistance from management. It solidifies the union position, gives it security. We would be the last to deny that our union considers that it has gained a big advantage with the signing of the agreement. Seldom, however, do we stop to realize the gains that management makes, at least in our circumstances.

Our own gains must be examined from the viewpoint of where
we stood before the agreement. We had recognized unions, but had
set no ground rules—no requirement of a majority, no recognition
of management rights, no exclusions from the bargaining unit.[2]
The mere establishment of these ground rules helped management.
And the agreement by the union to these ground rules is also
significant.

But more important, in our opinion, is our increased ability to
demand responsible action from the union. We believe that management gets the kind of union it deserves. If management wants to be
tricky, it will bring to the fore union leaders who are tricky in return. If management holds the union to every comma of the laws and
rules, unions will hold management just as tight. But if management
is fair and open, it is setting a climate to get fair and open responses
from its employees collectively, just as it can get such responses
individually.

We are trying to impress our employees—union and others—with
the fact that both management and rank-and-file must be sensitive
to public opinion. We cannot believe that the public approves of
bickering, trickiness, and constant wrangling. To the extent that
labor and management work together for the good of the citizen—not
in collusion, but in cooperation toward better service—we can expect
the support of the public. Formalized, well-understood, properly
communicated working relationships between management and unions
can foster such cooperation.

---

[2]Dues check-off had been established pretty much by horse-
trading. The unions wanted the security; we wanted the straight
dope on union membership. We charge five cents for each monthly
deduction.

Chapter 10

Municipal Labor Relations in Wisconsin:

A New Program

ARVID ANDERSON

The State of Wisconsin has been a pioneer in the enactment of labor legislation during the twentieth century. The Workmen's Compensation Statute of 1911 and the Unemployment Compensation Statute of 1932 were models copied by other states. In 1937, Wisconsin was one of the first states to adopt a "little Wagner Act."

That law was amended in 1939 by the passage of the Employment Peace Act which, in turn, was the forerunner of the federal Taft-Hartley Law in 1947. In 1959 and 1962, Wisconsin again ventured into a new field of labor legislation by enacting a comprehensive labor-relations code governing the conduct of municipal employer-employee relations.[1]

The 1959 Statute

The 1962 statute amended a 1959 law which conferred upon employees of local units of government the right to form and join labor organizations and to be represented by such labor organizations in conferences and negotiations with their municipal employers on questions of wages, hours, and conditions of employment. It also provided that such municipal employees had the right to refrain from any and all of such activities.

A municipal employer was defined in the 1959 statute as meaning any city, county, village, town, metropolitan sewerage district, school district, or other political subdivision of the state. It does not apply to employees of the state government. Municipal employees as defined in the statute include any employee of a municipal employer except city and village policemen, sheriff's deputies, and county traffic officers.

The earlier statute provided certain specific prohibited practices on the part of municipal employers. They were directed to

---

Arvid Anderson is a Commissioner of the Wisconsin Employment Relations Board, Madison.

[1]Wisconsin Laws 1961, Chapter 663, Section 111.70.

refrain from interfering with, or restraining, or coercing municipal employees in their right of self-organization and their right to seek representation. The municipal employers also were prohibited from encouraging or discouraging membership in any labor organization by discrimination in hiring, tenure, or other terms or conditions of employment.

Similarly, municipal employees individually, or in concert with others, were prohibited from coercing, intimidating, or interfering with the rights of other municipal employees to join or to refrain from joining a labor organization.

The 1962 Statute

The 1962 statute implemented the 1959 act by providing for a means of enforcement of the prohibited practices by proceedings before the Wisconsin Employment Relations Board. This board is a three-member commission with a civil service staff similar to the National Labor Relations Board. Unlike the NLRB, however, the Wisconsin Board does not investigate and prosecute complaints. This is the responsibility of the parties.

The 1962 statute also provides that questions of representation that might arise between a municipal employer and a labor union can be determined by a secret ballot election to be conducted by the Wisconsin Employment Relations Board. The statute further provides that municipal employers and their employees might avail themselves of the mediation services of the state labor agency upon the request of both parties. It specifically prohibits the right to strike in public employment.

Fact-Finding Provisions

The means of resolving deadlocks in conferences and negotiations is also provided in the statute by the establishment of a fact-finding procedure. Fact finders are empowered to make non-binding recommendations for the settlement of disputes.

Proceedings in fact-finding cases are limited to those situations in which a labor union had been certified by the Wisconsin Employment Relations Board, or had been recognized by the municipal employer as the representative of the employees. Fact finding may not be applied in disputes involving discharge or discipline cases where civil service provisions exist.

The statute also provides that, where a local employer through ordinance or otherwise had established fact-finding procedures substantially in compliance with the 1962 statute, the state agency cannot initiate action on the fact-finding petition.

Interestingly enough, law enforcement officers, who are exempted from a general coverage of the statute, are permitted to avail themselves of the fact-finding proceedings. The procedure applies in a circumstance where a majority of the members of a police, sheriff, or county traffic officer department petitions the governing body for changes or improvements in wages, hours, or working conditions and designates a representative to appear before the governing body.

Statutes Evidence of Growing Interest

The enactment of the 1959 and 1962 Wisconsin statutes is symbolic of the sharply increasing public interest in municipal employer-employee labor relations. In Wisconsin, it was the culmination of a legislative effort on the part of representatives of public employee labor unions for the past fifteen years.

It has been the public policy of this country for the last twenty-five years in the private sector of our economy to encourage collective bargaining by state and federal statutes. This is exemplified by the enactment of the Wagner Act in 1937, and by the passage of the Wisconsin Labor Relations Act, a "little Wagner Act," in the same year. As mentioned above, this was amended in 1939 to create the Employment Peace Act, the forerunner of the Labor-Management Relations Act of 1947 on the national scene.

The enactment and the subsequent developments flowing from such statutes increased the demand of public employees to enjoy the same rights and privileges conferred upon private employees. The basic argument for the encouragement of collective bargaining in public employment has been summarized as follows:

> A government which imposes upon private employees
> certain obligations dealing with their employees may
> not in good faith refuse to deal with its own public
> servants on a reasonably similar basis, modified of
> course to meet the exigencies of public service.[2]

Fear of Bargaining-Equals-Strike

However, the encouragement of collective bargaining among public employees always raises a number of concerns, particularly about strikes in public employment. The concern over the extension of union organization and collective bargaining to the area of public

---

[2]American Bar Association. Second Report of the Committee on Labor Relations of Governmental Employees, 1955.

employment may be summarized as follows: unions mean collective bargaining; collective bargaining means strikes; the right to strike in public employment should not exist; and therefore there is no need for public employee unions or collective bargaining in public employment.

This concern led to a Wisconsin legislative effort in 1947 to enact a statute similar to the Condon-Wadlin Act in the State of New York which prohibits strikes by public employees and provides for certain penalties.[3] Legislative representatives for public employee unions combated the 1947 proposal, which was sponsored by the state Chamber of Commerce, by attempting to introduce amendments to the bill. These would guarantee to public employees the right to organize, the right to bargain, and the right to utilize fact finding.

The 1947 union proposal embraced the prohibition of the right to strike, except in those cases where the recommendations of the fact finder were disregarded or where there was a breach of an agreement. The legislation failed to pass.

Early Legislative Efforts

In 1951, the public employee unions succeeded in securing legislative passage of a bill which guaranteed the right of public employees to form and join unions, but did not define an employee so as to exclude policemen. Governor Kohler vetoed that bill on the ground that police should not be participants in the labor movement.

In 1953, 1955, and 1957, similar efforts were made without success by the public employee unions to pass legislation protecting the rights of public employees to organize and to bargain collectively. In 1955, an interim Legislative Council committee had been established to study the subject, but concluded after its investigation that there was no necessity for legislation at that time.

Opposition to the enactment of the 1962 statute included a number of traditional craft unions who were less than sympathetic with the objectives of public employee unions. They resisted the provisions permitting the selection of a bargaining representative until a compromise was worked out whereby, in the determination of collective-bargaining units, it was specifically provided that craft employees would not be included in the same collective-bargaining unit as other employees.

For example, if an electrician was employed in the maintenance department of a municipal employer, that electrician could not be

---

[3]Condon-Wadlin Act, N. Y. Civil Service Law. Sec. 22A, Ch. 391, Laws of 1947.

included in the same bargaining unit with other non-craft maintenance employees. However, the craft employee could be represented by the same labor organization, if he so desired, but only in a separate bargaining unit.

The 1962 statute, as first proposed, empowered the Wisconsin Employment Relations Board to serve as an arbitrator to determine grievances which would arise during the term of the collective-bargaining agreement. That provision was stricken from the bill prior to passage. A provision relating to mediation was modified so as to be applicable only upon the joint request of both parties.

A further amendment to the statute provided that contracts between municipal employers and unions could not be binding, except where language to that effect was specifically contained in the agreement. The last significant amendment related to fact finding. It respected the home rule desire of some municipal employers by providing that, where a local ordinance which was substantially in compliance with the fact-finding procedures of the state statute was in effect, the state agency should not initiate fact-finding proceedings.

Passage of Statute Raises Questions

The practice of collective bargaining in public employment, or at least the representation of public employees by labor unions, has existed in Wisconsin and elsewhere for many years without statutory encouragement or protection. However, the enactment of the recent Wisconsin statute calls attention to a number of questions affecting labor relations in the public service:

1. Do public employees have the right to strike or picket in support of their demands for improved wages, hours, or conditions of employment?

2. Should the right to strike in public employment be protected, limited, or prohibited?

3. Do all public employees have the right to join a labor organization of their own choosing?

4. Do public employers have the duty to recognize labor unions as the bargaining representative for their public employees?

5. Can a public employer grant recognition to a labor organization as the exclusive bargaining agent for certain of its employees?

6. Do public employers have the duty to bargain collectively or to engage in conferences and negotiations with representatives of their employees on wages, hours, and conditions of employment?

7. Can public employers be required to enter into a collective-bargaining agreement with a labor union?

8. Do public employees have the right to avail themselves of grievance procedures to resolve complaints over their conditions of employment?

9. May public employers and employees or their representatives agree to submit to arbitration grievance disputes over contract interpretation or terms of employment?

10. May public employers and employees or their representatives use mediation services to resolve public employer-employee disputes?

11. What is the role of fact-finding in public employer-employee disputes?

The passage of the 1959 statute and the amendment to that law in 1962 provide some answers to these questions for Wisconsin municipal employers and employees.

Administration of the Statute

Section 111.70 of the Wisconsin Statutes is comparatively brief for the reason that much of the machinery for administering the law is contained in Chapter 111, the Wisconsin Employment Peace Act, and is incorporated by reference into Chapter 111.70. For example, the procedure for the enforcement of prohibited practices is the same as that which applies in private employee disputes. Also, the proceedings in representation cases to determine bargaining representatives are to be in accordance with the procedures outlined in the Employment Peace Act for private employers, insofar as applicable.

After the passage of the statute, the Wisconsin Employment Relations Board appointed an advisory committee composed of an equal number of representatives of municipal employers and municipal employee unions to advise it on the formulation of procedural rules for the administration of the statute. A series of formal and informal meetings was held by the board on the preparation of rules for administering the statute. The rules were formally adopted on August 1, 1962.

They governed such subjects as the conduct of hearings, the processing of unfair labor practice or prohibitive practice complaints, the mediation of labor disputes, and procedures in fact-finding cases. Even prior to the formal adoption of the procedural rules, the board began to receive a number of election petitions.

The Question of Representation

It had been estimated that approximately a hundred municipal employee cases would be filed annually with the board. Some seventy cases have already been filed during the seven months since the law was passed, most of them within the last four months. As might be expected, nearly all of the cases involve representation questions. It is the opinion of the board that the flood of these cases will continue for some time.

The elections now being conducted do not, for the most part, represent new organizational efforts on behalf of public employee unions, but rather confirm existing union activity. For a number of years the practice of representation of municipal employees by labor organizations has existed to some degree throughout the state of Wisconsin at various levels of government. Labor unions are using the opportunity of the new statute to secure certification of the fact that they represent a majority of such employees by the conduct of secret ballot elections. As a consequence, the labor unions which have petitioned for representation have won all but two of the elections conducted to date.

A more objective comparison and evaluation of public employee sentiment toward labor unions among unorganized public employees will have to wait. The passage of time will determine whether the statute has resulted in the certification of labor unions as the representative of many public employees who are not now presently represented by a labor organization.

May Have "Day in Court"

The increase in union activity has met some resistance from municipal employers and the Wisconsin Board already has had occasion to find one of them guilty of prohibitive practices.

Green Lake County and its Highway Commissioner, after a formal hearing, were held to have discharged two employees of the County Highway Department for the purpose of discouraging union organization. The county was ordered to reinstate the employees and to make them whole for the time lost. It was also to cease and desist from further interfering with the organizational activities of its employees. The county has notified the board of its intention to comply with the order.[4]

---

[4]Green Lake County. Decision No. 6061, Wisconsin Employment Relations Board, July 27, 1962.

The board has been presented with a number of unique questions concerning representation. It has found that the representative of the union selected by a majority of the employees in a bargaining unit is the exclusive representative of such employees for the purposes of engaging in collective conferences and negotiations with their municipal employer.

The 1962 statute did not use the term "exclusive bargaining representative," but the board has determined that that is the only practical certification to make inasmuch as the Employment Peace Act, under which the proceedings for the determination of bargaining representatives are made, provides that the representative selected by the majority of the employees shall be the exclusive collective-bargaining representative.

It is not unlikely that this question will ultimately be the subject of litigation for it has been argued that government cannot exclusively bargain with a labor union or any other organization on behalf of its employees for the purpose of determining governmental employment policies.

There seems little question that a public employer cannot refuse to hear the views of interested citizens and non-represented employees on questions of wages, hours, and conditions of employment. Whether a municipal employer owes to such non-represented employees and interested citizens anything more than the right to a hearing, however, is doubtful.

When Is a Unit Not a Unit?

The Employment Peace Act, under which the questions of municipal employee representation are to be determined, defines a collective-bargaining unit as including all of the employees of the employer. If, however, a majority of such employees engaged in a single craft, division, department, or plant shall vote by a secret ballot to constitute themselves as a separate bargaining unit, they may be so considered.

Thus, the statute confers upon municipal employees considerable discretion in determining whether they wish to be a part of an overall unit or a smaller collective-bargaining unit. It has the added proviso that, in public employment, craft employees may not be included in the same bargaining unit as other employees.

The board has been presented with some complex unit problems. For example, petitions have been filed in eleven different departments of the Division of Public Works of the City of Milwaukee. Within those departments numerous other petitions have been filed on behalf of crafts and other specialized groups of employees.

In a few such cases it has been surmised that petitions are filed by specialized groups of employees, not so much for the purpose of seeking representation rights under the statute, but to exclude themselves from representation by a larger group of employees. As an illustration, a petition for representation has been filed by a group of doctors and nurses in the City of Milwaukee employed by the Public Health Department, while another petition by a public employee union is pending for an overall unit of the Public Health Department.

Considerations in Certifying a Unit

The public employees' statute contains no exclusion for supervisory employees; however, the Wisconsin Employment Peace Act does. Complicated questions arise as to who is or who is not a supervisor in public employment, particularly in larger governmental units employing large numbers of professional employees.

As a general proposition, the board includes as supervisory employees those persons who have the authority to effectively recommend the hiring, firing, promotion, and transfer of employees or who spend fifty per cent or more of their time supervising other employees. Salary schedules are considered in evaluating the supervisory status of employees. The board has noted the tendency among public employers to designate as supervisors persons whose duties are to supervise an activity rather than other people--a supervisor of a playground or of elections, for example.

Also, the board has excluded from collective-bargaining units confidential employees; that is, employees who are secretaries to the personnel officer or the principal executive and who have confidential information about management decisions regarding the employment policies of the employer. The definition of "confidential" does not extend to such other generally confidential subjects as the patient records in a hospital.

The Wisconsin Board has adopted the following definition of a craft. "Employees are engaged in a single craft when they are a distinct and homogeneous group of skilled journeymen craftsmen, working as such together with their apprentices and/or helpers."[5] The board has considered that professional employees, such as teachers, constitute a craft within the meaning of the statute and, therefore, may constitute themselves as a separate collective-bargaining unit.

---

[5]Winnebago County Hospital Case. Decision No. 6043, July 27, 1962.

Purpose Must Be Clear

The board has made it clear that it will refuse to certify a bargaining unit based on the extent of organization. The unit must be
appropriate under the statutory criteria. This means that a labor
union cannot, because it represents six employees in a public works
department, petition for an election to represent such employees and
at the same time seek to exclude from voting on the question of
representation twelve other employees, who may not belong to the
union, working in similar classifications for the same department.

The Wisconsin statute does not define a labor organization, nor
does it have any filing requirements as a prerequisite to utilizing
the act. The employee representative does not even have to use the
name "union" or "labor organization"; however, the purpose must
be to represent employees in conferences and negotiations with their
municipal employer on questions of wages, hours, and working conditions.

Although we have discussed only the question of and the right to
representation, the statute specifically provides that the employees
have the right to refrain from representation. From this it follows
that, regardless of any other constitutional questions that might be
involved, a public employee in Wisconsin, who is subject to the law,
cannot be required as a condition of employment to belong to a labor
organization as a condition of his municipal employment. In private
employment this would be described as a "right-to-work law."

Once a labor union has been selected as the representative of
the majority of the employees in a collective-bargaining unit, it has
the right to engage in conferences and negotiations with the municipal employer. The time period and the subjects of negotiations are
governed in part by statute. Statutory deadlines for the adoption of
budgets necessarily limit the time during which bargaining can be
commenced. Municipal budgets must be adopted in time for tax rates
to be assessed.

Reducing the "Fish-Bowl" Effect

Negotiations in public employment have frequently been carried
on in public as contrasted to private collective-bargaining sessions.
Negotiations take the form of lobbying before committees, or appearances before legislative bodies.

Any experienced practitioner or observer of collective bargaining realizes that there can be very little genuine collective bargaining in a legislative arena. The temptation on the part of public
officials and representatives of public employee labor organizations
and taxpayer groups to make political statements for the consumption

of their constituents is too strong to be resisted. Hence, any realistic attempt to compromise the issues in negotiation are lost.

There has been arising in some communities the practice of assigning to legislative and personnel committees the responsibility for carrying on some of the functions of collective bargaining. In this connection, it should be noted that a provision has been made for the utilization of the mediation services of the Wisconsin Employment Relations Board to assist the parties in collective bargaining.

An opinion of the Attorney General of the State of Wisconsin has significantly provided that mediation proceedings under the Wisconsin statute concerned with a labor dispute involving a municipal employee and a municipal employer does not require that mediation proceedings be open to the public. This ruling was requested because of a Wisconsin statute which provides that all meetings of all state and local boards shall be publicly held and open to all citizens at all times.[6]

At this writing, we have had the experience in only three mediation requests affecting municipal employers. In two instances, the disputes were resolved; the third is pending before a fact-finder. It is much too early to observe whether the municipal employers and employee organizations will avail themselves of mediation services and, if they do, whether such services will prove to be effective in assisting the resolution of municipal employer and employee labor disputes.

Municipal Employers Question Obligation

The new statute would appear to create a duty on the part of municipal employers to negotiate with municipal employee representatives over questions of wages, hours, and working conditions. It is anticipated that there will be some legal challenges to the responsibility of municipal employers to negotiate with labor organizations.

Some municipal employers argue that the statute is merely permissive and does not impose an obligation upon municipal employers to actually engage in negotiations and collective bargaining. No such court tests have been brought to date. Of course, the duty to negotiate does not mean that an agreement can be compelled; but if an agreement is reached, the Wisconsin statute does provide that such agreement shall be reduced to writing in the form of an ordinance, contract, or a resolution.

This latter provision would seem to answer the argument that the fixing of the conditions of work in the public service is a

---

[6]Attorney General's opinion, March 8, 1962.

legislative function and that neither the executive nor the legislature may delegate such functions to an outside group. The statute does provide that such agreement may include a term for which it shall remain in effect not to exceed one year and that such agreement shall be binding on the parties only if the express language to that effect is contained therein.

Bothersome Feature

A feature of the Wisconsin statute, which has been the most controversial to date, has concerned the fact-finding provisions. Since the statute specifically prohibits the right to strike by public employees, the public employee unions sought to include a fact-finding provision with the authority to make recommendations, which are advisory only, in the event that the parties to a labor negotiation were unable to resolve their differences.

The fact-finding procedure may be invoked by either the employer or the union whenever it is determined after a reasonable period of negotiations that the parties are deadlocked or that the employer or the union fails or refuses to meet and negotiate in good faith at reasonable times and places to arrive at a settlement.

The board is required to investigate a petition for fact-finding to determine whether the conditions have been met. If so, it appoints a fact-finder whose duty it shall be, after a hearing, to make written findings of fact and recommendations for the solution of the dispute and cause these to be served on the municipal employer and the union.

The statute provides that the cost of fact-finding is to be borne equally by the municipal employer and the labor organization. In the establishment of the procedural rules for the administration of the fact-finding provision, the board adopted the minimum state bar fee of $150 a day for the services of a fact-finder and a hearing, and $100 a day for preparation. The thought here is that the fee is high enough to command competent fact-finders and also high enough to discourage frivolous use of the procedure.

It is the feeling of a number of municipal employer groups that the fact-finding provisions could result in an interference of home rule in that local employment policies will be influenced by persons from outside the community. Accordingly, the fact-finding provision was enacted only after the statute was amended so that the Wisconsin Board could not initiate fact-finding proceedings in any case when the municipal employer, through ordinance or otherwise, had established fact-finding procedures substantially in compliance with this sub-chapter.

Extensive negotiations have been carried on between representatives of the League of Municipalities and the representatives of the

Wisconsin State Council of State and Municipal Employees. The result has been an agreement on a suggested model ordinance to be adopted by municipalities who may wish to implement their own fact-finding procedures. The model ordinance is being circulated among various municipalities for their consideration.

It is too early to state whether such ordinance will be adopted by the various municipalities and, if so, to what extent it will be utilized in preference to the state procedure.

Political Factors Present

The philosophy behind the fact-finding procedure is that public opinion will support the recommendations of the fact-finder and lead to a solution of the dispute.

It should be emphasized that the basic reason for the fact-finding procedure is the belief that in public employment, lacking the right to strike, employment policies are determined largely as the result of political decisions rather than economic decisions. The right to strike in private employment is an economic weapon designed to bring economic pressure upon a private employer to settle a dispute. However, this reasoning overlooks political persuasion which, I believe, to be the primary factor in determining public employment policies.

Public employee representatives through appearances at public hearings, through the press, and by the use of lobbyists, apply political pressure on the legislature, the city council, the county board, and their executives in an attempt to influence public employee negotiations. I submit that this is not an evil. When ethically practiced, it is completely consistent with the nature of representative government.

Political factors are present in the negotiation of many private labor disputes and in most major disputes having considerable public impact, but economic factors are of primary concern. Economic facts cannot be, and are not, ignored in public negotiations, but the primary emphasis is on political persuasion. Whether this theory is correct or not will be given a test under the fact-finding provisions of the Wisconsin statute.

Statute Answers Some Questions

In summary, the Wisconsin statute has given a number of answers to some of the important questions involving public employer-employee relations.

It has determined that public employees, other than state employees, have the right by legislative protection to join labor

organizations and to be represented by labor organizations in collective conferences and negotiations with their municipal employers on
questions of wages, hours, and working conditions.

It has specifically provided that such employees do not have the
right to strike.

While the statute does not expressly provide that public employers must recognize such labor organizations as the bargaining
representative for their public employees, the right of representation would appear to be meaningless without such co-relative obligation on the part of public employers.

The Wisconsin Board in administering the statute has determined
that the labor organization selected as the representative by a majority is to be the exclusive bargaining agent. This question may be
ultimately determined by the courts or by further legislation.

It would also appear that public employers have the duty to engage in conferences and negotiations with representatives of their
municipal employees on wages, hours, and conditions of employment.
Furthermore, if they reach an agreement on such questions, they
have the responsibility of reducing such agreement to writing either
in the form of an ordinance or resolution, or an agreement.

Time Will Tell

One area not resolved by the statute is whether a municipal
employer and a labor union may agree to arbitrate the disposition
of grievances arising under the terms of a labor agreement or
municipal ordinance. For example, if an employee believes that
under the terms of a labor agreement he should have been promoted
to a vacancy on the basis of seniority and qualifications, can that
issue be submitted to an arbitrator?

While the statute does not empower the state agency or the
municipal employer to provide arbitration services, this would not
necessarily mean that the municipal employer and the labor union
could not provide a grievance procedure up to, and including, arbitration for the disposition of grievances which arise during the term
of a labor agreement.

The new Wisconsin statute and its administration will provide a
laboratory test over the next few years to determine whether the
statutory encouragement of collective bargaining in public employment is in the public interest and will lead to a more stable and
equitable solution of governmental labor-relations problems.

PART IV
Management-Employee Relations in State and Local Government

Introduction

In Chapter 11, Mrs. Batson reports on a survey of current practices in state and local governments. Her material comes from a survey made by the Public Personnel Association during late summer, 1962. Coverage of the survey was sufficiently broad to gather information on practices in the largest states, counties, and cities. Mrs. Batson's selection of quotes illustrates the variety of agency practice and the range of views among public personnel officials.

You will want to reach your own conclusions about what Mrs. Batson says. Her analysis, plus an examination of the raw material she reviewed, lead me to these observations.

1. Personnel officials are not sitting on the side-lines. Regardless of whether the system of negotiation with employee groups be "formal" or "informal," in most cases personnel officials do take active part in the process.

2. Despite rising pressure for state and local governments to bargain collectively (in the industrial sense) the practice is not now widespread in relation to the total number of state and local jurisdictions.

3. Most personnel officials prefer to deal informally with employee organizations; they believe this system is preferable to formal collective bargaining.

4. Most personnel officials believe their present system adequately serves employee and management, but their minds are not closed to refinements in present practice.

5. "Formal" negotiations are a fairly recent feature of employee-management relations in state and local government; the system gained some momentum in the late 50's and early 60's.

Chapter 12--"Examples of Policy Statements and Agreements"--speaks for itself. I thought it desirable to offer sufficient material to give a good understanding of the subjects covered in negotiation. This in particularly pertinent when seeking answers to questions like these: Do collective negotiations differ from, and/or cover the same subjects as a civil service merit system? Also what other, if any, topics and areas should be the subject of negotiation?

Chapter 13--"The Independent Public Employee Association"--deserves special comment. The importance of this subject arises in part from such matters as: union-employee association relations; the goals of employee associations in comparison with unions; the techniques, tactics, and strength of independent organizations.

I believe the material in Chapter 13 reflects an objective approach. It holds special interest because its author, Mr. Joseph Krislov, served at one time as a legislative representative of a government employees' union, but now writes from the vantage point of academic halls.

Chapter 14--"Public Employee Unionization in Texas"--contains only part of a longer work by Mr. Chester A. Newland on the same subject. I urge readers to examine the full account cited in the Bibliography. The major portion of Mr. Newland's chapter comes from the conclusions and summary of his longer work. I believe they deserve study by management and employee organizations.

Chapter 15--"Independent Municipal Employee Associations in California"--differs from the one just mentioned. The former presents facts in the body of his article. Mr. Richard L. Harris draws on facts being gathered for a comprehensive study of this subject. His contribution is somewhat more impressionistic and interpretative in the sense that he offers a number of personal observations based on data he cannot share with us at this time. Again, it seems to me, Mr. Harris gives all parties some incisive ideas about how local officials look upon their management relations--particularly with independent associations in contrast with unions.

K.O.W.

Chapter 11

A Survey of Current Practice

ELEANOR R. BATSON

How widespread is the practice of the different approaches to
management relations with organized public employees that were
described in Part III? The Public Personnel Association made an effort to obtain such information from a cross-section of state and local
governments.

Two questionnaires were used. The first asked if a formal arrangement existed for dealing with unions. If so, what officials typically represent management? What role does the personnel agency
play? A follow-up questionnaire went to those agencies that reported
they had no formal arrangement. These governments were asked to
make open-end responses to several questions that would explain
their particular procedures. PPA promised that neither the respond-
ent nor the agency would be identified in any report of results from
the second questionnaire.

Information was received from 94 public agencies: 24 of the 50
states; 51 of the 132 cities with populations of 100,000 or more, 18
metropolitan counties, and four special jurisdictions. (The Montana
Highway Department and the Montana Merit System Agency made
separate reports.) Replies from the four special agencies are not
included in the analysis of the data. At the end of this chapter there
is an alphabetical list of respondents, by type of jurisdiction.

The first review of the questionnaires and supporting documents
disclosed that dealing with employee organizations is not an all-or-
nothing proposition. Variations in practice are almost infinite. They
blend subtly from the extreme of absolutely no organized groups, and
therefore no relations, to almost total collective bargaining in the
industrial sense. Statistical treatment of such subtle variations of
practice is difficult. For this reason, much of the information obtained by the questionnaires is presented by quoting replies that best
reflect middle and extreme positions.

Eleanor R. Batson, formerly Director of Publications of the Public
Personnel Association, now residing in Kalamazoo, Michigan, is a
free-lance editor and writer in the field of public administration.

Formal Programs

The agency's rating as to whether its program is formal or informal was accepted for purposes of reporting questionnaire replies. This was necessary since answers to questions depended on management's opinion of its practice. It needs to be pointed out, however, that some procedures rated "informal" are supported by administrative memoranda, policy statements, or legislation. Some agencies might rate them formal. Differences of opinion apparently stem from a different interpretation of formally authorized relations and formally conducted relations.

For example, a county described its "informal" program this way:

> Under state law, public agencies are required to hear the views of employee organizations and give consideration to their requests. Our method of handling their requests varies in accordance with the individual situation. The most common pattern, however, is the establishment of a committee to which the employee organizations have representation and management has representation.

Extent of Formal Programs

Twenty-one agencies, some 22 per cent of all respondents, reported they had a formal arrangement through which management negotiates with employees. Sixty-three governments described their programs as informal. Ten said there were no organized employees or so few that contacts were practically nonexistent. Answers by type of jurisdiction were:

	States No.	States %	Counties No.	Counties %	Cities No.	Cities %
Formal program . . .	5	20	4	22	12	24
Informal program. . .	14	56	13	72	36	70
No program.	6	24	1	6	3	6
Total . . .	25	100	18	100	51	100

Procedures like those of Philadelphia, described in Part III, are obviously formal; and some respondents also reported agreement-type programs, for example, New York City and the State of Rhode Island. Here are some other types of "formal" practice:

Illinois

The executive officer of the Department of Personnel meets with all labor organizations making a claim of representation of the employees of the State of Illinois; union demands are obtained; surveys of area wages are made; information as to ability of operating agencies to pay is solicited; and the total picture is placed upon the Governor's desk with comment and/or suggestion. The Governor may instruct the Director of Personnel to bargain further or he may approve or disapprove the Director's suggestions.

Flint, Michigan

Prior to and including 1961, representatives of the organized employee groups attended the meetings of the Flint City Commission and made their demands directly to the City Commission. The groups made subsequent appearances at which they made their appeals and arguments to the City Commission. Following the 1961 negotiations, the City Commission established a policy that the City Commission would conduct a special meeting with the representatives of the organized employee groups at which each group would merely present a list of their demands. The demands or requests would be referred to the City Manager and the City Manager and the Finance Director would then conduct the necessary negotiation meetings with representatives. The Manager and the Finance Director would attempt to reach a satisfactory agreement with the employee representatives. If a satisfactory agreement was reached this agreement would be presented to the City Commission in the form of a recommendation by the City Manager. If a satisfactory agreement could not be reached, the employee groups would then again go directly to the City Commission.

Los Angeles County

Employee organization representatives have the right to meet and communicate with County management. Matters such as working conditions and grievances are frequently negotiated at the department head level. Where matters cannot be resolved at this level, they may then be taken by the employee representative to either the Chief

Administrative Office or the Civil Service Commission, depending on the scope of the problem and the jurisdiction of these staff agencies.

Problem areas, wherein the corrective action requested by the employee representatives would require action of the Board of Supervisors, are negotiated with the Chief Administrative Officer or his authorized representative, usually the Chief of the Personnel Division. Such areas generally pertain to salaries; fringe benefits; other matters covered in the Salary Ordinance such as bonus compensation, and overtime; staffing patterns; and matters covered by the Administrative Code such as meals, travel, and uniform allowances. Also, all matters pertaining to the preparation and modification of the "Management-Employee Relations Policy" and areas contained therein are the responsibility of the Chief Administrative Office. Agreements entered into between the Chief Administrative Office and employee organizations are, of course, not binding upon the Board of Supervisors.

Who Negotiates for Management?

What official or officials typically represent management in negotiations with organized employees? Replies were tabulated by type of jurisdiction because of organizational differences. Seven different officials or groups of officials (boards, commissions, councils) were named by states, five by counties, and twelve by cities.

When the actual functions of these management representatives are considered, negotiation appears to be principally the responsibility of personnel administrators, city managers, department heads, finance and budget directors, and legislative committees.

More than one of these individuals or groups is usually involved. See, for example, the variety of officials named in the Flint and Los Angeles County statements quoted above.

Role of the Personnel Agency

Respondents were asked to describe in some detail the activities carried on by the personnel agency as an adjunct of negotiation. Their replies show that states, cities, and counties all rely on their personnel departments to collect and interpret information and to analyze the proposals of employee organizations. The personnel department may also make recommendations or help negotiators work out compromise solutions. Typical personnel department activities are:

Nevada

The State Personnel Department conducts salary, benefits, and practices surveys and prepares recommendations for improved laws, rules and procedures and for changes in wages and fringe benefits. Recommendations are subject to possible review at formal Employee-Management Committee meetings, monthly departmental meetings, and Personnel Advisory Commission meetings, along with formal and informal meetings with employee representatives, legislative representatives, and other interested parties.

Springfield, Massachusetts

The Personnel Director participates in negotiations and acts as a resource person for the Personnel Policy Board which the mayor and city council designated as the official "management bargaining agent."

Philadelphia

The Personnel Department conducts wage surveys and costs as to the financial aspects of Union demands during its annual negotiations for certain requests, particularly with respect to fringe benefits. It also conducts studies and research and obtains information with respect to prevailing practices, and if agreement is reached, prepares the necessary amendments to the Civil Service Regulations to reflect the revised policy.

Informal Programs

All of the 63 states and local governments that describe their relations with organized employees as "informal" recognize the right of employees to form or to join an employee organization. One city puts it this way:

It is hereby declared to be the policy of the City of_____, subject to and within the limits of the City Charter, applicable provisions of State law, the Municipal Code, and rules of the Civil Service Commission, to assure employees full freedom of association in bona fide and responsible unions, to represent them for the purpose of orderly presentation and adjustment of grievances, and, at appropriate times, to present their proposals concerning the terms of their employment including wage, hours, and working conditions for their fair and timely disposition.

How Do Employees Present Their Views?

If there is no formal method for dealing with employees, what is an "appropriate" time or way for employee groups to make proposals to management? Here are some answers to this question. They range from listening to employee representatives to seeking their opinions. (As was explained earlier, agencies will not be identified.)

States

Each employee organization has the privilege of requesting meetings with the Personnel Director to discuss problems which they feel should be brought to his attention. No problems that fall within the administrative prerogatives of an agency or institution head and no problems which are covered by the established Grievance Procedure are entertained.

While the State of   does not formally recognize any unions of employee organizations, we are aware of the existence of both in the State and consider suggestions and recommendations that occasionally come from them. Their views are not solicited as such, but are welcomed.

Counties

Fortunately, so far, our relations with employees are such that the representatives of the employee groups have come to us and asked advice as to how to achieve their aims rather than demand of us that we comply with them.

While there is no formal recognition, employee representatives attend all meetings of the Civil Service Commission and nearly all meetings of the Board of Supervisors. They are free to propose any matters that are appropriately brought before either of these bodies, or to question actions that are pending.

Cities

This Commission is contacted quite frequently by representatives of employee groups relative to personnel transactions. Our Commission listens attentively to their presentations and where a legitimate complaint is voiced, the Commission takes appropriate action.

Employee representatives can feel free and do walk in at any time to express their views. They are in regular attendance at City Council meetings and almost always take the floor to express their views on pertinent subjects and occasionally go directly to the City Manager. They have organized an Employees' Joint Council which is made up of representatives from about six different employee groups. At the Manager's request, they have agreed to meet with me (the personnel officer) monthly to discuss common problems.

Employee groups deal directly with the Civil Service Commission. They are notified routinely by the Commission secretary or members of the Civil Service Staff of matters of interest to them. Their representatives are recognized by the Commission in the same way that any other person wishing to be heard is recognized.

Some years ago we felt there was a need for the various employee organizations to present a common point of view to us on pending matters of broad employee interest, where this was possible. The organizations also felt such a need, and they formed a committee of representatives of all groups having any substantial numbers of city employee members. This committee has been highly effective. It has enabled us to inform all groups quickly and effectively of proposed changes and the reasons behind them. The committee has been very reasonable in its deliberations, and often has been a positive aid to the Civil Service staff, both in supporting formal proposals or in suggesting alterations or compromise on other matters before they reached the formal stage. It is only fair to add that the committee has opposed, often successfully, some of the Civil Service recommendations presented to it.

Do Employee Organizations Lobby?

Absent formal negotiation with management, do employee organizations turn to legislators to secure their demands? Surprisingly, perhaps, few respondents described the activity as a problem from the viewpoint of management. Several comments indicated that the agency expected employee groups to deal directly with members or committees of legislative bodies on pay and fringe benefit questions. Lobbying in its traditional sense seems to take place mostly at the state level.

States

Representatives of the employee groups deal directly with members and committees of our Legislative body. In the past, the subjects dealt with have been largely in the area of across-the-board salary increases and working hours; also, on matters pertaining to the State Retirement Plan.

During legislative sessions the state employees association sponsors specific legislation designed to benefit employees.

The state employees association has a lobbyist registered at each legislative session.

The employees association carries on extensive lobbying activities while the legislature is in session and may make contacts with the Governor and his staff.

Counties

Representative committees occasionally petition the governing bodies for general salary increases or changes in working conditions. These are matters within the jurisdiction of the governing bodies and there is no reason, therefore, for them to petition the Personnel Board.

It is rather common for representatives of employee groups to lobby with our County delegation in the State legislature in the interest of amending our civil service law. In some instances such proposed amendments have been favored by the Personnel Board, but more often such changes have been opposed by the Board on the grounds that they would weaken the merit system and were not in the public interest.

Cities

Representatives of organized employee groups sometimes do go directly to the City Council on such matters as pay and fringe benefits. The Council usually refers the matters presented to the City Manager for study and report.

During the salary survey conducted by the Administrative Office for Board consideration earlier this year, the employee association manager also conducted a salary survey for presentation to the Board at the same time. Although the Board simply accepted and filed this report, since it was generally more liberal in recommendation than the administrative report and had also received considerable publicity, it had the effect of hastening the adoption of the administrative recommendation in toto by the Board, which probably would not otherwise have occurred.

Representatives of the employee groups sometimes deal directly with the legislative body. This is done primarily in the matter of wages, fringe benefits, and matters of policy which affect the various unions and employee groups.

The normal procedure, however, is that the initial negotiations for wages, fringes, and other policy matters are
conducted through the Personnel Office. Generally, the
direct approach to the Council does not take place unless
the employee representatives feel that they are not making satisfactory progress or unless they feel that a little
personal pressure might be necessary to get the Council
to accept what has already been agreed on between my
office [the personnel officer] and themselves.

What Is Role of Unions in Grievance Procedures?

It is generally agreed that the principal reason employees join
unions is economic--to gain better wages and fringe benefits. Next
on the list is security. Many employees have difficulty communicat-
ing with management. They want someone to speak for them when
they have grievances or face disciplinary action or dismissal.

Responses indicated agencies recognize that the individual
employee is at a disadvantage vis-à-vis management. A number of
informal agencies have formal grievance procedures that spell out
the rights of employees and the role of unions; some reported plans
to systematize policies. The interest that employee organizations
take in this aspect of employee relations is evident in the following
quotations. However, in the handling of grievances, as in lobbying
activities discussed above, there seems to be some difference between the role of state employee associations and the role of employee organizations that operate in city and county government.

States

There is no state-wide grievance procedure although
some departments have such procedures in effect.

Organized groups or union members can be represented
before the state civil service commission if the representative is an attorney.

Generally speaking, the Associations are not active on
matters of individual grievances. By and large, individual grievances are handled by department or agency
heads, and in other cases, the employee may come directly to the State Personnel Director. Occasionally, the
Executive Secretary may present, either in writing or
in person or both, an individual grievance.

In the only instance of which we are aware that the State
Employees Association took part in a grievance, they
provided an attorney and paid the transportation cost of
the grievant to appear at the Personnel Board hearing.

The state employees association has an Executive Secretary and an Assistant who work directly with department heads and with the personnel office in an attempt to clear up any grievances brought out by members.

Counties

The employee organization has a grievance committee which hears employee complaints. The committee asks both sides to present their case and then decides whether to pursue the problem further with the department involved and with management.

An attempt is made on employee grievances to have them follow the chain of command within their own particular department. Any employee, or their representative, may present their grievance.

Cities

The usual procedure on a grievance is for the representative of the union to advise the employee to discuss the problem with his supervisor in the hope of getting a satisfactory arrangement developed to both the employee and the department. The union representative is heard by the Personnel Department or the City Manager's office after this procedure has been followed and no satisfactory answer reached.

Depending on the nature of the grievance, the employee group participation will vary from merely bringing the matter to management's attention and accepting management's decision on it, to actively participating in the formulation of the policy within which the decision is made.

Each employee group has a legal counsel on permanent retainer. If it is determined there has been a possible infringement of the laws of the City, the group will assist an individual in his grievance and provide legal representation before the Civil Service Commission or City Manager.

There is no formal grievance procedure as yet; however, this office, at the request of the City Manager, is developing a formal grievance procedure. At the present time grievances are handled informally with the department head or the Personnel Director.

Evaluation of Informal Programs

Sixty-five per cent of the state and local governments that provided information for this survey stated their relations with organized employees were informal. Thus, this approach is currently majority practice. The last question asked was: "Do you think your arrangement for dealing with organized employees is good or not? Why?" Readers will recognize immediately that the Public Personnel Association would not have been able to obtain the kinds of honest answers quoted below without the promise of anonymity.

The difficulty of trying to treat statistically the variety of informal practices was pointed out at the beginning of this chapter. It was impossible to codify the multitudinous and subtle differences of opinion about the effectiveness of procedures. Neither was it possible to select comments that could be said to represent middle and extreme positions, as was the case with some practices.

Generally speaking, respondents expressed at least moderate satisfaction with their arrangements. The real importance of these program evaluations is that they provide an insight on this aspect of public administration that cannot be obtained by "adding up" practices.

States

The relationship between the State Personnel Department and the two Employee Associations has, generally speaking, been good. We think it quite natural, however, that the two organizations have taken considerable credit for bringing about improved or new personnel policies and programs when we in Personnel feel that these accomplishments are more correctly accredited to the Administrative Branch of our government. Questions have been raised by some who believe that Employee Associations whose membership is made up of supervisory and management employees, as well as the working employee, is not a good arrangement. We in Personnel, I believe, generally consider this question as academic.

We have always had excellent working relationships with the organization and have found it very useful on many occasions.

We have found our informal arrangements for dealing with the organized employee groups satisfactory. Whether or not they share this feeling is unknown.

Counties

We think our arrangement for dealing with employee organizations is a good one since employees are not forced to join such organizations in order to be heard.

Although no formal procedure exists for dealing with employee organizations, the informal atmosphere in which problems have in the past been aired, and solved in our opinion, has been very satisfactory.

Our present informal arrangements are quite satisfactory since we have been able to accomplish a great deal for the benefit of both the employer and employee in a very cooperative atmosphere.

At present our policy is to keep a pulse on trends and if we see the need for a more formal procedure we will establish one.

We feel that our present policy for dealing with employee organizations is satisfactory. We think this feeling is supported by the fact that there has been no overt effort on the part of employee groups to obtain greater recognition.

Cities

We feel that our arrangements for dealing with the organized employees are satisfactory because the cooperation and friendly attitude of the representatives has increased remarkably during the past four years. We admit, however, that the arrangements can be improved and we are constantly striving to do so.

To date, the arrangement for dealing with the employee association has worked quite satisfactorily, due in considerable measure to the capabilities and integrity of the manager, and to some extent to the lack of any major points of unreconcilable disagreement so far. Continued success depends on a number of things: improved communications both up and down; honesty and sincerity on the part of the Board and other representatives of management in dealing with the association; open, straightforward discussions and consideration of problems and requests with a serious attempt to understand the viewpoint of each other and the full ramifications of the problem; temperate philosophy and reasonableness in demands, approach, and solution to problems on the part of the association; and continuing integrity, honesty, and good judgment in the leadership and management of the association.

The time may come when we are forced into negotiation, but it appears to be in the distant future as the present plan seems to be working well enough that both sides are satisfied.

On the whole our arrangement for dealing with organized employees is satisfactory. Union activity among municipal employees is relatively new in this area and is obvious only during the period each year when the annual budget is being prepared.

Our arrangement for dealing with organized employees
is satisfactory under the present circumstances; however,
my personal opinion is that some more formal recognition of their activities would benefit both the city and the
employees.

In the main, we believe the way the city deals with employee organizations is good, even though we are disap-
pointed when their representatives take a short-sighted
rather than a long-term view. We certainly have no desire to see it restricted by anything resembling formal
collective bargaining. Not only do we think such an arrangement would be improper for a government agency,
but we also think the employees so represented would
lose more than they would gain.

There exists at present a very harmonious working relationship among the various interested groups. Insofar
as this office is concerned, it does not appear advantageous
to formally recognize these groups and provide for negotiated contracts. The civil service commission is charged
with protecting the rights of both the City and the employee
and can do this best by having direct access to the employee.

It is my opinion that our arrangements for dealing with
organized employees is good in our particular situation
because we have some strong Union representatives who
would like to take control of management decisions away
from department heads. This, however, is not true in
all cases because certain of our Union representatives
are quite cooperative with management.

We believe we are on the right track. Fortunately our
organizational representatives in all cases seem to have
a professional frame of mind, a desire to cooperate
reasonably toward our major goals.

List of Cooperating Governments

The following is a list of the 94 state and local governments that
furnished information on procedures for dealing with organized employees. They are listed alphabetically by type of jurisdiction.

States

Alabama
Alaska
California
Colorado

Connecticut
Florida (merit system)
Illinois
Iowa (merit system)
Kansas
Kentucky

Louisiana
Maine
Maryland
Minnesota
Mississippi (merit system)
Missouri
Montana (highway dept.)
Montana (merit system)
Nevada
North Carolina
Pennsylvania
Rhode Island
Utah (merit system)
Washington
Wisconsin

Counties

Alameda, Calif.
Arlington, Va.
Chatham, Ga.
Contra Costa, Calif.
Dade, Fla.
Jefferson, Ala.
Kern, Calif.
Los Angeles, Calif.
Milwaukee, Wisc.
Mobile, Ala.
Monroe, N. Y.
Multonomah, Ore.
Nassau, N. Y.
Ramsey, Minn.
Riverside, Calif.
San Bernardino, Calif.
San Diego, Calif.
San Mateo, Calif.

Cities

Akron, O.
Albuquerque, N. M.
Amarillo, Tex.
Berkeley, Calif.
Buffalo, N. Y.
Canton, O.

Cincinnati, O.
Charlotte, N. C.
Cleveland, O.
Dallas, Tex.
Dayton, O.
Des Moines, Ia.
Detroit, Mich.
Duluth, Minn.
Elizabeth, N. J.
Flint, Mich.
Glendale, Calif.
Grand Rapids, Mich.
Hartford, Conn.
Honolulu, Hawaii
Houston, Tex.
Jacksonville, Fla.
Long Beach, Calif.
Los Angeles, Calif.
Louisville, Ky.
Milwaukee, Wisc.
Minneapolis, Minn.
Nashville, Tenn.
New Orleans, La.
New York, N. Y.
Omaha, Nebr.
Pasadena, Calif.
Peoria, Ill.
Philadelphia, Pa.
Phoenix, Ariz.
Providence, R. I.
Richmond, Va.
Rockford, Ill.
Sacramento, Calif.
St. Louis, Mo.
St. Paul, Minn.
St. Petersburg, Fla.
San Diego, Calif.
San Jose, Calif.
San Luis Obispo, Calif.
Seattle, Wash.
Spokane, Wash.
Springfield, Mass.
Tacoma, Wash.
Tampa, Fla.
Tucson, Ariz.

Chapter 12

Examples of Laws, Policy Statements, and Agreements

PPA's survey of management-employee negotiations in state and local government showed that the majority of reporting jurisdictions deal with employee organizations informally. In these jurisdictions the views of organized employees are either solicited or welcomed, but government officials reserve the right to make final decisions about personnel policy. Only a small minority of those who returned questionnaires said either that employee organizations did not exist in their jurisdiction or they did not deal with such groups in any manner.

About one-quarter of the governments reported they had adopted some sort of formalized procedure for dealing with employee organizations. All types of local governments from all parts of the country were represented in this group. "Formal" procedures ranged all the way from a written grievance program that spelled out the role of employee organizations and their representatives to agreements signed by a governor or the chief executive of an agency.

The documents reproduced here were selected to show the variety of methods being used to establish uniform procedures for cooperation between management and employee organizations. The seven documents are:

1.   California bill approved by Governor, July 17, 1961;

2.   Resolution adopted by Sacramento City Council, April 13, 1961;

3.   Policy statement of City of Cleveland, March 1, 1962;

4.   Policy statement of County of Los Angeles;

5.   Agreement between the State of Rhode Island and the American Federation of State, County, and Municipal Employees, AFL-CIO, effective June 14, 1962;

6.   Agreement between the Housing Authority of the City of Atlanta, Georgia, and the Building Service Employees International Union, AFL-CIO, effective February 22, 1962; and

7.   Grievance Procedure of the City of Elizabeth, New Jersey, effective January 1, 1962.

1. California Bill Approved by Governor, July 17, 1961

Assembly Bill No. 2375

CHAPTER 1964

An act to add Chapter 10 (commencing with Section 3500) to Division 4 of Title 1 of the Government Code, relating to public employee organizations.

[Approved by Governor July 17, 1961. Filed with Secretary of State July 18, 1961.]

The people of the State of California do enact as follows:

Section 1. Chapter 10 (commencing with Section 3500) is added to Division 4 of Title 1 of the Government Code, to read:

Chapter 10. Public Employee Organizations

3500. It is the purpose of this chapter to promote the improvement of personnel management and employer-employee relations with the various public agencies in the State of California by providing a uniform basis for recognizing the right of public employees to join organizations of their own choice and be represented by such organizations in their employment relationships with public agencies. Nothing contained herein shall be seemed to supersede the provisions of existing state law and the charters, ordinances and rules of local public agencies which establish and regulate a merit or civil service system or which provide for other methods of administering employer-employee relations. This chapter is intended, instead, to strengthen merit, civil service and other methods of administering employer-employee relations through the establishment of uniform and orderly methods of communication between employees and the public agencies by which they are employed.

3501. As used in this chapter:

(a) "Employee organization" means any organization which includes employees of a public agency and which has as one of its primary purposes representing such employees in their relations with that public agency.

(b) "Public agency" means the State of California, every governmental subdivision, every district, every public and quasi-public corporation, every public agency and public service corporation and every town, city, county, city and county and municipal corporation, whether incorporated or not and whether chartered or not.

(c) "Public employee" means any person employed by any public agency excepting those persons elected by popular vote or appointed to office by the Governor of this State.

3502. Except as otherwise provided by the Legislature, public employees shall have the right to form, join, and participate in the activities of employee organizations of their own choosing for the purpose of representation on all matters of employer-employee relations. Public employees also shall have the right to refuse to join or participate in the activities of employee organizations and shall have the right to represent themselves individually in their employment relations with the public agency.

3503. Employee organizations shall have the right to represent their members in their employment relations with public agencies. Employee organizations may establish reasonable restrictions regarding who may join and may make reasonable provisions for the dismissal of individuals from membership. Nothing in this section shall prohibit any employee from appearing in his own behalf in his employment relations with the public agency.

3504. The scope of representation shall include all matters relation to employment conditions and employer-employee relations, including, but not limited to, wages, hours, and other terms and conditions of employment.

3505. The governing body of a public agency, or such boards, commissions, administrative officers or other representatives as may be properly designated by law or by such governing body, shall meet and confer with representatives of employee organizations upon request, and shall consider as fully as it deems reasonable such presentations as are made by the employee organization on behalf of its members prior to arriving at a determination of policy or course of action.

3506. Public agencies and employee organizations shall not interfere with, intimidate, restrain, coerce or discriminate against public employees because of their exercise of their rights under Section 3502.

3507. A public agency may adopt reasonable rules and regulations for the administration of employer-employee relations under this chapter (commencing with Section 3500).

Such rules and regulations may include provisions for (a) verifying that an organization does in fact represent employees of the public agency (b) verifying the official status of employee organization officers and representatives (c) access of employee organization officers and representatives to work locations (d) use of official bulletin boards and other means of communication by employee organizations (e) furnishing non-confidential information pertaining to employment relations to employee organizations (f) such other matters as are necessary to carry out the purposes of this chapter.

For employees in the state civil service, rules and regulations in accordance with this section may be adopted by the State Personnel Board.

3508. The governing body of a public agency may, in accordance with reasonable standards, designate positions or classes of positions which have duties consisting primarily of the enforcement of state laws or local ordinances, and may by resolution or ordinance adopted after a public hearing, limit or prohibit the right of employees in such positions or classes of positions to form, join or participate in employee organizations where it is in the public interest to do so.

The right of employees to form, join and participate in the activities of employee organizations shall not be restricted by a public agency on any grounds other than those set forth in this section. This section is not applicable to any employee subject to the provisions of Chapter 4 (commencing with Section 1960) of Part 7, Division 2 of the Labor Code.

3509. The enactment of this chapter shall not be construed as making the provisions of Section 923 of the Labor Code applicable to public employees.

2. Resolution Adopted by Sacramento City Council,

April 13, 1961

RESOLUTION No. 485

WHEREAS, a high level of municipal service has been provided the people of Sacramento by employees dedicated to the public welfare; and

WHEREAS, a wide variety of state legislative proposals have been introduced dealing with the rights of public employees; and

WHEREAS, there are basic and fundamental distinctions between public and private employment; and

WHEREAS, the people are entitled to a high level of uninterrupted municipal service essential to the public health, public safety and public welfare; and

WHEREAS, a basic policy governing municipal employee relations is essential to employee morale, the administration of city business and particularly to the general public;

NOW, THEREFORE, BE IT RESOLVED by the City Council of the City of Sacramento that:

1. Except as otherwise provided by the City Council, city employees shall have the right to form, join, and participate in the activities of employee organizations of their own choosing for the purpose of representation on all matters of employer-employee relations, for other mutual aid and protection, and for the improvement of governmental service. City employees shall have the right to refrain from joining or participating in the activities of any employee organization.

2. Employee organizations shall have the right to represent their members, either individually or collectively, in their employment relations with the city.

3. The scope of representation shall include all matters relating to employment conditions and employer-employee relations, including, but not limited to, wages, hours, and other terms and conditions of employment.

4. The governing body of the city, or such administrative officers or other representatives as may be properly designated by such governing body, shall meet and confer with either individual employees or representatives of employee organizations upon legitimate and reasonable request, and shall consider such presentations as are made by the individual employee or the employee organization on behalf of its members prior to arriving at a determination of policy or course of action.

5. The City Council and city administrative officers will not interfere with, intimidate, restrain, coerce or discriminate against public employees because of their exercise of their rights under Paragraph (1).

6. The city may require representatives of employee organizations to submit to the City Manager evidence of their official status with the employee organization and verification that the employee organization does, in fact, represent employees of the city.

7. In the exercise of their right to represent employees as herein provided, representatives of employee organizations shall be given access to work locations, opportunity to communicate with employees, and information pertaining to

employment relations, subject to reasonable regulation by the City Manager to avoid the disruption of public business.

8. Nothing herein contained shall be deemed to authorize the establishment of the terms and conditions of city employment by other than duly enacted laws, statutes and ordinances, nor to authorize the delegation of the Council's legislative functions to any person or group not directly responsible to the electorate of the city.

9 Strikes and picketing by city employees which disrupt or suspend municipal service will not be permitted.

_____

Mayor

_____

City Clerk

3. Policy Statement of City of Cleveland, March 1, 1962

PERSONNEL MEMORANDUM #62-4

CITY OF CLEVELAND
OFFICE OF PERSONNEL ADMINISTRATION

TO: All Directors & Commissioners

FROM: Office of Personnel Administration

SUBJECT: Labor Relations Policy

The attached statement of policy confirms in writing the long established working relationship with City employee unions, which has heretofore been an oral understanding.

Its purpose is to promote orderly and equitable policy for dealing with all employees in accordance with sound labor relations principles and consistent with the requirements of the public service.

Grievance Procedure - Adjustment of grievances is a normal part of the supervisory job. The labor relations policy puts in writing a general guide as to the channels to follow. Supervisors are expected to listen to grievances, consider them and be willing to explain their decisions. If the question raised involves a matter beyond the authority of the supervisor, the grievances should be referred to the next higher level.

Union Check-off - Voluntary monthly dues check-off privileges are now available for employees belonging to unions which have requested and been granted check-off. The following unions have requested and been granted this privilege:

1. American Federation of State, County and Municipal Employees, Local No. 100

2. Association of Cleveland Firefighters, AFL-CIO, Local No. 93

3. City, County & Waste Paper Drivers and Helpers Union, Local No. 244

4. Fraternal Order of Police, Cleveland Lodge No. 8

5. International Association of Machinists Local No. 1363 (Auto Mech.)

6. International Brotherhood of Firemen & Oilers, Local No. 52

7. International Union of Operating Engineers, Local No. 589 (Stationary Engineers)

8. Journeyman Plumbers' Union, Local No. 55

9. State, County, Municipal and School Board Employees, Local No. 1099

F. Robert Meier
Personnel Administrator

March 1, 1962

CITY OF CLEVELAND

STATEMENT OF CITY LABOR RELATIONS POLICY

It is hereby declared to be the policy of the City of Cleveland Administration, subject to and within the limits of the City Charter, applicable provisions of State law, the Municipal Code, and rules of the Civil Service Commission, to assure employees full freedom of association in bona fide and responsible unions, to represent them for the purpose of orderly presentation and adjustment of grievances, and, at appropriate times, to present their proposals concerning the terms of their employment including wage, hours and working conditions for their fair and timely disposition.

The City Administration agrees to give prior notice to the Unions regarding changes in, or institution of rules and regulations pertaining to working conditions and an opportunity for discussion of same wherever possible.

In the event of any difference concerning the interpretation or application of established policies and procedures on working conditions, the procedure to be followed is as follows:

(a) The question shall be discussed between the representative of the union and the supervisor having responsibility for the matter in question; and upon failure to agree

(b) Between the representative of the union and the head of the Division (Commissioner); and upon failure to agree

(c) Between the representative of the union and the Department Director; and upon failure to agree

(d) Between the representative of the union and the City Personnel Administrator, who shall serve in a mediating capacity for the purpose of endeavoring to achieve agreement on the issue under discussion.

It is to be understood further, that the right of an employee or employees to present their own requests, or adjust their own grievances shall not be impaired.

Employees of the City of Cleveland shall have the right to join a union or to refrain from doing so. There shall be no discrimination against any employee for belonging to a union or for not belonging to a union.

March 1, 1960

4. Policy Statement of County of Los Angeles

COUNTY OF LOS ANGELES

MANAGEMENT-EMPLOYEE RELATIONS POLICY

PREAMBLE

The function of County government is to provide services for the protection and welfare of the people of Los Angeles County. It is imperative, therefore, that every County officer and employee conscientiously devote himself toward the fulfillment of the responsibilities inherent in these functions in a manner which will deserve the confidence and respect of the public. Moreover, an obligation rests upon every County officer and employee to render honest, efficient and effective services in the performance of his duties.

In order to accomplish these purposes, it is the policy of the County to foster the establishment and application of procedures which will facilitate the continuation of the harmonious and cooperative relationships which exist among County management and employees.

The Management-Employee Relations Policy of the County of Los Angeles finds its foundation in the County Charter, the Salary Ordinance, the Administrative Code and the Civil Service Rules. Within the framework of these laws, each employee of the County of Los Angeles, or of any district of which the Board of Supervisors is the governing body, has certain rights and obligations. This Management-Employee Relations Policy expresses an interpretation of these rights and obligations and the provision of a basis for their uniform application throughout the County service.

I. MANAGEMENT-EMPLOYEE COMMUNICATIONS

A. Each employee shall be orientated to his job and to the County service under a planned program administered by each department head.

B. The levels of responsibility and authority within the departmental hierarchy shall be clearly set forth and made known to all personnel so that there is a thorough understanding on the part of each employee as to the limits in which he may operate and how far his authority and responsibility extends. However, an employee may be assigned other duties temporarily as long as such assignment is not unsafe or illegal.

C. Each department shall have a continuing program of management-employee communications to inform each departmental employee as to the policies, objectives, and responsibilities of the department which relate to his job in the interest of a common understanding and good management-employee relations.

II. PERSONNEL DEVELOPMENT

A. Each department head shall emphasize maximum development and utilization of employee skills on his present job.

B. Career opportunities in the County service shall be made known to all employees.

III. HEALTH AND SAFETY

Each department head is charged with the responsibility of maintaining a safe and healthful work environment for his employees, in terms of the work performed by the department.

IV. DISCIPLINE

A. Each department shall have a manual which sets forth, in the form of rules and regulations, a list of possible causes for disciplinary action. Such rules are to cover, but shall not be limited to, attendance, attention to work, inefficiency, insubordination, personal misconduct, safety. Within practical limits, possible disciplinary action which may be anticipated as a result of infraction of departmental rules and regulations shall be set forth.

B. It is the right and responsibility of each employee to know the rules and regulations of his department.

C. All complaints or charges brought against any employee involving violations of rules and regulations shall be thoroughly investigated by personnel whose responsibility it shall be to discover all pertinent facts in the matter and present them in a comprehensive report. The person making the investigation shall be equally diligent in establishing facts which tend to support the employee under investigation as those which tend to incriminate him.

V. GRIEVANCES

A. Each Department shall have a policy insuring all employees equal rights in their relationship with management.

B. It is the right of each employee to know the specific procedures including the lines of authority to follow to present his problem and to protect his interest as related to personal problems and/or grievances.

C. An employee may present his grievance to County management on County time. The use of County time for this purpose shall not be excessive nor shall this privilege be abused in any other manner.

VI. REPRESENTATION

    A.   Each employee of the County of Los Angeles shall have the right to organize, join, or refrain from joining any employee organization of his choice.

    B.   The rights of an employee are in no way augmented or changed by joining or not joining an employee organization.

    C.   Any organization of County employees has the right to communicate with County employees in a responsible manner not tending to mislead employees and when no cost to the County is involved.

    D.   Any representative of an employee organization shall inform the Department Head or his designated representative before contacting County employees on County facilities.

    E.   County buildings and other facilities may be made available for use by County employees for group meetings in accordance with established policy and procedures for such use.

    F.   Any organization of County employees shall have the right to communicate and meet with County management on problems relating to its members provided such meetings do not disrupt County business and provided such organization is in a position to represent the problem.

    G.   Employee organizations, in representing County employees, shall follow the same chain of command as that required of individual employees.

    H.   In order to represent County employees to County management, each employee organization shall file with the Chief Administrative Officer an annual statement containing the following information:

        Name and address of the organization.

        Names and titles of the officers.

        Number of County employees, by departments and classifications, who are members of the organization.

        Names of organization representatives who are authorized to speak on behalf of its members.

    I.   Any organization of County employees may have the regular dues of its members deducted from employees' paychecks under the conditions prescribed by law and the Board of Supervisors.

5. Agreement Between the State of Rhode Island and

AFSCME, AFL-CIO, June 14, 1962

AGREEMENT

WHEREAS the efficient administration of state government and the well-being of its employees require that orderly and constructive relationships be maintained between employee organizations and the Executive Branch of state government; and

WHEREAS the signatories hereto desire to encourage a more harmonious and cooperative relationship between the State of Rhode Island and its employees by procedures which will facilitate free and frequent communication between said state and its employees; and

WHEREAS it is the purpose of the signatories to this agreement to maintain and improve the present high standards of service to the people of the State of Rhode Island and to improve morale and personnel relations through a stabilized relationship between the State of Rhode Island and the American Federation of State, County and Municipal Employees, AFL-CIO as the representative of its members who are employed by the state:

NOW THEREFORE by this agreement entered into this 14th day of June 1962 by and between the Governor of the State of Rhode Island, as chief of the Executive Branch of the government of the State of Rhode Island, and the American Federation of State, County and Municipal Employees, AFL-CIO, referred to hereafter as the Union, it is hereby agreed as follows:

ARTICLE I

RECOGNITION

Section 1.

The Governor agrees that all departments of the Executive Branch of state government shall recognize and deal with the Union as the representative of its members in the Classified Service of the State of Rhode Island in accordance with Chapter 36-11 of the General Laws (P.L. 1958, Ch. 178) with respect to the hours and working conditions of its members. The Governor will recognize and deal with the Union as the representative of its members in all matters pertaining to the Salary Adjustment Fund.

Section 2.

Each and all matters covered by this Article and all other Articles of this agreement are governed by and limited by the provisions of all existing or future laws of the state and regulations issued in accordance therewith, including all existing and future Personnel Rules which may be applicable and this agreement shall at all times be applied subject to such laws and regulations.

Section 3.

The heads of departments retain the right, in accordance with applicable laws and regulations, (a) to direct employees of their respective departments, (b) to hire, promote, transfer, assign, and retain employees' positions within their department, and to suspend, demote, discharge or take other disciplinary action against employees, (c) to relieve employees of duties because of lack of work or for other legitimate reasons, (d) to maintain the efficiency of state government operations entrusted to them, (e) to determine the methods, means and personnel by which such operations are to be conducted; and (f) to take whatever action may be necessary to carry out the work of their departments in situations of emergency.

Section 4.

The Union agrees that its members employed by the state will not strike or assist or participate in any strike against the State of Rhode Island.

Section 5.

The Union agrees that it will not discriminate with regard to the terms or conditions of membership because of race, color, creed or national origin.

ARTICLE II

SENIORITY

The Governor agrees in principle with the concept of Seniority, and further agrees that this principle should be applied wherever practicable at the discretion of each department head with respect to:

Section 1.

a.   Promotional Appointments

b.   Vacation Schedules

c.   Any other questions of preference among employees that may arise but are not specifically mentioned hereinabove.

Section 2.

Seniority shall be by classification and shall be based upon the length of service in the promotional line and shall date from the first date of employment in the promotional line. Layoffs and rehiring shall be conducted on the basis of total seniority to the extent permitted by the Merit System.

Section 3.

Choice of working shifts, vacation shifts, vacation periods and days off scheduled shall be based on seniority within each department as far as the operating needs of the department permit. Should any situation arise in which a department finds it necessary to deviate from the principle of seniority with respect to working shifts, vacation periods and days off and members of the Union are affected, said department shall notify the President of the local Union in writing as to the reasons for the changes.

ARTICLE III

GRIEVANCE PROCEDURE

There shall be a grievance procedure to facilitate the solution of members' problems and it shall be understood to be:

Section 1.

a.   An aggrieved member shall discuss his problem with his shop steward and immediate supervisor who shall attempt to settle the problem within 48 hours.

b.   If the problem is not solved then it shall be reduced to writing and the aggrieved and the grievance committee of his local union shall meet with successive levels of supervision designated by the Appointing Authority in efforts to solve the problem. Each supervisor so designated shall answer within 48 hours.

c.   If the problem is still not solved the Department Head shall grant a hearing to the aggrieved and the Union committee and render a decision within 7 working days after said hearing.

d.   If the problem is still not solved, it shall be submitted to a person designated by the Governor who shall hear the aggrieved and the Union committee and prepare recommendations to the Governor with all possible speed.

e.   The Governor may meet with the aggrieved and Union committee and/or render a decision at his earliest convenience and his decision shall be final.

f.   The grievance procedures provided for in this section shall not be available to any member of the Union who fails to bring his grievance to the attention of his supervisor within thirty (30) days after the occurrence or after he has knowledge of the situation, condition or action giving rise to the grievance.

g.   Nothing in this Article shall diminish or impair any rights which would otherwise be available to any employee, whether or not such employee is a member of the Union, under the Merit System or any other laws or regulations of the State of Rhode Island.

Section 2.

a.   Union stewards shall, upon application to their supervisor, be granted reasonable time off during working hours to investigate and adjust grievances; provided however, that this privilege is extended with the understanding that the time will be devoted to the prompt handling of grievances and will not be abused. In the event a department head believes that stewards are spending an undue amount of their working time in handling grievances the department head shall have the right to correct such abuse. Before the department head takes any disciplinary action to correct such abuse he shall discuss the same with the President of the local Union.

b.   Officially requested or approved consultations and meetings between heads of departments and their agents, and representatives of the Union shall, whenever practicable, be conducted on official time.

c.   No Union steward or committee member shall be discriminated against or reprimanded by any supervisor as a result of the performance of legitimate Union responsibilities.

ARTICLE IV

RULES GOVERNING WORKING CONDITIONS

If the need should arise Appointing Authorities, as designated by the Governor or their representatives and the Union shall establish mutually satisfactory rules governing working conditions not specifically covered by existing statutes or personnel rules.

ARTICLE V

TERMINATION

Section 1.

This agreement shall be effective June 14, 1962 and shall continue in effect until December 31, 1962 and shall remain in effect thereafter from year to year unless terminated by the Governor, or by the Union on sixty (60) days written notice.

Section 2.

Any amendments or modifications to this agreement entered into by the parties after the expiration or anniversary date of this agreement shall be retroactive to said expiration or anniversary date.

Section 3.

Should any provision of this agreement, or any application thereof, become unlawful by virtue of any Federal or State Law, such provision of this agreement shall be modified by the parties to comply with the law, but in all other respects the provisions of this agreement shall continue in full force and effect for the life thereof.

ON BEHALF OF THE EXECUTIVE BRANCH FOR THE AMERICAN FEDERATION
OF STATE, COUNTY & MUNICIPAL
EMPLOYEES, AFL-CIO

John A. Notte, Jr., Governor
of Rhode Island

President, R. I. State Project

Secretary, R. I. State Project

6. Agreement Between the Housing Authority of the

City of Atlanta and BSEIU, AFL-CIO, February 22, 1962

AGREEMENT BETWEEN THE HOUSING AUTHORITY OF
THE CITY OF ATLANTA AND LOCAL 231, BUILDING
SERVICE EMPLOYEES INTERNATIONAL UNION, AFL-CIO

THIS AGREEMENT is made and entered into this 22nd day of February, 1962, by and between The Housing Authority of the City of Atlanta, hereafter called the Employer, and Local 231, Building Service Employees International Union, AFL-CIO, hereafter called the Union.

I.

PURPOSE

The general purpose of this Agreement is to provide for the efficient maintenance of all buildings and grounds under the jurisdiction of the Employer and to further to the fullest extent practicable the safety and employment of employees, economy of operation, protection of property and to establish harmonious relationships between the Employer and its employees and to provide for a mutual understanding between the Employer and the Union regarding wages, rates of pay, hours of employment and other conditions of employment.

II.

RECOGNITION

The Employer recognizes the Union as exclusive collective bargaining representative of all non-supervisory maintenance and custodial employees of the Employer engaged in the maintenance of and custodial service to all buildings and grounds under the jurisdiction of The Housing Authority of the City of Atlanta.

III.

METHOD OF EMPLOYMENT

The Union agrees to furnish to the Employer competent and satisfactory help for all job classifications covered by this Agreement, and the Employer agrees to give full consideration to applicants for employment which are referred to it by the Union. In the event the Union is unable to furnish competent employees within twenty-four (24) hours, the Employer may employ from other sources.

IV.

HOURS OF WORK AND OVERTIME PAY

The scheduled work week shall consist of forty (40) hours per week, and all work performed in excess of eight (8) hours in one day or in excess of forty (40) hours during the scheduled work week shall be paid for at one and one-half ($1\frac{1}{2}$) times the regular rate of pay.

All work performed on a Sunday or holiday as such shall be paid for at one and one-half ($1\frac{1}{2}$) times the regular rate of pay, with the exception of firemen who are regularly scheduled to work on Sundays and holidays.

V.

WAGE RATE

The wage rate of the job classifications of all employees covered by this Agreement shall be as determined by the Public Housing Administration as the result of a survey for the following classifications:

The wage rate which has been approved by Mr. Burdett of the Public Housing Administration is as follows:

Job Title	Per Annum	Per Hour
Maintenance Mechanic	$4,576.00	$2.20
Maintenance Aide (A)	4,097.60	1.97
Maintenance Aide (B)	3,660.80	1.76
Maintenance Aide (C)	3,265.00	1.57
Fireman	3,203.20	1.54
Laborer	2,527.20	1.23

VI.

HOLIDAYS, VACATION AND SICK LEAVE

The following days shall be recognized and observed as paid holidays:

> New Year's Day
> July 4
> Labor Day
> Memorial Day (May 30)
> Armistice Day (November 11)
> Thanksgiving Day
> Christmas Day

For pay computations an employee for a holiday shall be paid eight (8) hours' pay at straight time and a holiday shall be considered as a twenty-four (24) hour period of a standard day on which the holiday begins, except that if a holiday falls on a Sunday it shall be observed on the following Monday.

If an employee is scheduled to work on a holiday and does not work as scheduled he shall not receive the holiday allowance unless the absence is excused for cause.

In order to be eligible for holiday pay an employee must work the last scheduled work day before the holiday and the first scheduled work day following the holiday, unless his absence is excused by the employer.

Vacation and sick leave shall be as follows:

One working day vacation and one working day sick leave for each month of employment; sick leave shall be cumulative to forty-eight (48) working days, and vacation to twenty (20) working days. Employees taking vacations must have the prior consent of the Project Superintendent. Sick leave in excess of three (3) days will be allowed only on a doctor's certificate.

VII.

VACANCIES, LAYOFF AND REHIRING

In filling positions or vacancies and in layoffs and rehiring the principle of seniority will be observed, provided the employee is qualified to perform the duties of the job.

VIII.

NO STRIKE, NO LOCKOUT

The Union agrees that it will not call, condone, or sanction any strike, slow-down or work stoppage. The Employer agrees that it will not cause or sanction any lockout of its employees.

IX.

GRIEVANCE PROCEDURE

If any employee has a complaint of unjust treatment in the interpreting or application of the provisions of this Agreement or that he has been discharged or laid off without just cause, the aggrieved employee or employees accompanied by his or their Union representative shall present the grievance within five (5) working days to the Superintendent of the employee or employees.

The Superintendent to whom the grievance is submitted shall, within three (3) working days, give an answer in writing to the grievance.

Failing satisfactory settlement, the grievance shall be reduced to writing within three (3) working days from the time of the Superintendent's answer (failure of the Superintendent to answer within time allowed shall automatically put the grievance in the next step) and referred to the Union Grievance Committee composed of three (3) employee members and served upon the Employer's Technical Director who shall discuss the matter with the Grievance Committee of the Union duly authorized to discuss grievances at this level and an earnest attempt shall be made by both parties to settle the grievance; however, if the grievance is not settled within three (3) working days it shall be referred to the Labor Relations Representative of the Field Office of the Public Housing Administration who shall attempt to adjust the matter within five (5) working days and failing satisfactory settlement the grievance shall be submitted to arbitration.

X.

ARBITRATION

Any controversy referred to arbitration shall be heard and decided by Dr. Walter Buckingham, Director, Department of Industrial Management, Georgia Institute of Technology, who is agreed upon as the Impartial Arbitrator by both parties during the life of this Agreement. The parties do hereby agree that the decision of the Impartial Arbitrator shall be final and binding. Should it be determined that an employee has been treated unjustly the Impartial Arbitrator shall have the authority to order the employee reimbursed the amount of net pay lost by him and in the case of discharge, layoff or suspension, reinstatement with or without the net pay lost by him. The expenses and compensation of the Impartial Arbitrator shall be borne equally by the Employer and the Union.

XI.

TERM OF AGREEMENT

This Agreement shall take effect February 22, 1962, and continue in full force and effect through February 21, 1963. It shall automatically renew itself and continue in full force and effect for further periods of twelve (12) months unless either party serves a written notice upon the other party to terminate or modify the Agreement not less than sixty (60) days prior to February 21, 1963.

If this agreement is automatically renewed beyond February 21, 1963, then said written notice may be served not less than sixty (60) days prior to any subsequent anniversary date.

IN WITNESS WHEREOF, the parties have executed this Agreement the day and year aforesaid.

THE HOUSING AUTHORITY OF THE
CITY OF ATLANTA, GEORGIA

By_____
    Executive Director-Secretary

_____
Technical Director

BUILDING SERVICE EMPLOYEES
INTERNATIONAL UNION, LOCAL 231,
AFL-CIO

By_____
    NEGOTIATION COMMITTEE

7. Grievance Procedure of the City of Elizabeth, N.J.,

January 1, 1962

CITY OF ELIZABETH, NEW JERSEY

GRIEVANCE PROCEDURE

EFFECTIVE--JANUARY 1, 1962

BY ORDER OF THE BUSINESS ADMINISTRATOR:

PURPOSE

The purpose of this administrative regulation is to assure employees that their grievances will be considered fairly, rapidly and without reprisal. It is expected that the procedure set forth below will encourage employees to discuss with their supervisors matters pertaining to conditions of municipal employment as they affect individual employees.

The primary purpose of any grievance is to determine what is right, rather than who is right. Therefore, grievances must be considered objectively and in an atmosphere of mutual assistance. This cannot be done if a spirit of conflict enters into the consideration of a grievance. The basic purpose of city government is service to the community; this service cannot be achieved if the supervisors and/or employees fail to recognize that the true purpose of a grievance procedure is to help achieve this basic objective.

POLICY

It is the policy of the City of Elizabeth to provide a procedure for the presentation and mutual adjustment of points of disagreement which arise between employees and their supervisors.

DEFINITION OF GRIEVANCE

A grievance is a complaint, a view, or an opinion pertaining to employment conditions, or relationships between an employee and a supervisor or to relationships between the employee and other employees.

Grievances are concerned with work conditions, light, heat, sanitary facilities, safety, type and location of work assignment, work load and attitude of supervisors. Problems relating to salaries, fringe benefits, overtime and overtime pay, position classification and employee status, discharge, suspension, reduction and retirement are not considered grievances.

Any employee or group of employees who present a grievance can do so with freedom from coercion, reprisal or discrimination.

This grievance procedure, in no way, affects any civil service action which the employee may decide to use.

PROCEDURE FOR PRESENTATION OF GRIEVANCES

I.   DISCUSS WITH SUPERVISOR:

  A.   The employee or his representative shall first take his grievance to his immediate supervisor who shall make a decision and advise the employee within three (3) working days. The employee shall so inform the immediate supervisor that this is a grievance and expects an answer within the three (3) working-day limitation. It is not necessary nor desirable that the grievance be presented in writing to the supervisor.

  B.   Supervisors are encouraged to consult with their superiors or any other individual who may be qualified to offer their assistance or information which will aid the supervisor to reach a fair and mutually equitable decision.

II.   APPEAL TO APPOINTING AUTHORITY:

  A.   If the grievance is not resolved by the immediate supervisor to the satisfaction of the employee, or if a decision is not made by the supervisor within three (3) working days, the nature of the grievance and the desired solution may be submitted in writing by the employee or his authorized representative to the appointing authority.

  B.   The appointing authority shall have the responsibility of settling the grievance and shall inform the employee in writing, of his decision within seven (7) working days of the appointing authority. A copy of this decision shall be sent to the Business Administrator.

III.   APPEAL TO GRIEVANCE COMMITTEE

A.   If the disposition of the grievance by the appointing authority is not satisfactory to the employee, or if a decision is not made within seven (7) working days, the employee or his representative, after this seven (7) working day period may write to the Business Administrator and request a Grievance Committee to be convened on this grievance.

B.   The Business Administrator shall convene the Grievance Committee within five (5) working days after receipt by him of a request for a hearing. This request must be filed by the employee or his authorized representative within five (5) working days after the receipt of the appointing authority's decision; but in any case, no later than ten (10) working days after the original request was sent to the appointing authority.

C.   Prior to making his decision, the appointing authority shall interview the immediate superior and the employee involved on the concerned grievance.

D.   Each respective Grievance Committee shall be composed of five (5) members, appointed by the Business Administrator, namely:

   1.   The Chairman--Business Administrator or his authorized representative.

   2.   The appointing authority or his authorized representative, concerned with the grievance before the Committee.

   3.   The employee or his authorized representative concerned with the grievance.

   4.   Member of City Council.

   5.   One employee appointed by the Business Administrator from a previously, prepared list.

E.   Each of the following employee organizations shall appoint two (2) of its members to serve on the Grievance Committee during the calendar year.

   1.   Firemen's Mutual Benevolent Association.

   2.   Building Service Employee's International Union.

   3.   Elizabeth City Hall Employee's Association.

   4.   Policemen's Benevolent Association.

   5.   Civil Service Local #8.

   6.   Elizabeth Fire Fighters' Association.

      (a)   The only requirement of the above representatives is that they be a full-time employee on the payroll of the city government.

F. The employee appointed by the Business Administrator to serve on the Grievance Committee shall not be a member of the same employee group that is presenting the grievance.

G. The Business Administrator shall schedule a hearing to be held within five (5) working days, at a suitable time and place, and shall so notify the Committee selected.

IV. DECISION OF GRIEVANCE COMMITTEE

A. Within ten (10) days following a conclusion of the hearing, the Grievance Committee shall supply the appointing authority with four (4) copies of its report and recommendations, as approved by the majority of the committee.

B. Upon receipt of the Committee's report, and its recommendations, the appointing authority shall put into writing, within five (5) working days, the course of action he intends to follow and shall forward one (1) copy of his decision and one (1) copy of the Committee's report and recommendations to the Mayor; one (1) copy of each to the employee, and one (1) copy of each to the Business Administrator. The fourth copy shall be retained by the appointing authority.

C. The decision of the appointing authority, following consideration of the report and recommendations of the Grievance Committee shall be final and the employee shall have no further right of administrative appeal.

Chapter 13

The Independent Public Employee Association: Characteristics and Functions

JOSEPH KRISLOV

Administrative and legal opposition to the unionization of government employees has declined in the past decade. Several states and a number of cities have enacted legislation guaranteeing the right of employees to join unions; the federal government has also promulgated a new labor relations' program. Despite this more favorable organizational climate, the unionization of state employees will encounter opposition from independent public employee associations in a number of states. These associations have considerable membership, and in a few states have organized at least half of the full-time employees. Moreover, some of them have been in existence for more than twenty-five years, and two of them have been in existence for fifty years. It would seem, therefore, that they warrant some recognition and analysis as employee organizations.

To obtain information for such an analysis, the author sent a brief questionnaire to thirty state-wide public employee associations.[1] Twenty-five associations in twenty-three states filled out and returned the questionnaire, and also supplied copies of their constitutions, and of any formal agreements, grievance procedure, and insurance progams. These materials and the completed questionnaire are the basis for this article. The twenty-five associations claimed a dues-paying membership of 355,000—318,000 of whom were state employees and 37,000 local government employees (see table, p. 175). The five non-responding associations probably had a membership of 37,000.[2] Hence, the thirty known associations probably had a total estimated dues-paying membership of 392,000.

Several conclusions emerge from an analysis of the information supplied by the associations. First, the associations have succeeded in organizing significant numbers of state employees, but have made little progress (with one exception) in organizing local government employees.[3] Second, the structure and government of these associations is not too different from those of unions, but the dues are

---

Reprinted from Industrial and Labor Relations Review, July, 1962, by special permission of the publishers.

Joseph Krislov is a member of the faculty of McCoy College, the Johns Hopkins University, Baltimore, Maryland.

generally lower. Third, some of the associations have probably developed into effective employee organizations; others seem to be so poorly financed as to preclude any effectiveness. Fourth, 'membership recruitment' and 'legislative representation' appear to be the major staff functions. If the association provides a group insurance program or handles grievances, a minor proportion of staff time is devoted to either or both of these activities. Fifth, considerable antipathy exists between associations and the organized labor movement, and it seems unlikely that the associations will seek affiliation with the organized labor movement.

Jurisdiction, Membership, and Extent of Organization

In seven of the twenty-five associations, both state and local government employees were eligible for membership; in the other eighteen, membership was limited to state employees only.

Almost all of the twenty-five associations permitted membership of employees who would normally be considered 'management' in private industry[4]—that is, elected officials; officers appointed directly by the governor, mayor, or legislature; and department heads. Of the seven associations which organized both state and local government employees, only two limited membership to civil service employees; three denied membership to elected officials and to those appointed directly by the governor or mayor; and two permitted all public officials of the state and political subdivisions to join (one association specifically included elected officials). Of the eighteen associations limiting membership to state employees only, eight permitted all state employees to join (three specifically included elected officials). One association excluded elected officials; four associations excluded elected officers and those appointed by the governor; one excluded elected officers and all members of the armed forces of the state; and one association excluded "heads of departments, heads of institutions, officers elected by the people, or the legislature and members of legislature." Of the three remaining associations, two limited their membership to specific departments; one admitted to membership only employees of the Highway Department and the other admitted to membership only employees of the Highway and Prison Department. And the third association admitted to membership only employees "covered by the State Personnel Act."

The two associations in New Jersey appear to be competitive organizations. The two in North Carolina, however, apparently cooperate and have agreed on a jurisdictional division, one association admitting to membership only highway and prison employees and the other organizing all other state employees. The constitution of the latter organization, however, clearly indicates that all state employees are eligible for membership.

Membership, Annual Dues, Number of Active Chapters, and Year of
Organization of Independent Public Employee Associations.[1]

Name of Association	Membership	Annual Dues	Active Chapters	Year of Organization
California State Employees' Association.............	89,086	$12.00	145	1931
Colorado State Civil Service Employees' Association ...	5,152	12.00	31	1928
Connecticut State Employees' Association...........	11,374	8.58	159	1941
Hawaiian Government Employees' Association				
All members................................	9,342	27.00	5	1934
State....................................	4,361			
Local...................................	4,981			
Idaho State Employees' Association................	1,226	12.00	7	1959
Illinois State Employees' Association...............	10,276	3.00	31	1921
Indiana State Employees' Association..............	2,000	3.00	19	1953— reorganized in 1957
Kansas Highway Employees' Council...............	(2)	(2)	(2)	1958
Michigan State Employees' Association.............	13,400	10.40	86	1950
Montana Public Employees' Association				
All members...............................	3,500	1.00	(3)	1945
State....................................	2,500			
Local....................................	1,000			
Nevada State Employees' Association...............	690	12.00	8	1955
New Hampshire State Employees' Association	3,400	7.80	4	1941
New Jersey Civil Service Association				
All members................................	20,000	(4)	(4)	1911
State....................................	5,000			
Local....................................	15,000			
Council of State Employees (New Jersey)...........	5,000	5.00	6	1948
Civil Service Employees' Association (New York)				
All members................................	96,000	10.40	200	1910
State....................................	81,000			
Local....................................	15,000			
North Carolina State Employees' Association........	10,083	3.00	12	1946–1947
North Carolina State Highway and Prison Employees' Association........................	8,396	4.00	100	1947
Ohio Civil Service Employees' Association				
All members................................	15,440	7.50	56	1938
State....................................	14,676			
Local....................................	764			
Oregon State Employees' Association...............	11,128	10.80	85	1943
Rhode Island State Employees' Association..........	3,600	13.00	11	1945
South Carolina Employees' Association.............	6,200	1.00 to 3.00	(5)	1943
Texas Public Employees' Association...............	22,016	5.00	75	1946
Utah State Public Employees' Association...........	2,563	12.00	(6)	1959
Vermont State Employees' Association..............	2,491	7.28	18	1944
Washington State Employees' Association...........	2,000	12.00	(7)	1956

(1) All data as of July 1, 1961. Excludes associations in the following states with estimated memberships as follows: Alaska—400; Florida—600; Maine—6,000; Maryland—12,000; and Massachusetts—18,000.

(2) The Kansas Highway Employees' Council reported that it represented some 4,000 highway employees; its by-laws provide that "there shall be no dues collected." The membership was organized into seven sectional groups.

(3) The Montana Public Employees' Association reported that it had no chapter organization.

(4) The New Jersey Civil Service Association reported an annual per capita tax of $1.00 for affiliation with the state association. The association had twenty-two subordinate councils, organized primarily on county lines. A 'typical' council had a $6.00 dues; $1 is paid to the state organization, the other $5.00 is retained by the subordinate council.

(5) If annual salary less than $2,000, dues is $1.00 yearly; if annual salary is over $2,000 but less than $3,000, dues is $2.00 yearly; if annual salary is more than $3,000, dues is $3.00 yearly. Three active subordinate units were reported, one of which was organized in early 1961.

(6) The Utah State Public Employees' Association reported that it had no chapter organization.

(7) The Washington State Employees' Association reported that it had no chapter organization, but that it had seven district organizations.

Only five of the seven associations that included local government employees within their jurisdictions reported any local government membership. The combined local government membership
constituted but 10 percent of the total membership of the responding
associations, but the proportion for the five associations reporting
such membership varied. About three-fourths of the membership
of the New Jersey Civil Service Employees' Association are local
government employees, as compared with a bare majority for the
Hawaiian Government Employees' Association. In Montana, local
government employees constituted about one-third of the membership of that association. And in New York and Ohio, local government employees constituted about 15 and 5 percent, respectively, of
the membership of these two associations (see table).

In Hawaii, the association has organized more than half of the
estimated number of full-time local government employees. The
associations in each of the other four states have organized a much
smaller proportion, certainly no more than 15 percent. And in one
state, the association's membership is less than 1 percent.

The twenty-five responding associations reporting a total dues-
paying state employee membership of 318,000; it is believed that the
membership of the non-responding associations is concentrated
among state employees. Hence, it can be concluded that approximately 350,000 state employees are members of the thirty known
associations. These 350,000 members probably constitute around
25 percent of the estimated full-time state employees (as of July 1961).

In each state the proportion of the estimated full-time state employees who were association members varied, but the associations
in California and New York have succeeded in organizing more than
75 percent of the estimated number of full-time state employees.
Associations in Connecticut, New Hampshire, North Carolina,[5]
Oregon, and Vermont have probably succeeded in organizing more
than half of the estimated full-time state employees in their respective states.

Structure, Government, and Dues

The typical structure of an association does not differ substantially from that of a union. Nineteen associations had a local organization, usually called a 'chapter' (see table). A chapter was typically
defined as "an autonomous organization of persons qualified for
membership in the Association which holds an unrevoked charter";
generally, from seven to twenty-five members could petition for a
charter. Two associations reported no local unit organizations, and
one reported that it is now developing local unit organizations. The
three remaining associations reported subordinate units which were

organized on a broader base than the typical chapter; that is, as
sectional groups, district organizations, and county units, respectively.

Of the nineteen associations with chapters, ten had subordinate
units similar to the 'intermediate body' of unions.[6] Nine associations had intermediate bodies organized on a geographic basis; one
association had intermediate bodies organized into the following
groups: education, highway, institutional, and departmental. The
associations' constitutions suggest that these intermediate bodies
may play a significant role in the administration and government of
the associations.

The association's constitutions frequently provide for considerable direct participation by the membership in policy making. The
three associations which had no local unit organization held annual
meetings of the membership. In addition, four other associations
hold annual meetings of the membership. Seventeen associations
held conventions, attended by delegates from the local unit organizations and, frequently, from the intermediate bodies as well.
Fifteen of these seventeen associations hold annual conventions; two
reported holding conventions every two years.

The association's officers are usually elected at the convention,
although four associations elect officers by a secret mail ballot. In
addition, one association elects its vice-president by a secret mail
ballot; the vice-president then automatically succeeds to the presi-
dency the following year. Officers are usually elected for a one-year
period, but a few associations which hold annual meetings elect officers for a two-year period.

The governing body between conventions usually consists of officers and several additional board members, who are frequently
representatives of the intermediate body. These additional board
members are typically elected by their respective districts or
geographic units; they usually have longer terms than the officers.
The associations' constitutions suggest that these governing boards
meet often and may, therefore, play a significant role in developing
policy. By constitutional provisions, seven of these governing boards
were required to meet monthly. Three or four meetings a year, however, seems to be more common.

More than half of the constitutions specify that the governing
board may employ full-time employees. The constitution may also
outline the duties, responsibilities, and authority of the major full-
time employee (typically called executive secretary, executive director, or general manager).

Compared with unions, dues are low[7] (see table). The associations in Hawaii and Kansas are atypical; Hawaii had $27 annual dues,

Kansas had no dues. In addition to Hawaii, seven other associations had annual dues of at least $12 a year; while three had annual dues of from $10 to $12 a year. Five reported dues of from $5 to $10, and eight reported dues of less than $5. Only eleven of the twenty-four associations reported having dues deducted, but the membership of these eleven associations accounted for almost 70 percent of the total association membership. Only one association reported any initiation fee, which was $1.

The constitutions of eleven associations did not indicate whether any division of the dues is made between the association headquarters and subordinate bodies (the three associations without any subordinate units are of course excluded). In the absence of any constitutional provision, it seems likely that subordinate units do not receive any share of the dues. Moreover, the constitutions of at least three associations suggest that subordinate units are authorized to establish their own dues. Ten associations definitely provided for the distribution of dues to the subordinate units, with eight allocating 75 percent or more of the dues to the association headquarters; the remaining proportion was allocated to the local unit organizations. One association, however, allocated a portion of the dues to the intermediate body.

Recognition, Grievances, and Legislative Activity

Only one association claimed 'formal recognition' and supplied as evidence a statute guaranteeing the right of state employees to organize, and to present grievances. If the guarantee of the right to organize and to present grievances is the equivalent of formal recognition, then associations in other states could have made similar claims because they, too, have been accorded these rights by statute or by executive order.[8] Of course, formal recognition usually implies more than a statutory right to organize and to present grievances; it usually implies a 'right' (sometimes an 'exclusive right') to be consulted on all matters of interest to the organization's members. In the past decade, unions in government have become more vocal in their demands for formal recognition[9]; nevertheless, the responding associations evidently have been either uninterested in or unable to secure formal recognition.

All of the twenty-four other organizations, however, indicated that they were accorded 'informal recognition.' As specific examples of informal recognition, four associations reported that they selected the employee members of official state committees, such as management-labor councils and retirement boards; three reported that management officials 'consulted' with them; and one reported that their officers were given time off for association business. Despite these evidences of informal recognition, the responses to the question,

"Is your association consulted on all major personnel matters affecting your membership?", indicate some lack of consultation.
Eleven associations reported that they were not consulted on all
major matters; two replied with a qualified yes, and twelve, yes.

Associations were also asked to indicate if management discouraged or encouraged employees to join. Seven associations reported that employees were sometimes discouraged from joining;
ten reported that employees were encouraged to join. When asked
to describe management's specific acts, the associations typically
reported that department heads either encouraged or discouraged
participation. Two associations reported that certain employees
(state police and employees in the offices of the secretary of state,
attorney general, and governor, respectively) were forbidden to join.

Nine associations reported that they did not handle individual
grievances; one reported handling grievances other than those involving discipline; and fifteen reported handling grievances.[10] Four
of these fifteen associations reported handling four hundred or more
grievances per year; four reported one hundred or more; and the
remaining seven reported fewer than one hundred or failed to supply
any specific figure. Six associations reported that a formal grievance procedure had been established by law or executive order, and
supplied the statute or executive order establishing the procedure.
The grievance procedure typically permitted four appeals after the
immediate supervisor's decision, including a final appeal to the
state personnel board or to the governor.[11] Three additional associations indicated that they had a formal written grievance procedure,
but did not supply the document. One association reported that it had
a grievance procedure in one department only; the remaining five
reported no formal grievance procedure. These five associations
reported handling grievances informally with supervisors and department heads.

Ten associations indicated that they had initiated and supported
legal action in the courts for 'individuals or groups' having grievances, but only three reported ten or more such suits in the past five
years. Typically, these suits involved discipline, classification, or
salary problems.

All associations reported some legislative activity, including
drafting, sponsoring, and lobbying for the passage of legislation.
Seventeen associations reported that they participated frequently
with state administrative officials and legislative leaders in drafting 'agreed bills'; four reported only occasional participation in
drafting agreed bills; and four indicated no such participation. Although these replies suggest that associations have considerable
influence on legislation, they seem inconsistent with the replies
received on the extent of consultation. It seems unlikely that

administrative officers who did not consult on all major personnel matters would permit employee representatives to participate so actively in drafting legislation. On the other hand, the association's influence may be concentrated on legislative rather than administrative officers.

Other Association Activities, Staff, and Staff Activities

Associations were asked to report on four other activities: strikes, political activity, insurance programs, and communications with their membership.

Ten associations reported that they have a constitutional provision or convention resolution prohibiting strikes by their members. However, none of the fifteen associations which did not prohibit strikes reported authorizing a strike within the past decade. It would seem therefore that, even if an association does not have a written policy prohibiting strikes, it rarely, if ever, authorizes a strike.

Only one association replied affirmatively to the question: Does your association support candidates for state offices? That association's board of directors recommended candidates to the membership and then publicized the recommendation in the association's publication. Three other associations reported furnishing the membership with the voting records of political candidates. The remaining twenty-one associations indicated no political activity.

Eleven associations reported offering their membership the opportunity to participate in a group insurance program, typically life insurance. (At least one association provides a death benefit financed from membership dues.) In addition to life insurance, at least four associations also offer other programs, such as disability protection or a hospital, medical, and surgical program.[12] These insurance programs are usually underwritten by a life insurance company, and undoubtedly make available to members protection at a lower cost than would have been possible on an individual purchase. (Four associations volunteered the information that they administered a credit union; perhaps other associations perform this function.)

To communicate with members, twenty-three of the twenty-five associations issued a publication which was 'mailed at regular intervals.' Two reported a weekly publication; twelve reported a monthly publication; four, biweekly; four, quarterly; and one, yearly. Many associations also reported issuing weekly bulletins summarizing legislative developments when their respective state legislatures were in session.

In implementing these activities, associations are undoubtedly hampered by lack of staff. The relatively low dues' structure is of course reflected in the full-time staff that associations can employ. Only three associations reported more than ten professional staff members. Most associations reported from two to five staff members; three reported only part-time staff; two (including Kansas) reported no professional staff.

Seventeen associations were able to supply estimates of the percentage of time the professional staff devoted to various functions. Some of these seventeen associations had one or more employees who devoted full time to the insurance program; others did not. In reporting their estimates of staff activity, most associations reported the time devoted to the insurance program separately. For the others, the time devoted to other activities was recalculated (excluding the insurance program) to provide a basis for comparison. Since association membership is required before one can enroll in the insurance program, it can be argued that the 'insurance activity' is also a 'membership recruitment' activity.

For the six associations which did not handle grievances, membership recruitment and legislative representation combined usually accounted for more than 50 percent of the professional staff time. Membership recruitment constituted 50 percent or more of the staff time for two of the six associations; legislative representation constituted a high of 35 percent for two associations. Public relations, research, and administration completed the remaining proportions of staff time, with considerably more staff time devoted to public relations or administration than to research.

For the eleven associations which reported handling grievances, the proportion of staff time devoted to grievances is small. Seven of the associations reported less than 10 percent; two reported proportions as high as 25 and 30 percent, respectively. Seven associations reported 20 percent or more for membership recruitment; four reported more than 25 percent, with a high of 55 percent. The proportion of staff time for legislative representation was reported as low as 6 percent but as high as 60 percent, with 20 or 25 percent being typical. Combined, these three activities—grievances, membership recruitment, and legislative representation—typically accounted for more than 65 percent of staff time. Public relations, research, and administration accounted for the remaining proportions, with the same pattern as was indicated by the associations not handling grievances.

It can be concluded, therefore, that membership recruitment and legislative representation are the two major staff activities, with grievances (when they are handled), public relations, research, and administration constituting the remaining activities. Because the administration of the insurance program varied, it has not been possible to estimate the proportion of staff time devoted to it. For associations who actually participate in the program's administration, the staff time may be significant; for associations who do not participate in the administration, the staff time may be negligible.

Associations and the Organized Labor Movement

Associations were asked whether other employee organizations represented state employees and to estimate the membership of these organizations. The American Federation of State, County, and Municipal Employees, AFL-CIO (AFSCME) was mentioned by associations in sixteen states. Almost all of the associations claimed that their membership equalled or exceeded their estimate of AFSCME's membership. The Building Service Employees' International Union was reported as representing a few hundred state employees in each of two states, while the International Brotherhood of Teamsters was reported to represent an unknown number of state employees in a third state. The Hawaiian Government Employees' Association reported that the United Public Workers, the American Federation of Teachers, and the Hawaiian Education Association also represented state and local employees within their state. Their estimated membership of these three organizations, combined with their own membership, suggest that almost all state and local employees in that state belong to an employee organization.

The affiliated unions regard associations as 'company unions.'[13] Whether they are or are not dominated by management cannot be satisfactorily investigated except by close contact with each association. Consequently, this study can supply only limited data which would be relevant to that issue. In response to the question, "Have there been any attempts by 'management' to guide or influence the policies or programs of your association?", four associations reported affirmatively. Their replies were as follows: one reported attempts to influence legislative policy; one reported attempts to influence their position on a constitutional amendment on Civil Service; a third reported that department heads had attempted to control policy; and a fourth reported that there were attempts at control but did not describe them. Moreover, as indicated previously, department heads were eligible for membership in almost all of the associations and encouraged employees to join in sixteen states. It would seem therefore that employees who would not be eligible for membership in employee organizations in private industry may play active roles in these associations. Whether this fact means that these employees control association policy and that associations are company unions remains open for further research.

Antipathy toward labor unions is, in turn, manifested by the associations. Six had constitutional provisions forbidding affiliation with any labor organization; a seventh association's constitution provided only that it "may affiliate with a self-governing body of state employee associations"; and an eighth association's constitution provided that any proposal to affiliate would require a two-thirds' affirmative vote by both the board of directors and the convention. Moreover, two associations indicated that a nucleus of state employees who had been members of a union had disaffiliated and were instrumental in establishing their respective associations. It would seem unlikely, therefore, that many associations will seek voluntarily to affiliate with the organized labor movement.

Summary

Obviously, this exploratory study, based primarily on the associations' responses, is not sufficient to establish definitive conclusions. Further investigations will be needed to evaluate the independence and effectiveness of associations. Studies which would determine the extent of 'political' and 'supervisory' influence, as contrasted with the influence of rank-and-file members, would be particularly valuable. An analysis of the occupations and job classifications of an association's officers, executive board members, and chapter leadership would be helpful; but even more revealing, would be an evaluation of an association's program and activities. Do the associations, as charged by the unions, tend to support policies which provide greater benefits for supervisory and higher paid employees? Do they, as charged by the unions, neglect the interests and needs of the lower paid employees? Does the supervisory influence, as charged by the unions, explain the associations' limited emphasis on grievances?

Coupled with a study of an association's program should be some evaluation of the organization's effectiveness. What influence (if any) has it had in improving the wages, hours, and working conditions? How have employees represented by an association fared as compared with federal employees, other state employees, local government employees, and industrial workers? Do associations which handle grievances accept the difficult as well as the simple problems? And after accepting the grievances, do they have the resources and the ability to resolve them in favor of the employee?

A case study of an association and a union of about equal size in a single state could be extremely significant. Among the questions for research are: (1) Who are the members of each group? (2) How many and why do employees join both organizations? (3) What is the extent of rank-and-file participation in each organization? (4) Who are the leaders of each organization? (5) How do the two organizations' programs and activities differ? (6) How do their methods differ? (7) Which organization is more influential in the legislature? (8) Why? (9) Which is more effective with the administration?

(10) Why? (11) Do both organizations handle grievances? (12) Do they differ in the types of grievances handled? (13) Which organization receives the 'better press'? (14) Why? (15) To what extent does each organization participate in the broader social and economic problems of the state?

Finally, studies of associations must concern themselves with the future of this form of employee organization. Is it correct, as has been predicted here, that few associations will seek to affiliate with the organized labor movement? If the associations do not affiliate, will the organized labor movement launch a serious attempt to raid and absorb the associations? And if the organized labor movement does attempt to raid the associations, which of them will be absorbed and which will survive? Undoubtedly, the weaker, poorly financed associations will be inviting targets, but the information reported by the associations suggests that some of them may be able to resist the labor movement's organizational efforts. It would seem, therefore, that these associations will continue to be the spokesman for significant numbers of state employees for some time.

Notes

[1]The names and addresses of most of the thirty associations are available in a listing supplied by the Assembly of Government Employees entitled Directory—Independent Public Employees Associations. The assembly, organized in 1955, is a loose federation of these associations. Copies of the listing may be obtained from the Colorado Civil Service Employees' Association, 1280 Sherman Street, Room 212, Denver 3, Colo.

[2]Based on estimates made by the Assembly of Government Employees, see ibid.

[3]There are, of course, an unknown number of local employee associations. For a study of these groups in California, see California State Employees' Association, Formal Systems of Representation for California Public Employees, September 1960.

[4]For a discussion of the status of supervisors in public employment, see New York City Department of Labor, Organization and Recognition of Supervisors in Public Employment, Serial L.R.5, August 1955. A report of a federal task force on labor relations recommended that "no unit should be established for purpose of exclusive recognition which includes" supervisory personnel; see Report of the President's Task Force on Employee-Management Relations in the Federal Service: A Policy for Employee-Management Cooperation in the Federal Service, Nov. 30, 1961, p. 28.

[5]The membership of both associations in that state were added to obtain this estimate.

[6]Herbert Lahne, "The Intermediate Body in Collective Bargaining" Industrial and Labor Relations Review, Vol. 6, January 1953, pp. 163-179. See also, Ligouri Alphonsus O'Donnel, "An Inquiry into Union Structure: The Intermediate Body," Dissertation Abstracts, Vol. 22, September 1961, pp. 761-762.

[7]Data on union dues are available in Report for Fiscal Year 1960 (Washington, D.C.: U.S. Department of Labor, Bureau of Labor-Management Reports, 1960), p. 26.

[8]See "Trends in Labor Legislation for Public Employees," Monthly Labor Review, Vol. 82, December 1960, pp. 1293-1294.

[9]See my "The Union Quest for Recognition in Government Service," Labor Law Journal, Vol. 9, June 1958, pp. 421 ff., and Wilson R. Hart, Collective Bargaining in the Federal Civil Service, 1961, chaps. 8 and 9.

[10]Academic students of labor relations in some of these states have informed the writer that the associations are not aggressive in handling grievances. One association informed the writer that "we do not urge grievances."

[11]Almost all union contracts in private industry provide for the final disposition of grievances by an appeal to a neutral third party; some unions in government have been able to secure agreements which also provide for arbitration of grievances. See Jonas Silver, "Union Agreements with Municipalities," Monthly Labor Review, Vol. 56, June 1943, p. 1167, and Robert L. Stutz, Collective Dealing by Units of Local Government in Connecticut" (Storrs: University of Connecticut Labor-Management Institute, Bulletin No. 8) May 1960, pp. 21, 23. Charles Killingsworth reported that the American Federation of State, County, and Municipal Employees had supplied him with a list of more than seventy cities which had agreements providing for arbitration of grievances by neutrals. See his "Grievance Adjudication in Public Employment," American Arbitration Journal, Vol. 13, No. 1 (1958), p. 9.

[12]One association reported a health insurance program for retired members.

[13]See, for example, Solomon Barkin, The Decline of the Labor Movement and What Can Be Done about It, 1961, p. 34.

Chapter 14

Public Employee Unionization in Texas

CHESTER A. NEWLAND

Unionization of public employees is one of the most important recent developments in public personnel policy and practice in the United States. While the most publicized activities have occurred in Northern States, a dramatic growth of unions has also taken place in the South and West. This study examines one aspect of this development in the State of Texas: the growth and activities of broad-jurisdiction public employee unions.

This investigation was completed as a personal project by the author to help satisfy a need in Texas for objective information about this trend in public personnel management. The purpose has been to collect and analyze essential facts, while avoiding involvement in internal municipal and union affairs.

Texas city officials and union leaders willingly provided assistance at every stage of this research. Lengthy interviews were permitted by numerous persons, and access was often provided to union and municipal records. A high regard was generally demonstrated for the academic responsibility for research and critical analysis of public affairs in Texas.

Current Union Status

The status of labor organization in public employment in Texas has been defined in narrowly restrictive terms by state statutes since 1947.[1] Disruptive public employee strikes in Galveston (1942) and Houston (1946) influenced adoption of this legislation. Strikes and organized work stoppages by public employees are now expressly forbidden, just as in jurisdictions outside of Texas which adopted restrictive labor legislation in the late 1940's.

But Texas law is more inclusive and adverse to unionization of public employees than the laws common to many other states.

Adapted from the pamphlet of the same title published as Public Affairs Series Number 50 by the Institute of Public Affairs, the University of Texas, 1962, by permission of the Institute.

Chester A. Newland is Associate Professor of Government at North Texas State University.

Collective bargaining contracts between governmental jurisdictions and their employees are declared illegal. No labor organization may be recognized by public officials "as the bargaining agent for any group of public employees."[2] At the same time, the 1947 legislation recognized rights of employees to belong to labor organizations and to present grievances individually or through "a representative that does not claim the right to strike."[3]

Texas courts have sometimes been called on for interpretation of state law concerning public employee unions, but several political subdivisions of the state have contributed more to the elaboration of the law in actual practice through their dealings with employee groups. A realistic understanding of Texas law concerning public employee unions requires examination of handbooks of municipal personnel regulations and local government policy statements on employer-employee relationships. For understanding of the extent of public employee unionization and its importance in Texas it is also necessary to examine actual political and administrative relationships between governments and employee groups in several political subdivisions and to note activities of employee groups of the state capital.

The principal union described in this paper is the American Federation of State, County, and Municipal Employees (AFSCME), an affiliate of the AFL-CIO. Other broad-jurisdiction unions described include competing AFL-CIO affiliates, independent unions and associations, and one Teamsters Union local. Organizations of firemen and policemen are not examined in this study, although the AFL-CIO Fire Fighters and the non-affiliated Texas Municipal Police Association and Texas Police Association are major employee organizations.

On October 16, 1961, the AFSCME celebrated its silver anniversary as an AFL chartered international union. One Texas local also traces its date of earliest organization back to the first year of the AFSCME's official birth. At the close of the International's first quarter-century, Texas locals totaled eighteen with a membership of approximately 2,500.

It is difficult to arrive at exact statistics on Texas locals of AFSCME. The number of active locals fluctuates due to disbanding, suspension, reorganization, and creation of new locals. AFSCME Texas membership records for 1960 showed seventeen active locals, one disbanded local,[4] and one suspended local.[5] The active locals were organized among employees of ten cities,[6] four counties,[7] and two school districts.[8] One local included members employed by more than one political jurisdiction.[9] In 1958, an AFSCME local was chartered among employees of the Texas Department of Agriculture, but it continued for only a couple of months.

Today, no broad-jurisdiction union exists among state employees. By the end of 1961 only one Texas local in addition to those listed above had been chartered, bringing the total to eighteen; the most recent local is in Fort Worth.

Several factors in the development of broad-jurisdiction public employee unions in Texas, as examined in the preceding survey, may be briefly summarized under three topics: (1) union goals, methods, and personnel; (2) union rights and restrictions in actual governmental practice; and (3) elements of union power and weakness. Two larger problems of public employee unionization which are evident from this investigation of Texas experience are also noted below.

Union Goals, Methods, and Personnel

Public employee unions in Texas seek objectives which are commonly sought by other elements of organized labor in the state, with improvements of wages and hours a foremost goal. But certain union aims stand out in this survey and deserve the attention of responsible officials. Job security is the prime objective of public employees. Union organization is relied upon as a defense against rotation out of government service due to political spoils. This objective is especially sought by county employee unions, and it was also obvious in the early development of the city employee unions of El Paso and Houston.

Machinery for employee group participation in redress of individual grievances is another major objective sought by public employee unions. Hospitalization and death insurance programs constitute a third major goal. In addition to these benefits, public employees groups have generally sought (1) improved working conditions, (2) position classification, (3) education and training programs for supervisors and subordinate employees, and (4) leave, vacation, holiday, and retirement programs.

Public employee unions rely upon a variety of methods to achieve their objectives. Even before limitations were imposed by the state legislature in 1947, strikes were rarely resorted to by public employees, but crippling municipal strikes in Galveston and Houston contributed to pressures to pass the present restrictive statutes. Since 1947 the strike has not been employed. However, a brief walkout by AFSCME members did occur in Port Arthur in 1955, and informational picketing was used by the AFSCME Local in Texas City in 1960. The unions in the last two instances were apparently restrained from further action by the present Texas law.

A chief instrument of the public employee unions is political influence. One outstanding characteristic of the unions in this survey, with the exception of the present Galveston city unions (one Teamsters and one Independent, both of which were first established

with broad union affiliation) is their heavy dependence upon the local
Central Labor Unions or Trades Councils for political support. Affiliation with the main body of organized labor is a critical source of
public employee union power in Texas. These unions also rely upon
public relations techniques to win community support. However,
educational efforts by these unions are usually aimed directly at
government officials in the form of information favorable to the employees represented.

Wherever permitted by government officials, Texas public employee unions rely heavily upon checkoff of dues for maintenance of
membership. Although Texas law requires individual authorizations
before dues deduction may be commenced, periodic re-authorization
is not required. Signing of authorizations by new employees may become routine, as they apparently were for some years in El Paso,
and old authorizations may be used even after increases of union
dues, as in the Jefferson County Local. Without dues checkoff, sur-
vival by public employee unions is difficult.

Union welfare programs are relied upon to gain employee support. When provided through local unions, group health and death
insurance programs serve both to broaden and to maintain union
membership. They also tend to induce elected officials and top
supervisors to affiliate with union locals. Union representation of
employees in accident liability and traffic court cases also appeals
to employees where the city governments fail to meet this need.

Jurisdictional disputes between public employee unions have
occurred in Texas, and exclusive recognition has sometimes been
openly sought. The Houston City Employees Union (Hod Carriers)
was able to delay extension of the checkoff privilege to the Houston
AFSCME Local when it raised a question of raiding and conflicting
jurisdiction. The El Paso City Employees Union approved a motion
in 1959 which supported efforts to gain exclusive bargaining rights.
The Texas City AFSCME sought to establish a principle of majority
representation. But that AFSCME Local is the only one in Texas
which includes policemen and firemen as well as city hall and public
works employees. The possible conflict with fire fighters has been
avoided in Texas City by membership of firemen in both AFL-CIO
unions since 1958.

Three generalizations about union leadership are supported by
this investigation. First, native union leaders are most effective
in Texas; antipathy toward outsiders is strong among local government officials and community leaders. Second, union leaders in
Texas have often lacked broad knowledge and understanding of local
government and of personnel management concepts and practices.
However, knowledge of local personnel practices and politics has
frequently been adequate to counterbalance this need. Third,

factional and individual personality conflicts within union organizations have hindered union growth as much or more than any other single factor, as, for example, in Galveston, El Paso, Houston, Texas City, and Austin.

It should also be noted in summary that some public employee union leaders in Texas have commanded considerable local respect both in performance of their union duties and in community services generally.

Union Rights and Restrictions

Legal rights and restrictions of public employee unions in Texas have been analyzed here only in the limited context of actual government practices. A realistic understanding of the existing meaning of Texas legal provisions is possible as a result.

This investigation reveals that, in practice, the following rights of public employee unions are generally recognized and exercised in Texas local governments where unions exist: (1) employee organization; (2) affiliation with organized labor generally; (3) checkoff of union dues; (4) group grievance representation before administrative and policy branches of government, including bargaining-type conferences on working relationships; and (5) individual grievance representation before administrative and policy branches of government.

Restrictions which are imposed and observed in practice are: (1) no right to strike; (2) no collective bargaining to formulate a labor contract; and (3) no exclusive representation agreements.

Of the above legal relationships, one remains the subject of controversy. The legality of the checkoff is sometimes questioned (as in Beaumont, Dallas, and Fort Worth), although actual practice in Texas over a long period of years overwhelmingly supports it.

Union Power and Weakness

Sources of union power and causes of weakness have been suggested already in summaries above. Public employee unions in Texas derive power from the wants and needs of their members for improved benefits and working conditions, particularly from demands on local governments to provide job security, employee participation in grievance machinery, protection from hazards of sickness and death, and contemporary wage-hour standards. However, despite employment conditions, public employee unions in Texas exist and are effective only when organized labor generally is powerful in the same community. Political influence has been essential to public employee union success in Texas, and for such influence public employees rely primarily on support by local Central Labor Unions and the State AFL-CIO.

Broad-jurisdiction public employee unions have been unsuccessful in attracting a broad membership even in heavily unionized areas of Texas. Firemen are organized separately, and the fire fighters constitute the strongest public employee group in Texas local government. Except in Texas City, policemen have also remained aloof from employee groups outside their own departments, and these police associations are powerful in Texas' largest municipalities.

City hall and county courthouse employees are seldom attracted to the unions. Consequently, the broad-jurisdiction public employee unions in Texas are composed primarily of equipment operators, drivers, common laborers, and waste collectors. Such membership, when predominant, tends to discourage participation of office personnel, who may feel that they belong in a different class from "outside employees." This constitutes a peculiar difficulty in union organization, since office and public safety employees are the largest and fastest growing employee groups in local governments.

A shortage of union leaders trained in local government, politics, and personnel processes may also be considered a weakness. Organization of "inside employees" in local government in Texas has only been successful when such employees have supplied their own leadership. Related major weaknesses of broad-jurisdiction public employee unions in Texas have been changing leadership, internal factionalism, and failure to establish an effective framework for statewide action. Personal power struggles have obstructed union growth among Texas public employees. Competing broad-jurisdiction unions also undercut each other in local government.

Current Major Problems

Two problems of public employee unionization in Texas deserve separate consideration: (1) involvement of public employees in politics, especially through affiliation with organized labor; and (2) recurrent espousal by union and government officials of the extremes of "bilateral binding negotiations" and "unilateral sovereign action" as the alternatives in public employee relationships.

Involvement of public employees in politics is illustrated at several points in this survey. The problem is connected with the right of public employee unions (the fire fighters as well as the unions examined here) to affiliate with organized labor generally. Such affiliation is thought essential to union power in most communities, since the public employee unions in Texas have generally felt required to have some source of political strength to gain the sympathetic hearing of government officials. Consequently, public employees or their union representatives regularly participate in preelection screening of candidates for public office, and, at least as members of the Central Labor Unions, frequently endorse favorites for election.

Actual campaigning is generally left to relatives and members of other unions, but poll tax drives and "educational" efforts to explain the positions of candidates are engaged in directly by public employees. Sometimes political action is even more open, as in Texas City in 1960. Thus public employees may become involved in elections of their political superiors, although employee unions have generally stated that their objectives include the elimination of political considerations as conditions of employment in subordinate positions.

Political rotation in office may be eliminated, but pro-union factionalism does not differ significantly from other political partisanship. This has especially been true in Texas' political system where factionalism predominates in local politics. It should be recognized that union and political leaders have been unable to divorce politics from this aspect of local government in Texas. The desirability of exploiting or restricting such political participation by government or union action might then be clearer to the employees, unions, governments, and interested publics.

A second problem which is evident in Texas is the continued tendency of some union and government officials to insist upon extreme alternatives in personnel relationships. Unions generally desire binding bilateral bargaining, and government officials often insist upon unilateral government prerogatives. Both of these positions may be unrealistic in Texas today. Collective bargaining contracts between governments and unions are illegal, and no drastic departure from that position is foreseeable in Texas. On the other hand, despite political theories of sovereignty and legal provisions prohibiting binding labor-management contracts, effective personnel administration today often requires reliance upon joint labor-management consultation and bilateral communication.

As extreme positions are discarded, developments in Texas indicate a general trend toward acceptance of the following principles of personnel management: (1) periodic and regular consultation between employee representatives (union and non-union) and government officials, and (2) the prevailing local wage concept. Difficult problems remain in the development of the first of these points.

Union representatives and government officials frequently disagree about who should participate in labor-management consultations. The interesting feature of this problem in Texas is that the principal point of dissension is often not over participation by various employee representatives but over who shall meet with them as agents of government. Union representatives have generally sought to go directly to political officials to resolve differences instead of going to responsible administrators and "following channels"—for example, in Texas City, where the mayor could be required to participate in the resolution of individual grievances from the first stage.

In short, as summarized above, behavior of public employee unions in Texas is frequently that of political pressure groups. This tendency of public employee unions appears to be an obstacle to development of administrator channels of group consultation in local government.

The political orientation of public employee unions in Texas may be due to several causes. One reason which is evident from this survey is the felt necessity of political power to accomplish union goals. Since public employee unions lack instruments of economic power, such as the strike, which is available to unions in private industry, they may turn more to politics. Also employees of local government who have formed unions have often been products of spoils systems in local Texas government.

Finally, local government officials (except city managers and other "professionals") are elected to office through political processes, and public employees are tempting sources of votes. The temptation may be particularly strong when a public employee union is affiliated with a politically active central labor organization.

Notes

[1] Vernon's Annotated Revised Civil Statutes of the State of Texas, art. 5154c.

[2] Ibid., sec. 2.

[3] Ibid., sec. 6.

[4] Jefferson County Institutional Employees Local 802. A duplication of AFSCME per capita tax membership records for Texas for 1960 (dated Jan. 19, 1961) was provided by Don McCullar, Business Agent, Local 1990, Houston, Texas.

[5] Corpus Christi Local 1619.

[6] Austin, Beaumont, Dallas, El Paso, Freeport, Houston, Nederland, Port Arthur, Texas City, and Waco.

[7] El Paso, Galveston, Harris, and Jefferson.

[8] Dallas Independent School District and Fort Worth Independent School District.

[9] Jefferson County Water Control Improvement District No. One, Local 1465, includes Groves and Port Neches.

Chapter 15

Independent Municipal Employee Associations in Californi

RICHARD L. HARR

Within the last few years much attention has been devoted to union-affiliated public employee organizations, and several articles in the professional public administration journals have dealt with the unionization of public employees and the growth of collective bargaining in municipal government. However, very little attention has been paid to the independent or non-affiliated public employee associations which exist in a number of municipal government jurisdictions throughout the United States.

In California, for example, over half of all the municipal employees in the state belong to independent public employee associations. Only a small minority of the total number of municipal employees in the state belong to public employee organizations affiliated with the general labor movement, and the majority of these unionized municipal employees are firemen who belong to the International Association of Fire Fighters, AFL-CIO.

The IAFF and the American Federation of State, County, and Municipal Employees are the only two union-affiliated public employee organizations that have attained any success in organizing municipal employees in California. Of the 373 city governments in California, approximately 40 have locals of the IAFF, and 20 have locals of the AFSCME. Over 250 cities have independent public employee associations.[1]

Unfortunately, no reliable data exist on the number of municipal employees belonging to independent public employee associations throughout the nation. However, it is probably safe to assume that many other states have more municipal public employees belonging to independent public employee associations than to union-affiliated public employee organizations.

Richard L. Harris is Research Analyst for the Institute of Government and Public Affairs, University of California at Los Angeles.

[1] An extensive coverage of the public employee organizations in California will soon be available in a book being written on this subject by Dr. Winston W. Crouch of the University of California, Los Angeles.

Despite the probability that independent public employee associations are more numerous than union-affiliated public employee organizations in municipal government, no recent attempt has been made to determine what their characteristics, functions, and objectives are. Little has been written about the kind of relationships these associations have with local municipal administrators and legislators. No articles have been published on the future of these associations, and absolutely nothing has been printed—outside of the union publications —about the problems the union-affiliated public employee organizations face as a result of these independent associations.

Four Factors

It is the intent of this article to try and correct what appears to be a somewhat unbalanced and distorted picture of the organized public employee groups in municipal government. For this reason, the scope here is limited primarily to a discussion of four basic factors which the author, in the course of studying the independent public employee associations in California municipal government, has come to believe decisively determine their development, character, and effectiveness.

These four factors are: (1) the employment conditions of the public employees in each municipal government; (2) the degree of political influence the municipal employees in each municipal government have in the local communities where they are employed; (3) the leadership of each independent municipal public employees' association; and (4) the attitude that the local government officials in each municipal government jurisdiction take toward these independent public employee associations.

Since no reliable information is available on the independent associations in municipal governments outside of California, there is no way to definitely confirm or deny the assumption that these four factors have been—and are—the key determinants in the development, character, and effectiveness of the independent public employee associations in municipal government throughout the entire nation. However, because these four factors seem so basic to the fundamental existence of the independent associations in California, it seems highly probable that these same four factors are basic to the development, character, and effectiveness of independent associations in other jurisdictions across the country.

For this reason, the author is convinced that the following discussion of these four determining factors will help to stimulate a greater interest in and understanding of these associations. Furthermore, it is entirely possible that much of what will be said about them will also relate to independent public employee associations in other levels of government.

Employment Conditions of Municipal Employees

To begin with, the employment conditions in each municipal government seem to be a key factor in the formation and development of independent municipal public employee associations. For example, the independent associations in California municipal government have originated largely out of the dissatisfaction of municipal employees with their employment conditions—that is, wages, fringe benefits, hours of work, and general working conditions.

As a result, these associations have been formed by municipal employees for the primary purposes of improving their wages, limiting their hours of work, acquiring various fringe benefits, improving their general working conditions, and occasionally even for the purpose of pressuring municipal governments into instituting civil service merit systems.

Furthermore, because of the occupational differences in the employment conditions of public safety employees (fire and police), at least four different varieties of independent municipal public employee associations have emerged: general municipal employee associations representing employees from every job classification and department within a municipal government; firemen's associations representing the exclusive interests of the firemen in each municipal government; police officers' associations representing the exclusive interests of municipal police officers; and occasionally policemen's and firemen's protective leagues in which both police officers and firemen are allied.

These four varieties exist because fire and police personnel in municipal government often feel that they have problems relating to their employment conditions that are peculiar to their respective occupations. Consequently, they feel that their interests can best be represented by their own individual associations.

On the other hand, occasionally both the firemen and the policemen within a municipal government jurisdiction feel that they have common interests relating to the improvement of their employment conditions. In such cases, they are likely to form policemen's and firemen's protective leagues.

The employment conditions within each municipal government also appear to determine the fundamental character of the independent associations within these governments. For example, in California the interest and active support of each association's membership seem to rely to a great extent on whether the members of that association are dissatisfied or satisfied with the progress their association is making toward the improvement of their employment conditions.

Thus, if the salaries and working conditions of the municipal employees are improved to their complete satisfaction by the efforts of their association and the beneficence of their municipal officials, the employees, instead of being stimulated to make more and more demands, tend to have less need for their independent public employee association.

In such instances, municipal employees in California frequently have allowed their associations to do one of three things: (1) lapse into a state of relative inactivity until some future date when the need for organization arises once again; (2) evolve into predominantly social and benevolent organizations; or (3) cease to exist altogether. On the other hand, if municipal employees, through their independent associations, are able to only partially improve the unsatisfactory employment conditions, it appears that they will continue agitating through their associations for improvement.

Finally, in cases where associations, over a considerable period of time, have failed to achieve the desired improvements, the associations have either been abandoned or they have evolved into loosely organized social and benevolent organizations.

Political Influence of Municipal Employees

The success of independent public employee associations in improving the employment conditions of their members apparently can be determined by the degree of political influence that municipal employees have in the communities where they are employed.

How can municipal employees, civil servants, have political influence? First of all, by being resident voters in the communities where they are employed. In California, employees of the municipal governments that have strict employee residence requirements collectively have a greater potential political influence in the community than those of municipal governments that have no residence requirements and only a few of their employees living in the community.

While it is true that the proportion of municipal employees in relation to the total number of voters in each municipality—especially in the larger cities—is very small, it is not just the number of votes the municipal employees themselves have that counts. What does count is the number of votes the local public employees are able to influence.

It would appear that a unified and well organized drive for public support by municipal employees, their relatives, and their friends can be very effective in any community where the municipal employees do not have an unfavorable public image and the issues at hand have merit. Undoubtedly, there are many communities outside of California—with restrictions upon the political activities of their

local public employees--that have had the opportunity to see how effective such campaigns for public support by local public employees
can be.

Various means can be used by independent municipal public employee associations to gain community support and to influence
municipal officials. The publication of newspaper articles and adver-
tisements asking the public to support the local municipal employees
in their stand for higher wages and working conditions, wining and
dining of important municipal officials, contributions to the campaign
funds of councilmen up for re-election, radio broadcasts and interviews in which the public employees are given a chance to state their
reasons for asking for more favorable employment conditions, employee demonstrations, and getting prominent community leaders to
endorse their demands are just a few of the tactics which can be used.

Municipal officials who refuse to recognize the independent public employee associations in their jurisdictions, unwittingly seem to
force these associations to become political pressure groups who
must take their demands to the electorate. For example, public employees in a number of California home-rule charter cities have been
forced to obtain some of their objectives by initiative legislation because they could not gain the recognition of their local officials. In
some communities they have become so effective as political pressure
groups that local officials often solicit their aid in influencing the
voters when proposals supported by the local officials appear on the
municipal ballot.

Need for Competent Leaders

Without competent leaders to keep the municipal employees functioning as a well organized and unified group, the potential political
influence in the community of any independent municipal public employee association would be limited and thus it would have no effective
influence with the local officials. Moreover, the internal vitality of
each of these associations, as well as its success in dealings with the
local legislature and administration, depends a great deal on competent leadership.

In California municipal government, the leaders of these organizations are the spokesmen for their associations. It is apparent that
their articulateness, their experience in organizing and directing
others, their tactfulness in dealing with both management and legislators, and their willingness to give up a great deal of their spare
time for association business have contributed to their associations'
effectiveness. The impression that local officials have of the independent public employee associations in their jurisdictions, it seems,
is usually determined by the impression the leaders of these associations have made.

Furthermore, if the association leaders are highly dedicated and aggressive, they appear to stimulate the active interest of the local employees in the independent public employee associations in their jurisdictions. On the other hand, when these leaders do not adequately speak for the interests of the municipal employees, they stand to lose the interest and support of the very group they claim to be representing.

Attitude of Municipal Officials

While all of the factors discussed in this article are interrelated, the fourth factor, which deals with the attitude of municipal officials toward the independent public employee associations in their jurisdictions, is probably more important than the other three combined.

In the first place, the development of each independent municipal public employee association appears to be decisively influenced by the amount of opposition, indifference, or encouragement it receives from the municipal officials. For example, when California municipal officials have actively discouraged their employees from organizing and joining their own independent associations, they have occasionally prevented their employees from successfully organizing these associations.

However, the denial of recognition to these associations more often has resulted in the associations becoming more demagogic, irresponsible, and obstructive. In each case, it would seem that the municipal officials lose. Even when they have succeeded in preventing their employees from organizing, they have found themselves faced with the problems of poor employee morale and an excessive turnover rate.

In some cases, those municipal officials who do not believe their employees have the right to organize give their employees no other alternative than to affiliate with one of the national public employee unions—such as the AFSCME. When, because of the unfavorable attitude of the municipal officials, employees cannot get the recognition of their interests through their own independent public employee associations, they may feel that, by affiliating with a union such as the AFSCME, other labor unions in their community will come to their support and put political pressure on the municipal government to recognize their interests.

However, the number of municipal government jurisdictions that continue to refuse to recognize the rights of their employees to organize is probably quite low compared to the number of municipal governments where independent public employee associations are recognized by both management and the local legislature.

Informal Recognition

If the municipal governments in California that recognize the independent public employee associations in their jurisdictions are any indication of what takes place in other jurisdictions throughout the nation, then probably a substantial number of municipal government jurisdictions that have independent public employee associations recognize and negotiate with these associations on an informal basis. This means that these municipal governments probably do not have legislation or formal written agreements with their independent associations that outline the extent or form of recognition and consultation that these municipal governments are to extend to these associations.

However, despite the fact that no formal consultation machinery exists in any municipal government jurisdiction in California, the independent public employee associations in a majority of these jurisdictions are regularly given hearings or consulted on such matters as salaries, hours of work, overtime provisions, retirement, medical and life insurance plans, vacations, uniform allowances, and sick leave provisions. Furthermore, these jurisdictions often provide payroll dues deduction for the associations. This service greatly enhances the financial stability of the associations.

As a result, even though the independent public employee associations in California municipal government are not formally recognized and negotiated with, they are, for the most part, informally accepted by both municipal management and legislatures. Under these conditions, most independent associations appear to be able to maintain the support of their members as well as to obtain improvements in their employment conditions.

Conclusion

Based upon the present situation in California municipal government, it seems unlikely that the unionization of public employees will spread to the majority of those municipal government jurisdictions where independent public employee associations are already doing a good job of promoting the interests of the local municipal employees. The national public employees' union does not seem to be able to offer the municipal employees in these jurisdictions anything more than the independent associations can offer. In fact, the national unions are handicapped in at least three ways.

First, they invariably must ask higher membership dues than the independents. This is because public employee unions, such as the IAFF and the AFSCME, require their locals to pay per capita dues to their international headquarters, the state labor federation, and to the Committee on Political Education (COPE).

Second, healthy independent public employee associations provide their members with quite liberal welfare benefits and life insurance plans. Consequently, the members of these associations cannot easily be lured away to join a union.

Finally, and of most importance, the average municipal government appears to prefer to deal with non-affiliated public employee organizations. For example, outside of those industrialized communities in California where organized labor is an important element in local politics, municipal government officials and local taxpayers generally take a negative view toward the unionization of public employees. I would venture to say that this is probably true in many other similar municipalities throughout the United States.

However, those municipal government administrators who do not want their employees to affiliate with a national public employees' union would do well to recognize the interests of the independent associations in their jurisdictions and allow the representatives of these associations, as spokesmen for the employees, to participate in the policy-making processes that determine the municipal employees' salaries, fringe benefits, and working conditions.

PART V
Management-Employee Relations in the Federal Government:
A New Program

Introduction

You will find public officials and government workers who believe 1961 ushered in a new era of employee relations in the U. S. public service. That year the President's Task Force on Employee-Management Relations in the Federal Service laid the groundwork for the now often-cited Executive Order 10988, signed by the President January 17, 1962. The two chapters in Part V emphasize a rather widely held view that the Executive Order stands as a milestone in the history of federal personnel administration. But, as we shall see, any novel institutional arrangement carries with it built-in problems.

In Chapter 16, John W. Macy, Jr., Chairman of the U. S. Civil Service Commission, gives a lively account of the new federal program. He brings the story through the period of a draft Code of Fair Labor Practices and a draft Standards of Conduct for Employee Organizations. Mr. Macy provides a detailed statement of the content of the new program and concrete actions taken to make it effective [to October, 1962].

Earlier I mentioned some features of the new federal program that hold high interest. The program represents a positive statement of federal policy... it provides for formal recognition of employee organizations... it reaffirms the right of employees to join organizations... it outlines specific areas for negotiation... it sets up machinery for the conduct of collective negotiation . . . it recognizes the superiority of Congress to deal exclusively with certain subjects outside the bargaining area . . . it underscores public interest as a guiding principle... it reiterates that federal merit-system principles must continue.

No one expected the new program to be self-operative. Leaders of federal employee organizations are most likely to find gaps in the program. For that reason I invited a number of persons who appeared before the President's Task Force to express their views in Chapter 17 on the strong and weak points of the program. I believe that what these men tell us will be of great interest to officials throughout the country who are faced with the question of how they should conduct their own relations with organized workers.

Representatives of organized employees generally support the objectives of the new federal program. A number cite specific provisions which in their judgment deserve attention and possible revision.

The most explicit call for a change comes from the National Federation of Federal Employees. Mr. Vaux Owen, President of that organization, makes a case for repeal of collective bargaining features either by executive or legislative action and elimination of the "conflict of interest" feature so management and supervisory employees can hold office in unions. Other union representatives call attention to a variety of matters of concern to them. Included are: determination of bargaining units; clarification of language about standards of employee conduct; acceptance of voluntary dues check-off; broadening areas of negotiation; de-emphasis on mechanics and re-emphasis on the spirit and philosophy of the program; encouragement rather than discouragement of union membership by management.

One might expect differences of opinions among employee organizations. A sharp contrast of views appears clearly in two brief quotations on a fundamental point: collective bargaining as a characteristic of industrial labor relations and its applicability to the public service.

Mr. Griner, newly elected President of the American Federation of Government Employees, discusses implications of the term "collective bargaining." He says:

> The whole hullabaloo over collective bargaining is nothing more than semantic nonsense. Consultation with union representatives on personnel policies and working conditions is merely another way of saying "collective bargaining." The alternative to collective bargaining, which means nothing more than group negotiation over problems of mutual interest and concern, is unilateral dictation.

Mr. Vaux Owen decries the tendency to look at industrial and public management as the same. As mentioned, he opposes the concept of collective bargaining, and further says:

> We now can well expect the progressive development of the practices associated with collective bargaining in private industry. Such practices include slow-downs, reluctance to sign collective-bargaining agreements, strikes, picketing, compulsory union membership, sweet-heart contracts, jurisdictional disputes and serious harm to innocent people and the public.

But all authors who contribute to Part V hold one common view: Success in the new federal program calls for responsible leadership within employee organizations and management.

K.O.W.

Chapter 16

Employee-Management Cooperation
in the Federal Service

JOHN W. MACY, JR.

More progress has been made in federal employee-management relations since June 22, 1961, than was made in any comparable period in the 80-year history of the federal civil service.

Major areas of progress include:

-- A new system of relationships with federal employee organizations;

-- Provision for veterans and non-veterans to have identical rights to appeal adverse actions to the Civil Service Commission;

-- Establishment of a new system of appeals in federal agencies; and

-- Development by the Civil Service Commission of improved instructions to be followed by federal agencies in employee grievance procedures.

The present charter for the conduct of federal employee-management relations, Executive Order 10988, is the end result of a long and sincere desire to bring order, consistency, and fairness to a myriad of varying approaches to the conduct of labor relations in government.

More than a score of separate bills on the subject of federal labor relations were introduced in the last session of Congress alone. As in previous sessions in recent years, they were sponsored by members of both parties. None were enacted into law.

Employee organizations in some form have existed in the federal service since the early 1800's. The attitude of federal agencies toward these organizations has varied from willing cooperation to passive acceptance to dour toleration to a reluctance to deal. There was a conspicuous absence of any government-wide policy as to what the attitude of the agency <u>heads</u> should be in dealing with employee organizations.

John W. Macy, Jr., is Chairman of the United States Civil Service Commission, Washington, D. C.

The President's Task Force

Against the backdrop of these conditions, President Kennedy appointed on June 22, 1961, a Task Force on Employee-Management Relations in the Federal Service. Membership of the Task Force was composed of the Secretary of Labor as Chairman; the Chairman of the Civil Service Commission as Vice Chairman; and the Postmaster General, the Director of the Bureau of the Budget, the Secretary of Defense, and the Special Counsel to the President as members.

In the memorandum which served as charter for the Task Force, President Kennedy said:

> The right of all employees of the Federal Government to join and participate in the activities of employee organizations, and to seek to improve working conditions and the resolution of grievances should be recognized by management officials at all levels in all departments and agencies. The participation of Federal employees in the formulation and implementation of employee policies and procedures affecting them contributes to the effective conduct of public business.
>
> I believe this participation should include consultation by responsible officials with representatives of employees and Federal employee organizations.

Task Force staff work included the collection and analysis of all available information on current practices, the review of past studies on the subject, and the scheduling of hearings in Washington and the field. Reports were submitted by 57 agencies which collectively employ 93 per cent of the federal work force. At the hearings held in Washington and in six principal cities, employee organization leaders and public witnesses expressed their views on the main issues facing the Task Force.

Questionnaires to agencies and employee organizations completed the fact-gathering which was published in six special reports that served as the basis for policy proposals.

Findings

It was revealed that union strength in government ranged from 82 per cent membership in the Tennessee Valley Authority to practically none in the State Department. Overall, an estimated 33 per cent of the federal work force was found to be affiliated with employee groups. This percentage approximated the extent of union affiliation in the nation's non-farm work force.

When Task Force members interviewed union leaders and asked: "What do you want?" the answer was: "Status, recognition, acceptance; the right to be consulted, and the right to represent our members."

Asked what is wrong now, union spokesmen replied: "We are not recognized. We are not consulted. And we are not given a proper role."

When federal agency spokesmen were asked what they wanted, they generally expressed satisfaction with the programs already in effect in their agencies, but frequently offered positive recommendations for improvement.

To establish even basic rules which would be in the public interest and satisfactory to all employee organizations and to the heads of all federal agencies would not be a simple task.

The Task Force looked to experience in industry and other public jurisdictions for guidance.

Public Interest Comes First

It became apparent that union recognition and collective bargaining in the United States had produced one of the best labor-relations systems in the world. But, not all the private-industry experience could be applied unchanged to the government.

In industry the system of relationships, rights, and benefits develop out of bargaining between an employer who can make a final determination on these matters and a union that can strike if its demands are not met.

Basic personnel structure, basic benefits, and basic employee rights in government are controlled by laws of Congress and regulations of the civil service system. The agency head must exercise his authority in a manner prescribed by the Congress and the President. These matters are not subject to bargaining; and the law properly prohibits federal workers from use of the strike.

The Task Force asserted that the first obligation of the federal service is to function in the public interest and to meet the program goals of government. Any program of employee recognition or cooperation must meet and be compatible with the basic principles of the merit system.

Managers would have to function as managers, the Task Force reasoned, and employee organizations would have to function as representatives of the interests of employees to the officials for whom the employees worked. By and large, employee unions wanted a clear line of demarcation between management personnel and rank-and-file employees. They did not want a conflict-of-interest situation in which a management official held union office.

Recommendations

On the basis of all these considerations, the Task Force developed a series of recommendations which established the proper roles of individuals, employee organizations, and agency management, and which spelled out the rights and responsibilities of each.

The individual's rights included the right to join or not join a union, the right to be heard, the right to have a representative of his own choosing in a grievance action, and the right to act in concert with his fellow employees in presenting his views to management and in participating in policy decisions which affect him in his job.

All these rights already existed in one form or another, but their reiteration in one broad statement of policy and with government-wide application was new. In many instances the nature of the proceeding was changed.

The group's rights included new status as a participant in the formation of policy—depending upon the strength of the organization—a recognized role in representing employees, and new responsibility.

This responsibility forbade the employee organization to discriminate. It required the organization to be free of corruption and undemocratic practices. And, when exclusive recognition was granted, it required the group to be responsible in representing all employees in a unit.

Agency management was given an important new opportunity to promote the effectiveness of the federal service through a rational system of cooperation with the elected representatives of their employees.

From the Task Force recommendations came two landmark directives, Executive Order 10987 on Agency Appeals and Executive Order 10988 on Employee-Management Cooperation. Signed January 17, 1962, these orders were effective July 1, 1962. Taken together, the two directives comprise what is probably the most significant development in federal personnel policy since the Veterans' Preference Act of 1944 became law.

Major Features of the Federal Policy

The following major features of the Task Force report and the Executive Order on Employee-Management Cooperation in the Federal Service form the policy substance which makes this Presidential action such a significant forward stride.

Right To Organize

Federal employees have the right to join or the right to refrain from joining bona fide employee organizations. Wherever any considerable number of employees have organized for the purpose of collective dealing, the attitude of the government should be that of an affirmative willingness to enter such relations.

Their right to join other organizations such as social or fraternal groups, employee councils, and veterans groups is not affected by this policy.

Forms of Recognition

Bona fide organizations of federal employees, which are free of restrictions or practices denying membership because of race, color, creed, or national origin, which are free of all corrupt influences, and which do not assert the right to strike or advocate the overthrow of the government of the United States should be recognized by government agencies.

Organizations of federal employees should be granted recognition essentially according to the extent to which they represent employees in a particular unit or activity of an agency. This recognition may be informal, formal, or exclusive.

Informal Recognition. Informal recognition gives an organization the right to be heard on matters of interest to its members, but places an agency under no obligation to seek its views. Informal recognition will be granted to any organization, regardless of what status may have been extended to any other organization.

An organization seeking informal recognition must meet the basic definition of an employee organization (i.e., not merely a social, religious, or fraternal organization), and must not engage in prohibited practices which apply to organizations seeking any degree of recognition.

Formal Recognition. Formal recognition will be granted to any organization with at least 10 per cent of the employees in a unit or activity of a government agency as members, where no organization has been granted exclusive recognition. Formal recognition gives an organization the right to be consulted on matters of interest to its members.

Exclusive Recognition. Exclusive recognition will be granted to any organization chosen by a majority of the employees in an appropriate unit. Exclusive recognition gives an organization the right to enter collective negotiations with management officials with the object of reaching an agreement applicable to all employees of the unit.

Such agreements must not conflict with existing federal laws or regulations, or with agency regulations, or with government-wide personnel policies, or with the authority of the Congress over various personnel matters. To receive exclusive recognition, an employee organization must meet the criteria for formal recognition, as well as have the support of a majority of unit employees.

Consultations and Negotiations

Scope. Consultations or negotiations, according to the form of recognition granted, may concern matters in the area of working conditions and personnel policies, within the limits of applicable federal laws and regulations, and consistent with merit-system principles.

Accordingly, an employee organization which has been granted formal or exclusive recognition may consult with or negotiate with management officials on matters of concern to employees.

Generally, negotiations may take place on policies in such areas of employee concern as working conditions, promotion standards, grievance procedures, safety, transfers, demotions, reductions in force, and other matters consistent with merit system principles. Negotiation should not include matters concerning an agency's mission, its budget, its organization and assignment of personnel, or the technology of performing its work.

In Event of Impasses. Impasses in negotiations between government officials and employee organizations granted exclusive recognition should be solved by means other than arbitration. Methods for helping to bring about settlements should be devised and agreed to by the agencies concerned.

Agreements and Services

Agreements between management officials and employee organizations granted exclusive recognition should be reduced to writing in an appropriate form. Decisions reached by management officials as a result of consultation with employee organizations granted formal recognition may also be communicated in writing to the organization concerned. Negotiations should be kept within reasonable time limits.

Bulletin boards should be made available to employee organizations. Officially approved or requested consultations with employee organizations should take place on official time. An agency may require that negotiations with an employee organization granted exclusive recognition take place on employees' time. No internal employee organization business should be conducted on official time.

If authorized by Congress, voluntary dues withholding may be granted to an employee organization, provided the cost is borne by the organization.

Grievances and Appeals

Employee organizations should have a recognized role in grievance systems. Advisory arbitration may be provided by agreement between an agency and an employee organization granted exclusive recognition.

A more uniform system of appeals of adverse actions should be established within each agency. Veterans and non-veterans in the competitive service should have identical rights to appeal adverse actions to the Civil Service Commission.

Union Shop

The union shop and the closed shop are inappropriate to the federal service and are not permitted.

Technical Services

Technical services to agency management required to implement the program will be provided by the Department of Labor and the Civil Service Commission. Upon request, the Secretary of Labor shall nominate a person or persons to make advisory determinations on appropriate units for exclusive recognition and to perform similar services. The Department of Labor and the Civil Service Commission have jointly prepared recommendations for standards of conduct for employee organizations and a code of fair labor practices for the federal service.

These elements, all incorporated into the Executive Order with the exception of the point bearing on dues withholding (which will require the action of Congress), are to be applied to all executive-branch agencies of government.

Progress to Date

The months between January 17, 1962, when the two Executive Orders were signed, and July 1, when they became fully effective, were active months for all federal agencies -- especially the Civil Service Commission and the Department of Labor which were given specific responsibilities for implementation of the program.

Guidelines were drafted and released by the commission to help the agencies understand the two orders. Orientation sessions were staged for management and supervisory groups to acquaint them with their new responsibilities under the orders.

The Task Force early in its deliberations reached the decision that paternalism by the government toward the unions should be studiously avoided. In line with this decision, government managers have not been providing training for union officials in the new program.

However, they are providing them with information, including the answers to questions the union leadership has asked. The unions received copies of the Executive Orders and the Task Force report published by the commission. Through periodic public reports, union leaders learned what the commission was doing to implement the program.

Training Program Begins

Training materials were prepared and an extensive program of education was conducted by the commission and the agencies. Instructions were given in Washington and the field to agency managers, beginning with the top executives who would be involved in the program.

Revised instructions on grievance procedures, new regulations on agency appeal systems, and guidelines on employee-management cooperation were prepared and distributed to federal agencies.

Staff work was completed on drafting standards of conduct for employee organizations and a code of fair labor practices for the federal service.

Conflict of Interest

Obviously no simple rule could be prepared to define which employees in which agencies would be involved in a conflict of interest if allowed to serve as agency managers and union officers. As intended by the Executive Order, specific rulings were ultimately made by the heads of agencies concerned. It is not unnatural that there were some differences in rulings from agency to agency, for the missions of agencies are greatly dissimilar and the degrees of management responsibility vary among individuals.

In two or three unions there was marked opposition to the application of conflict-of-interest standards. One union attempted to secure Congressional intervention and Presidential action to eliminate this portion of the Executive Order.

In cases where a conflict-of-interest situation might develop if a person with management responsibility continued to hold union office, a reasonable time was allowed for the incumbent official to remain in office until the union could select a replacement.

Existing Procedures Revised

Civil service rules and regulations were rewritten as necessary to incorporate the contents of the orders. Entire chapters of the Federal Personnel Manual, the "bible" of federal personnel administration, were edited and revised to incorporate all changes. Appeal rules and grievance procedures were specifically revised to conform with new policy standards.

Civil service inspection agendas were revised to incorporate the requirements of the new employee-relations program, including fact-gathering and evaluation of the programs established in the agencies.

Early Problems

Secretary of Labor Arthur Goldberg was able to report to the President in May, 1962, that plans were moving on schedule and that the program would be placed in effect by July 1. He said that there had been some problems, as anticipated, but none which could not be solved through continued cooperation on an administrative basis.

One of these problems arose when employee organizations filed for the varying degrees of recognition to which they felt entitled under the Executive Order. The question was one of interpretation: What constitutes a majority vote for exclusive recognition?

The order said: "Exclusive recognition will be granted an organization chosen by a majority of the employees in an appropriate unit." This statement contained profound impact because, under the system, if an employee organization is chosen by the majority of employees in an appropriate unit it becomes the only recognized representative of the unit.

The Temporary Committee on Implementation interpreted the statement quoted above to mean that a simple majority of those voting would decide the issue, provided that at least 60 per cent of those eligible voted.

However, if a union obtains an absolute majority of those eligible to vote, the 60 per cent rule would not apply.

On the matter of recognition, as in all other details of the program, the Civil Service Commission and the Department of Labor provided guidance but left the specific application to the judgment of the agency head concerned.

The Standards and Code

The program became operational July 1, as scheduled.

Next in the chain of progress came the issuance of the draft Standards of Conduct for Employee Organizations and the draft Code of Fair Labor Practices. These documents were submitted to agency heads and officials of employee organizations for review in July.

While there is a likelihood that some changes may be made before the standards and code are adopted, they covered the following topics in draft form.

Standards of Conduct for Employee Organizations

These standards would apply to every employee organization accorded or seeking formal or exclusive recognition, and would apply in every agency. They could also be applied to groups which seek or have received informal recognition.

No agency would accord formal or exclusive recognition to any employee organization which does not have clear provision for:

-- The maintenance of democratic procedures and practices, including provisions for periodic elections to be conducted subject to recognized safeguards and provisions defining and securing the right of individual members to participation in the affairs of the organization, to fair and equal treatment under the governing rules of the organization, and to fair process in disciplinary proceedings.

-- The exclusion from office in the organization of persons affiliated with Communist or totalitarian movements and persons identified with corrupt interests.

-- The prohibition of business or financial interests on the part of organization officers and agents which conflict with their duty to the organization or its members.

-- The maintenance of fiscal integrity in the conduct of the affairs of the organization, including provision for accounting and financial controls and regular financial reports or summaries to be made available to members.

Code of Fair Labor Practices

The code, like the standards, would apply to all federal agencies and all federal employee organizations. Under the code, agency management would be prohibited from:

-- Interfering with, restraining, or coercing any employee in the exercise of the rights assured by Executive Order 10988.

-- Encouraging or discouraging membership in any employee organization by discrimination in regard to hiring, tenure, or other condition of employment.

-- Sponsoring, controlling, or otherwise assisting any employee organization, except that an agency may furnish customary and routine services and facilities specified in the order where consistent with the best interests of the agency, its employees and the organization, and where such services and facilities are furnished on a non-discriminatory basis to employee organizations similarly situated.

-- Refusing to accord appropriate recognition to an employee organization qualified for such recognition.

-- Refusing to hear, consult, confer, or negotiate with an employee organization as required by the order.

Employee organizations would be prohibited from:

-- Coercing, intimidating, or interfering with employees in the enjoyment of their rights under the order.

-- Attempting to induce an agency management to coerce, intimidate, or interfere with an employee in the enjoyment of his rights under the order.

-- Coercing or attempting to coerce, or disciplining any member of the organization for the purpose of affecting, or as punishment or reprisal for, his discharge of his duties owed as an officer or employee of the United States.

-- Threatening, calling, or engaging in any strike, work stoppage, or slow down against the government of the United States.

No employee organization which is accorded exclusive recognition could deny membership in the organization upon the same terms and conditions generally applicable for other members to any employee in the appropriate unit except for failure to tender required dues and initiation fees uniformly required as a condition of acquiring and retaining membership. Employee unions could enforce discipline in accordance with their constitutions and by-laws which conform to the standards.

The standards and code will provide features for enforcement, hearings, and impartial review, with final decisions vested in the heads of agencies.

Discrimination

Agencies would process complaints that an employee organization is discriminating because of race, color, creed, or national origin under provisions of the code. Nothing in the code would limit or impair the jurisdiction or authority of the President's Committee on Equal Employment Opportunity.

A Look at the Future

The basic establishment of a federal program of employee-management cooperation is completed. The real challenge lies ahead.

How successful will agencies be in interpreting and applying the program and making it work? Will this program for improved employee-management cooperation help to provide a better federal service?

Heads of federal agencies and leaders of federal employee organizations have expressed a sincere interest in making the program succeed.

The next phase will present a particular challenge to the Civil Service Commission as the central personnel agency of the government and the administrator of the merit system. The commission will be called upon to provide the leadership necessary to assure continued effectiveness of the civil service system, using improved employee-management cooperation as an instrument for growth.

Success Assured

Indications are that the program will be a success.

Procedures for enforcement are incorporated in the order, the standards, and the code. Agency heads themselves are responsible for the operation of the program in their respective agencies, even though they will answer to the Civil Service Commission and the Department of Labor for certain matters of guidance and administration.

Through the commission's inspection program it will be ascertained that each department and agency does indeed have an employee-management program which reflects the letter and spirit of the Executive Order, the standards, and the code. From this review a periodic appraisal will be presented to the President.

Commission officials will evaluate the program execution in the various departments and agencies, will provide advice and assistance as necessary, and will continue to assist in the training of personnel who will administer agency labor-management programs.

The Labor Department will continue to advise agencies on standards of <u>exclusive</u> recognition and the definition of appropriate units as well as assist in the resolution of possible impasses between parties on unit determination and exclusive recognition.

On Firm Ground

It would be premature at this time to estimate the degree to which the program will improve labor-management relations in the government. It would be inaccurate to say that all agencies and all employee organizations are completely satisfied with every detail of the program.

Nevertheless, several positive, tangible accomplishments can be related. Collectively, they constitute some sound building blocks for a most effective program of employee-management cooperation in the federal service.

-- The federal government has, for the first time in history, a government-wide plan for employee-management cooperation. Many specifics of the plan have been employed in various agencies for some time, but now they have been incorporated into one single program.

-- There is in being a long-needed Presidential policy on the rights of employees to organize, to be recognized, and to take part in the making of policies which affect employees and working conditions.

-- Non-veterans now have the same rights as veterans in appealing adverse decisions.

-- Appeals procedures within agencies are more uniform.

-- Management now must consult with recognized employee organizations and, when appropriate, negotiate with them.

-- Employee organizations have a recognized role in grievance proceedings.

-- There is a clear definition as to who is "management" and who is "labor" in federal agencies, and a better understanding of the roles each should play in employee-management relations.

-- There is for the first time a code of fair labor practices which applies to management and unions, and
substantive standards of conduct to be followed by
federal employee organizations who have or want
official recognition.

-- Training of federal personnel in industrial relations
procedures, such as consultation and negotiation
techniques, has been intensified. This may be interpreted as a clear indication of government's willingness to cooperate with employee unions on a sus-
tained basis.

-- There is provision for voluntary arbitration in the
settlement of grievances, but the rules spell out
rather clearly that voluntary arbitration may not
be used as a "back-door" approach to challenging
agency policy. It is natural to expect that agency
policy might be influenced by specific decisions
reached in arbitration hearings, but the intent of the
program is that organization leaders will affect the
shaping of policy through a "front-door" approach --
when policy is being written.

-- The desirability of making provision for voluntary
withholding of employees' dues has been recognized,
but no action can be taken in this regard until
enabling legislation, which has been introduced, is
passed.

Conclusions

At this point an inventory is in order. Prudently we should ask:
How does the program now in existence measure up to what was expected of it?

We can arrived at program goals by stripping away the
"whereases" and "therefores" and examining the statements of
policy embodied in the preamble to Executive Order 10988:

"Participation of employees in the formulation and implementation of personnel policies affecting them contributes to effective conduct of public business."
They can participate.

"Efficient administration of the Government and the well-
being of employees require that orderly and constructive
relationships be maintained between employee organizations and management officials." Such relationships exist.

"Subject to law and the paramount requirements of the
public service, employee-management relations within
the Federal service should be improved by providing
employees an opportunity for greater participation in
the formulation and implementation of policies and
procedures affecting the conditions of their employment." This opportunity exists.

"Effective employee-management cooperation in the
public service requires a clear statement of the respective rights and obligations of employee organizations and
agency management." Such a statement exists, for the
first time, on a government-wide basis.

Throughout the new regulations runs the theme that the public
interest must be served. And nowhere in the directives does the
substance of the federal employee-management cooperation program
conflict with the merit principle.

Chapter 17

Union Views of the New Federal Program

ANDREW J. BIEMILLER

Director, Department of Legislation, AFL-CIO

The AFL-CIO wholeheartedly endorsed President Kennedy's declaration in his memorandum of June 22, 1961, to heads of departments and agencies of the federal government on the rights of federal employees to join and participate in the activities of employee organizations, seeking to improve working conditions and the resolution of employee grievances.

Spokesmen of the American Federation of Labor and of the Congress of Industrial Organizations, and, since the merger, the AFL-CIO itself, have urged legislative and executive action to secure more uniform recognition and effective implementation of such rights. We have taken the view that public employment is not so inherently different from employment in private industry as to require denial to employees of the federal government of the rights of organization and collective bargaining which have long been guaranteed by law to employees in private industry.

The right of employees in the federal government to join employee organizations had been recognized for postal workers directly, and for civil service workers inferentially, ever since the Lloyd-LaFollette Act was passed on August 24, 1912. Such a right has been guaranteed and implemented for many years for workers in private industry which affects commerce in a long line of federal statutes, including the Railway Labor Act, the Norris-LaGuardia Act, section 7(a) of the National Industrial Recovery Act, the National Labor Relations (Wagner) Act, and the Labor Management Relations (Taft-Hartley) Act, 1947.

Indeed, even before President Kennedy's June 22, 1961, memorandum some federal employees, such as those employed by the Post Office Department, the Government Printing Office, the Bureau of Reclamation in the Department of the Interior, some military and naval installations, the Tennessee Valley Authority, the Bonneville Power Administration, and other agencies, had for some time enjoyed a substantial measure of recognition and participation in the formulation and implementation of employee policies and procedures in these agencies. Extension and implementation of these rights to employees of the federal government generally, the AFL-CIO felt, was long overdue.

The AFL-CIO recognizes that there is a wide diversity of federal programs, a variety of occupations and skills in federal employment, and differing organizational patterns among federal departments and agencies, and that public service carries with it special obligations. Undoubtedly, these factors complicate the task of formulating policies and procedures to effectuate the rights of employee organizations in the federal service. It is doubtful, however, that the federal service presents any greater diversity than the private employments within which federal law has protected the right to organize and bargain collectively since 1935.

As to the special obligations of public service, the AFL-CIO testified before the President's Task Force on Employee-Management Relations in the Federal Service that it favored a limitation which would guarantee relationships with federal departments and agencies only for employee organizations that are free of restrictions or practices denying or classifying membership on grounds of race, color, religion, or national origin. It further testified that the labor movement is prepared to accept a requirement that only organizations which do not assert the right to strike against or advocate the overthrow of the government of the U.S. shall be entitled to enjoy such relationships.

In its testimony the AFL-CIO pointed out, however, that if collective bargaining is to be at all effective in the federal service an effective alternative will have to be found for the right to strike, which is an essential element of collective bargaining in private industry. The fact that Executive Order No. 10988 does not contain such an effective alternative is, we believe, one of the most serious deficiencies in the order.

We do not contend that every employee organization should have the benefit of government protection. In line with well-established AFL-CIO policy, we believe that only bona fide employee organizations should be entitled to such protection.

The types of bona fide employee organizations which federal employees should have a protected right to join are those national organizations and/or subordinate affiliates, made up in whole or in part of employees of the federal government, in which employees participate and pay dues (or any council composed of such organizations) and which have as one of their basic and central purposes dealing with the management of a government department, agency, activity, organization, or function concerning conditions of employment. They do not include organizations whose basic purpose is purely social, fraternal, or limited to a single special interest objective which is only incidentally related to conditions of employment. Nor should they include any organization sponsored by a department, agency, activity, organization, or facility of the federal government.

The AFL-CIO regards President Kennedy's Executive Order No. 10988 as a major breakthrough in assuring and implementing the rights of self-organization, recognition, and collective negotiation for employees in the federal service. We believe that it contributes significantly to the more efficient conduct of government business by encouraging government employees to participate through their organizations in the formulation and implementation of employee policies and procedures.

The organization rights which the Executive Order guarantees to federal employees are substantially similar to the organization and collective bargaining rights which employees of private employers have long been assured under the several federal statutes that define and implement our national labor policy. This order recognizes that employees through their organizations can and should have an opportunity to contribute to the efficient functioning of their respective departments and agencies.

It is our hope and expectation that federal employees will make full use of the rights and opportunities extended them by the President's order.

The Executive Order does not do all the things that we believe are necessary to put into effect a fully satisfactory program of employee-management relations in the federal service. It does not, for example, provide for voluntary withholding of employee organization dues, a practice long sanctioned for employees in private industry and specifically confirmed by the Taft-Hartley Act. The President's Task Force on Employee-Management Relations in the Federal Service recommended enactment of legislation to permit such dues withholding, and the Administration has recommended such legislation to the Congress. As yet, however, this legislation has not passed the Congress. We believe such legislation should be promptly enacted.

As time goes on, experience will, we believe, demonstrate the need for tightening up the procedures, principles, and safeguards contained in Executive Order No. 10988. It is of the utmost importance that the federal government no longer be the laggard in the field of labor-management relations but rather that it assume and hold the leadership in this most important field.

Insofar as implementation of President Kennedy's Executive Order No. 10988 through department and agency rules and regulations is concerned, we do not believe we have had enough experience with the operation of the order and the various departmental rules and regulations thereunder to enable us as yet to provide any useful or definitive comments. Indeed, the proposed Standards of Conduct for Employee Organizations and Code of Fair Labor Practices have not even been formally issued as yet. We have every reason to be confident, however, that the Administration is making a sincere and determined effort to see to it that the order is administered uniformly throughout the government and in conformity with its highly beneficial intent and purpose.

J. F. GRINER

National President, American Federation of Government Employees

Executive Order 10988 offers an unparalleled opportunity for management and non-management federal employees to demonstrate their ability to cooperate in the public interest and in the interest of those who have chosen the federal service as a career. It is a reasonable assumption that the public interest and the general interest of career employees are completely compatible. Neither can safely disregard the best interests of the other.

What has been seriously needed for a long time has been an orderly method of employee-management negotiations which would apply consistently throughout the departments and agencies and which would provide continuity of the most equitable and effective methods regardless of changes in top management positions.

In implementing the Executive Order, management officials in many instances have sought to promulgate regulations calculated to meet every possible contingency, and in so doing often have been too narrow in their interpretations of the intent of the order. Practically the entire emphasis has been placed on the technical provisions or mechanics of implementation to the exclusion of the spirit and the philosophy that prompted the issuance of Executive Order 10988. The paragraphs in the order headed by the word "Whereas" are of far greater importance than the relatively simple process of working out the mechanics of the program.

The title of the order speaks for itself. Unless there is "Employee-Management Cooperation in the Federal Service" in full measure, unless there is complete willingness to cooperate on the part of those charged with the responsibilities of management and the non-supervisory employees, the public service will suffer.

There has been, unfortunately, evidence of unwillingness or inability on the part of some management officials to carry out the order and enter into meaningful relationships with employee organizations. This hesitancy--and sometimes harassment--has manifested itself in a number of ways. Attempts have been made to invoke national security as an excuse for denying certain groups of employees their rights under the order when, in reality, national security was not a legitimate issue at all. Proposals have been made to exclude from union membership minor supervisors who have far more in common than they have in conflict with the employees working under them.

Steps also must be taken to rectify the lack of recourse from arbitrary decisions made by management officials in the field.

Another weak spot is the requirement in some agency policies that union representatives take annual leave to carry on negotiations with management when management believes that consultation or bargaining sessions have consumed too much time. It is interesting to note that the annual leave requirement applies only to union representatives. Management officials, apparently, can negotiate "on the clock" regardless of how much time the sessions consume. This can only lead to the conclusion that the working time of management officials is less useful to the government than that of rank-and-file employees.

A specific example of undue restriction is that of an agency which excludes from holding union office employees in civilian personnel offices. Another is the exclusion of "shorthand reporters, reporting stenographers, administrative aids and secretaries to management officials."

One of the most important aspects of the new program still in the formative stage is the Standards of Conduct for Employee Organizations and the Code of Fair Labor Practices for both union and management. This program imposes certain responsibilities on employee organizations and on management officials.

Section 3.2(2) of the proposed Code of Fair Labor Practices contains a provision that agency management is prohibited from "encouraging or discouraging membership in any employee organization by discrimination in regard to hiring, tenure, or other conditions of employment." In joining an employee organization an employee exercises a right that is guaranteed him under the Constitution of the United States and he assumes an individual responsibility that is concomitant with citizenship in a democracy.

Are we performing an act of good citizenship when we prohibit the encouragement of other citizens in such lawful pursuits? In view of the right of employees to join organizations and the protection of that right provided in Section 1 of Executive Order 10988, it would seem that emphasis should be placed on prohibiting discouragement of union membership.

When we examine objectively the logic and the necessity for organized effort in the light of our economic and social structure,

the tacit acknowledgment that there is nothing wrong with membership in an employee organization should serve to eliminate the prohibition against encouraging membership.

The insignificant effect in the rare instances in the past where
membership has been encouraged has been offset many-fold by the
widespread discouragement that has occurred. We continue to be
confronted by problems brought about by anti-union sentiment.

During the past years the emphasis has been placed on so-called
"neutrality" by management and personnel officials. The emphasis
has been so negative and so marked that "neutrality" in fact often
has become either opposition or discouragement. It has never been
interpreted to indicate encouragement.

The fact that the term "collective bargaining" has been used in
connection with the Executive Order appears to be a source of concern to many management officials. When we stop to consider that
there are in excess of 100,000 collective bargaining contracts in effect in private industry it must be apparent that this has become an
accepted method of orderly dealing between management and unions.

The American Federation of Government Employees has had two
collective bargaining contracts with the federal government for a
number of years. These contracts include a provision for arbitration, and arbitration has been resorted to on two occasions. In each
of these instances the consent of the head of the agency had to be
obtained, and the head of the agency had the legal right to accept or
reject the decision of the arbitrator. The decisions in each instance
were accepted with reasonable satisfaction to all concerned.

The important point is that collective bargaining is feasible in
the federal service; and while our experience has not been extensive
as to the number of contracts, it has covered a period of years which
has been long enough to prove its practicality and efficacy.

Collective bargaining is the foundation of any enlightened labor-
relations policy. It has our unqualified support. The whole hullabaloo
over collective bargaining is nothing more than semantic nonsense.
Consultation with union representatives on personnel policies and
working conditions is merely another way of saying "collective bargaining." The alternative to collective bargaining, which means
nothing more than group negotiation over problems of mutual interest and concern, is unilateral dictation.

Under the provisions of Section 13 (b) of the Executive Order,
the "President's Temporary Committee on the Implementation of
the Federal Employee-Management Relations Program" was established. We believe this committee, or a similar one, should be
established on a permanent basis in order to provide recourse for

both the departments and agencies and the federal employee organizations in arriving at solutions of the problems attendant upon interpretation and implementation of the order.

There are, unquestionably, problems to be worked out in the operation of President Kennedy's Executive Order. This is inevitable in any new program of such scope But we wholeheartedly support and applaud the President's program. The twofold aim of the American Federation of Government Employees, as stated in our constitution, is to promote "unity of action in all matters affecting the mutual interests of governmental civilian employees in general and for the improvement of governmental service." We believe President Kennedy's Executive Order will help us immeasurably in the pursuit of these worthwhile objectives.

B. A. GRITTA
President, Metal Trades Department, AFL-CIO

For a great many years, the Metal Trades Department, AFL-CIO, and its affiliated international unions have represented many thousands of federal employees consisting mainly of wage board or blue-collar employees in navy yards and other major naval installations, as well as in activities of other federal agencies throughout the country.

Our department and its affiliates have long urged the passage of legislation which would give to federal workers the same basic protections in their rights to organize and to bargain collectively through unions of their own choosing as are enjoyed by workers in private industry. Government agencies, we have long contended, should have a responsibility to bargain with the duly designated unions of their employees on all matters which come within the purview of the agency and to reduce the results of such bargaining to a written agreement.

When the President indicated his intention to issue an Executive Order on this subject and appointed a task force to hold hearings preliminary to the issuance of Executive Order 10988, our department and its affiliates played a vital role in the development of detailed testimony and information to assist in this endeavor.

Since the issuance of this order on January 17, 1962, we have kept in constant and close touch with the Secretary of Labor, who serves as Chairman of the President's Temporary Committee on the Implementation of Federal Employee-Management Relations Program. Our views, our comments, and criticisms have been given to him in detail on all his proposed regulations and standards to be issued. We have also made detailed comment and criticism in connection with implementation orders coming from the various departments and their bureaus.

There is no question but that the issuance of this Executive Order is a major and vital forward step in bringing to government workers a measure of collective bargaining and union recognition previously not extended to them.

During the first few months of its operation we have experienced a number of problems in connection with the application of the Executive Order which require clarification if its intent is to be carried out.

Section 6 (a) of the order indicates that appropriate bargaining units "may be established on any plant or installation, craft, functional or other basis which will ensure a clear and identifiable community of interest among the employees concerned."

This clearly establishes the fact that craft units may be recognized as appropriate units. The only limitations of the type of unit deemed appropriate are that such unit must assure "a clear and identifiable community of interest among the employees concerned" and not be based solely on the extent of organization.

Despite the provisions of this section of the Executive Order, various federal activities in several agencies or departments have taken predetermined and arbitrary positions that all employees of the particular activity, exclusive of supervisory, professional, and managerial employees, constitute the only appropriate unit for which a union will be recognized at the installation. This we view as contrary to the intent of the Executive Order.

Certainly there is nothing in Section 6 (a) to justify such a limited approach as to what constitutes an appropriate unit. It is our position that in implementing the Executive Order, all agencies, departments, and their subdivisions should reiterate the appropriateness of craft bargaining units and should take no action of any kind which would impair or foreclose the right of a craft union to seek and obtain exclusive bargaining rights for a unit composed of the workers of its craft.

It might also be noted that our Metal Trades Councils, for many years in some of the major installations, have been recognized informally as the spokesmen for wage board employees, and such a unit has the functional coherence and community of interest factors which outline its appropriateness. It should be granted when petitioned for.

Another problem to which we have directed our attention is the interpretation which has been placed upon that portion of the same section of the order which requires an agency to recognize a labor organization as the exclusive representative of the employees in an appropriate unit when it is otherwise qualified under the terms of the order and has been designated or selected by a majority of the employees of such unit.

The existing and historical practice observed generally in connection with the election process throughout our country and the policies which have been universally followed on this question of majority determination by the National Labor Relations Board in its election procedures, would lead one to believe that the same policies would be followed in implementing this part of Section 6 (a) of the order.

However, to our amazement we have noted that in implementing the order in each of the various departments and agencies, it has been determined that for a union to gain exclusive recognition through an election it must either (1) be designated by a majority of the employees in the unit eligible to vote in such election or, (2) be designated by a majority of the employees voting and the number voting being not less than 60 per cent of the eligible employees.

These limitations are unduly restrictive and discriminate in favor of the employee not voting. In other words, if there were 100 eligible employees and 60 cast ballots, with 31 voting for the union, it would be considered as being designated by the majority. However, if one of those 60 persons stayed away and only 59 votes were cast, then because 59 constitutes less than 60 per cent of the eligible workers the union would have to receive 51 votes to be considered as being designated by the majority.

This rule has been vigorously protested by the Metal Trades Department. The language of both Section 6 (a) of the Executive Order and Section 9 (a) of the National Labor Relations Act, as amended, read essentially the same on this point. Yet for some 27 years the NLRB has continuously followed the normal election rule that a majority of the eligible votes cast is all that is necessary for union certification, even though the total vote is less than a majority of the employees eligible to vote. Despite all this, the majority-of-employees-eligible-to-vote rule is being applied.

These are two of the most troublesome problems with which we have been concerned in the early months of the administration of this Executive Order. We are continuing our efforts to bring about a more appropriate interpretation on both of these matters.

As we move forward in our endeavor to negotiate agreements with federal activities where our exclusive bargaining rights have been established, we will doubtless experience other problems in the determination of the points on which we can bargain and the extent to which agencies may be willing to commit themselves in a written collective-bargaining agreement.

E. C. HALLBECK

President, United Federation of Postal Clerks, AFL-CIO

In 1962, organized federal employees had a rendezvous with history. Not since enactment, 50 years ago, of the Lloyd-LaFollette Act guaranteeing our right of appeal to Congress and our right to organize has there been a sequence of events in the federal labor-management field to equal in significance our newly won rights to bargain collectively on personnel practices and working conditions.

President Kennedy's Executive Order of January 1962 sets forth for the first time a government policy with positive approval of union activity within the federal service. Furthermore, the recent historic nation-wide bargaining elections--largest in labor history--have now confirmed the United Federation of Postal Clerks, AFL-CIO as the exclusive national bargaining agent of our craft, and five other postal unions as the exclusive national agents of their crafts.

These giant steps forward have particular significance for postal clerks inasmuch as our affiliation as a new national union with the American Federation of Labor in 1906 and our activities thereafter are generally regarded as having triggered the series of union-busting gag rules issued by President Theodore Roosevelt and President William Howard Taft. Prior to our AFL affiliation as a national body, this organization had maintained only a fragmented AFL relationship through individual locals.

It is also a fact of history that our agitation, with the help of Senator LaFollette, Congressman Lloyd, and the late Frank Morrison, then Secretary of the American Federation of Labor, helped bring about the ultimate enactment of the Lloyd-LaFollette Act in 1912.

Starting back in 1948, the Miami convention of the old National Federation of Post Office Clerks, AFL-CIO, was also first to call officially for union recognition in government--a resolve which Congressman George Rhodes of Pennsylvania answered by introducing in the House the first bill with this stated objective. It might not be an exaggeration to observe that Congressman Rhodes and I were perhaps the only two people in Washington then who believed such an objective had a prayer of ever being fulfilled.

Even though it was finally achieved by the exercise of President Kennedy's executive authority, I firmly believe that Congress sooner or later would have approved a formal labor-management law had the President not acted.

Finally, a word of tribute is due the new Justice of the Supreme Court, Mr. Arthur Goldberg, who, as Secretary of Labor, was in our judgment the principal architect of the Task Force Report and the Executive Order which flowed from it.

Having said all this, it must now be affirmed that the order and its governing regulations are only potentially powerful instruments for good in improving both the public service itself and the economic welfare of government workers. Neither the order nor its regulations are self-enforcing. It will thus be our responsibility to police it; and it will be useful only if, on the one hand, organized labor in government is sufficiently responsible to take advantage of its opportunities while recognizing management's right to manage, and if, on the other, management accepts the fact we are not fooling in our anticipation of profound changes in attitudes and practices.

The principal area of uncertainty now lies in the fact that federal employees both by law and through their own sworn forbearance lack the muscle to reinforce their minimum positions with any effective economic weapon, such as the right to strike. It would seem to us, therefore, that government managerial circles have even a greater obligation than private industry to be scrupulously fair. If they cling to some of the arbitrary attitudes that have long characterized federal bureaucracy, it is not impossible that we would consider new techniques which have been proved effective in the government service of other countries.

It is perhaps too early to pinpoint significant trends. The Post Office Department, for example, in establishing the ground rules for last summer's bargaining election, retreated at our insistence from its original determination that balloting results be derived from the total of those eligible to vote within crafts. We maintained successfully--and we believe correctly--that this was contrary to the established precedents under NLRB practices whereby the final determinations derive from the majority of those eligibles actually voting.

However, the department did not see eye to eye with our representations on unit determination that the ballot itself should not be open to every so-called postal employee organization, no matter how small or ineffectual. We maintained without success that the Executive Order's own provisions barred groups representing less than 10 per cent of any craft and, indeed, that the whole departmental theory of multiple recognition violated the spirit and letter of the Executive Order.

With respect to the proposed Standards of Conduct for Employee Organizations and the Code of Fair Labor Practices, called for under the Executive Order, we are in general favorably impressed with the purposes and intent of the draft. We have, of course, been subscribers to the AFL-CIO's own Code of Ethics since early 1958, and in that same year also devised our own Code of Disciplinary Proceedings in further compliance of ethical practices.

In at least two instances, however, the drafts prepared by the Labor Department and the Civil Service Commission strike us as defective or at least as requiring a somewhat more precise set of definitions.

Section 2.2 (b) of Part A, Standards of Conduct for Employee Organizations, as presently written would bar from union office "persons affiliated with Communist or totalitarian movements <u>and persons identified with corrupt interests</u>" (emphasis supplied). What constitutes a "corrupt interest"? What is meant by "identified"? Dictionary definitions of these terms are broad enough to encompass even a meaningless street corner or hotel lobby conversation or a luncheon or any type of association, however innocent.

While I cannot conceive of this problem affecting our own union, it is in principle a dangerously loose provision as written. Even the Landrum-Griffin Act requires, at the least, conviction of crime by an officer, and even this does not disenfranchise the union but merely disqualifies the individual.

Section 2.4 likewise appears to me to need some revision. This provides that an employee organization "shall not be required to furnish other evidence of its freedom from influences described in section 3 (a) . . . unless . . . the agency has cause to believe that the organization has been suspended or expelled from <u>or is subject to other sanction by another employee organization</u> or labor organization or federation of such organizations with which it had been affiliated because it has demonstrated an unwillingness or inability to comply with governing requirements comparable in purpose to those required by section 2.2 of this Part . . ." (emphasis supplied).

If the section applies solely to a local, a chapter, or a branch of a national or international organization, there is little room for objection. But the underscored phrase might be used by another or rival group without just cause. A simple revision could meet this objection by eliminating the phrase "another employee organization" from the sequence listed.

As we move forward in our new tandem relationship with management, I think the key phrase on both sides must be "<u>responsible leadership</u>." It is our responsibility to show management how things that must be done can be done better or, put another way, how better overall results can be obtained through mutual cooperation.

We are confident the Executive Order can bring about that mutuality of responsibility, and that in time this new and long-overdue chapter in federal labor-management relations can prove to be the best investment the federal government has ever made in sustaining morale and improving service to the American people.

Vaux Owen
President, National Federation of Federal Employees

The Independent National Federation of Federal Employees views Executive Order 10988 as a cause of a mixture of good and bad effects.

The word "cooperation" appears in the title of the order. The concept of cooperation has motivated the NFFE for many years. In its national constitution, cooperation with federal officials is specified as a means by which it attains its objectives. We welcome the opportunity under the order for consultation. Consultation can lead to cooperation. It can promote understanding.

The word "management" also appears in the title of the order. This indicates a concept that management in government is analogous to management in private industry. It is not. In private industry, management is primarily concerned with profit. In government, the officials are the servants of the people. The primary concern of officials is the administration of the laws of the country. This also is the primary concern of federal employees. The positions occupied by both officials and federal employees are in existence for the purpose of service to the people of the country, not merely for the benefit of the officials and the employees.

Self-interest in profit for management in industry has often worked in conflict with the interest of employees in better working conditions. There is no such self-interest in profit on the part of officials (management) in government.

The use of the word "management" in connection with employee relationships in government implies a conflict of interest which does not, and should not, exist. The economic conflict between capital and labor in the private sphere has no logical place in government service. The misconception that such conflict does exist in government service is the cause of the bad effects being brought about by the implementations of the Executive Order.

It is not surprising that this is so. The chief moving personality whose thinking is in the background of such implementations is the recent Secretary of Labor, Mr. Arthur J. Goldberg. Most of his life has been spent in the arena of the conflict between capital and labor in the private sphere. He was a labor lawyer with but little experience in government.

It was quite in keeping with his life pattern to look upon federal employee problems and their solutions as he had done with reference to problems of employees in private industry. In my opinion, he was deluded by his past associations. In pursuing his delusion he could count on the support of his former labor union employers in the private sphere.

The AFL-CIO affiliates could very well hope to bring thousands of federal employees into their dues-paying ranks and under their control. Tremendous political power could be grasped by the outside labor union leaders who have operated mainly in the private sphere. It can happen that as outside labor union leaders acquire power over federal employees, the control of the people over the means by which their government is operated will become weaker.

Under the influence of outside labor union thinking, "collective bargaining" has been introduced into the federal service. We now can well expect the progressive development of the practices associated with collective bargaining in private industry. Such practices include slow-downs, reluctance to sign collective bargaining agreements, strikes, picketing, compulsory union membership, sweetheart contracts, jurisdictional disputes and serious harm to innocent people and the public.

The advocates of collective bargaining in the federal service will deny these possibilities and point to the language in the order against strikes. But, language will not prevent strikes. There was a strong law against strikes in New York City but the union of teachers struck. Already a union of federal employees has asserted the right of concerted action short of a strike.

A conflict between employees and officials is being accentuated by the dictatorial rules which go far beyond the express provision of the Executive Order itself and prohibit certain employees from holding office in an employee organization. This is an unabashed denial of a membership right.

Because the Executive Order is being implemented to promote conflict rather than cooperation, we have asked the President to revoke that part of the order which is being construed to authorize "collective bargaining" in the federal service. We strongly believe our request is in the public interest.

Under the implementation of the Executive Order, and at variance with the order itself, 69% of the employees in a union may be forced to submit to representation for which they did not vote. This means federal employees will have to submit to representation by an outside labor union if 10% of the employees in the unit belong to such labor union and 21% of the non-members vote for such representation.

As national president of the NFFE, I made the following statement in my Report to the National Conference at Phoenix, Arizona, on September 10, 1962:

> Nevertheless, the NFFE has an abiding confidence that a majority of federal employees will not desire representation under "exclusive recognition" for which they have not voted.

*   *   *   *   *   *

In the light of this confidence the NFFE could very well adhere to a policy which might be briefly stated substantially as follows:

1. The NFFE will not engage in the "conflict-of-interest" practice of "collective bargaining."

2. The NFFE will not affiliate with any organization having members outside the federal service who engage in "collective bargaining."

3. The NFFE opposes "collective bargaining" by any other organization of federal employees because it believes "collective bargaining" will lead to the assertion of the right to strike and political pressure to repeal the law against strikes.

4. The NFFE opposes the use of force, or the threat or show of force, against the United States by any employee organization.

5. The NFFE opposes the concept that the so-called "rank and file" employees constitute a class which is in conflict with government officials and supervisors but believes all should cooperate under law for the public interest.

6. The NFFE will encourage its members, when they have grievances, to avail themselves of the established grievance procedures. It will continue to seek improvement in such procedures.

7. The NFFE will encourage one or more members in each local to study and train themselves to represent a fellow employee in grievance proceedings upon request of such fellow employee.

8.   The NFFE National Office in Washington, D. C., will
      continue to represent its members at the final appeal
      state in Washington as in the past.

The National Convention of the NFFE adopted on September 14,
1962, a resolution regarding Executive Order 10988 reading in part
as follows:

RESOLVED, That the NFFE request the President of the
United States to modify Executive Order 10988 by
eliminating Section 6 of the Order; and be it further

RESOLVED, That failing to obtain modification, the NFFE
initiate action through the Congress to pass legislation
which will negate the provisions of Section 6, E. O. 10988.

AND BE IT FURTHER RESOLVED, That our National
Officers exert every possible effort to have the "Conflict of Interest" element of E. O. 10988 eliminated and
replaced with a provision which would allow more
elasticity so that management and supervisory employees can hold office in employee unions.

Ashby G. Smith
President, National Alliance of Postal Employees

In at least one agency of the federal government a drastic change
in employee-management relations preceded and occurred independently of the President's appointment of a Task Force, its report, and
the resultant Executive Order 10988. In the Post Office Department,
a fruitful program of consultation between management and employee
unions had already been installed by Postmaster General Day at Departmental and Regional levels and was being introduced into local
offices.

Impending changes in postal policy affecting personnel were
communicated to national union offices. After studying them, union
officers met with postal management, voiced objections, and suggested changes. Frequently, revisions in the tentative plans were
made in accordance with union suggestions. At long last, postal administration was utilizing the judgment of its employees, the people
upon whom the activation of its program ultimately rests.

In this agency, then, the new employee-management program
embraced in Executive Order 10988 came when employee relations

were already of a high order. If this decree had done nothing more
than formalize the program and extended it over all federal agencies
it would have achieved a definite advance in the field of federal employee-management cooperation.

However, the Task Force and the Executive Order created a
much more complex arrangement and this complexity may well defeat the purposes of the program.

Contrary to the recommendation of the National Alliance of
Postal Employees and others to the Task Force, the principle of exclusive recognition was introduced into the federal service. Unions
obtaining exclusive recognition are given the right to "negotiate"
with management and to reach and sign agreements. The order by
its own terms so curtails the areas in which these negotiations can
take place that the value of the right becomes nebulous.

What exactly can be negotiated? To what extent can an agency
head, representative of the President of the United States, be bound
by agreements reached through negotiation? Which of his powers as
head of state can the President delegate to agency heads? These are
questions yet unresolved--questions which must be answered before
this new program is safely on foot.

These are questions for management, but the unions too must
face questions and find answers. Do the rights which a union obtains
with exclusive recognition compensate it for taking on the responsibility of representing all persons, members and non-members, in
the unit?

In the postal system where recognition is given at three levels,
the local office, the region and the department, as many as three
unions may have exclusive recognition in the same craft, one at each
of these levels. Also the same union may, in a given craft, have
three kinds of recognition, exclusive at one level, formal at another,
and informal at a third. Surely, here we have the basis for endless
confusion and jurisdictional disputes.

In the implementation of the order a major controversy in the
Post Office Department arose over the selection of the appropriate
unit of representation. The decision of the agency to base the unit
on craft gave an initial advantage to the craft unions over the industrial unions in the elections held to determine the employees'
choice.

This advantage increased when implementing orders changed
the original requirement that a union, to achieve exclusive recognition in a unit, must be selected by a majority of employees in that
unit. The change requiring only a majority of those employees who
voted, providing sixty per cent voted, clearly raised the question

of the propriety of giving a union exclusive recognition when it is the choice of a possible thirty-plus per cent of that unit's employee complement.

How representative is such a union? How responsive will it be to the needs of the employees?

The total effect of this grant of exclusive recognition is mitigated to some extent by the decision of the Post Office Department to exercise the option, given to agencies in the final sentence of Section 5 (a) of 10988, to give formal recognition at the national level to all national postal unions.

A number of salutary features appear in the order. The right of federal employees to join unions of their own choosing and the obligation of management to deal with representatives of these unions are clearly spelled out. The standards of conduct set forth have led to changes in documents and practices. Item 3 in Section 2 in the order, which excludes from recognition any organization that "discriminates with regard to the terms or conditions of membership because of race, color, creed or national origin," lays down a rule that has led to the hasty abandonment of dual locals and "Caucasion-only" clauses by several major postal unions. Careful policing is necessary to see if these actions mean a real change in policy and practices by these unions.

It is too early to attempt a mature judgment on this new experiment in employee-management relations. Experiment it is, for it is safe to say that the last word in this matter has not been said.

In federal agencies this brave attempt to formalize these relations was long overdue. It is possible that, in creating the order and the implementing directives, the terms of the National Labor Relations Act were too closely followed, and that insufficient consideration was given to the difference between government employment and employment in private industry.

Policing management to prevent favoritism among competing unions and policing unions to assure that they live up to their responsibilities under the order are matters that must be dealt with promptly and firmly if the program is to have a chance to succeed.

This Administration has made a bold beginning. If both the Administration and the government employee unions realize that it is only a beginning, if both retain flexibility and a willingness to adjust features that prove unjust or unworkable, if all approach the employee-management problem with a real desire to achieve a workable program, Executive Order 10988 could well mark the first step toward a program that will increase harmony and cooperation in federal employment to the benefit of employees, management, and the American public.

PART VI
Selected Bibliography

Notes

The literature in this field is extensive. This highly selective bibliography contains a number of references of recent date that deal with the theory and practice of management-employee relations. There are three exceptions, each being a classic in the field. The first, Employee Relations in the Public Service, remains, after twenty years, the best single comprehensive work. It covers ethical, theoretical, and (to a lesser extent) legal questions of importance. Spero's Government As Employer and Godine's The Labor Problem in the Public Service are both historical (and analytical) treatments; they provide essential perspective.

This bibliography contains many of the works recommended by the San Francisco Bay Area Chapter of the Public Personnel Association in its 1960 background study on collective bargaining in the public service. A special subcommittee of the Chapter served under the chairmanship of William F. Danielson, Director of Personnel, City of Berkeley, California. The report itself would be listed as an important source except for its limited circulation in mimeographed form.

Bibliography

Anderson, Arvid. "Labor Relations in the Public Service." Wisconsin Law Review, Vol. 4, July 1961, 601-635.

Avery, Robert S. "The TVA and Labor Relations; A Review." Journal of Politics, Vol. 16, August 1954, 413-440.

Barkin, Solomon. The Decline of the Labor Movement and What Can Be Done About It. Santa Barbara, Calif.: Center for the Study of Democratic Institutions, 1961.

Beal, Edwin F., and Wickersham, Edward D. The Practice of Collective Bargaining. Homewood, Ill.: Richard D. Irwin, Inc., 1959.

Berger, Harriet. "The Grievance Process in the Philadelphia Public Service." Industrial and Labor Relations Review, Vol. 13, July 1960, 568-580.

Case, Harry L. Personnel Policy in a Public Agency—The TVA Experience. New York: Harper & Bros., 1955.

Civil Service Assembly of the U. S. and Canada. Employee Relations
    in the Public Service. Chicago: The Assembly, 1942.
Cohen, Frederick. "Legal Aspects of Unionization among Public Em-
    ployees." Temple Law Quarterly, Vol. 30, Winter 1957, 187-198.
Cornell, Herbert W. "Civil Service Benchmark Court Decisions."
    Public Personnel Review, Vol. 17, October 1956, 215-224.
Dilworth, Richardson. "The Philadelphia Viewpoint on Exclusive
    Collective Bargaining." Mayor and Manager, Vol. 1, March 1958,
    5, 17.
Dotson, Arch T. "The Emerging Concept of Privilege in Public Em-
    ployment." Public Administration Review, Vol. 15, Spring 1955,
    77-88.
Gallagher, Donald. The Legal Aspects of Collective Bargaining for
    California Public Employees. Sacramento: California State
    Employees Assoc., November 1959.
Godine, Morton R. The Labor Problem in the Public Service: A Study
    in Political Pluralism. Cambridge, Mass.: Harvard University
    Press, 1951.
Goldberg, Joseph P. "Constructive Employee Relations in Government."
    Labor Law Journal, Vol. 8, August 1957, 551-556.
Hart, Wilson R. Collective Bargaining in the Federal Civil Service.
    New York: Harper & Bros., 1961.
Holland, Ann. Unions Are Here to Stay. Washington, D. C.: Society
    for Personnel Administration, February 1962.
International City Managers' Association. Negotiations with Municipal
    Employee Organizations. Chicago: The Association, September
    1958. (MIS Report No. 176)
Kaplan, H. Eliot. The Law of Civil Service. Albany, N. Y.: Matthew
    Bender & Co., 1958.
Klaus, Ida. "Labor Relations in the Public Service: Exploration and
    Experiment." Syracuse Law Review, Vol. 10, Spring 1959, 183-202.
National Civil Service League. Employee Organizations in the Public
    Service. New York: The League, 1946.
National Institute of Municipal Law Officers. "Workshop No. 4—Trends
    in Litigation Involving Municipal Officers and Employees." National
    Institute of Municipal Law Officers Municipal Law Review, 1958,
    528-556.
Newland, Chester A. Public Employee Unionization in Texas.
    Austin, Tex.: Institute of Public Affairs, University of Texas, 1962.
    (Public Affairs Series No. 50)
New York City Department of Labor. Labor Relations Series, March-
    December 1955. (1) The Right of Public Employees to Organize;
    (2) Recognition of Organized Groups of Public Employees; (3)
    Extent of Recognition and the Bargaining Unit in Public Employment;
    (4) The Ascertainment of Representative Status for Organizations
    of Public Employees; (5) Organization and Recognition of Supervi-
    sors in Public Employment; (6) The Collective Bargaining Process

in Public Employment; (7) Government as Employer-Participant in the Collective Dealing Process; (8) The Collective Agreement in Public Employment; (9) Unresolved Disputes in Public Employment.

Posey, Rollin Bennett. "Employee Organization in the United States Public Service." Public Personnel Review, Vol. 17, October 1956, 238-245.

President's Task Force on Employee-Management Relations in the Federal Service. A Policy for Employee-Management Cooperation in the Federal Service. Washington, D. C.: Government Printing Office, November 30, 1961.

Silver, Richard A. "Collective Bargaining with Public Employees." Personnel Administration, Vol. 22, January-February 1959, 27-34.

Simpson, Dorothy. Selected References on Collective Bargaining in the Public Service. Berkeley, Calif.: Bureau of Public Administration, University of California, April 15, 1960.

Smith, Oscar S. "Are Public Service Strikes Necessary?" Public Personnel Review, Vol. 21, July 1960, 169-173.

Spero, Sterling D. Government As Employer. New York: Remsen Press, 1948.

Stutz, Robert L. Collective Dealing by Units of Local Government in Connecticut. Storrs, Conn.: University of Connecticut, May 1960.

Sussna, Edward. "Collective Bargaining on the New York City Transit System, 1940-1957." Industrial and Labor Relations Review, Vol. 11, July 1958, 518-533.

"We Look at Us." Public Employee, Vol. 23, March 1958, 3-19.

Canadian Publications

Frankel, Saul J. "Employee Organization in the Public Service of Canada." Public Personnel Review, Vol. 17, October 1956, 246-252.

_____. A Model for Negotiations and Arbitration Between the Canadian Government and Its Civil Servants. Montreal: Industrial Relations Centre, McGill University Press, 1962.

_____. Staff Relations in the Civil Service: The Canadian Experience. Montreal: McGill University Press, 1962.

_____ and Pratt, R. C. Municipal Labour Relations in Canada. Montreal: Canadian Federation of Mayors and Municipalities and Industrial Relations Centre, McGill University, 1954.

Noble, George W. "Labour Relations in Canadian Municipalities." Public Personnel Review, Vol. 22, October 1961, 255-261.

Prives, M. Z. Unionism and the Merit System in Municipal Relations in Canada. Montreal: Canadian Federation of Mayors and Municipalities, September 1958.